An Overview of the Library Services and Construction Act– Title I

An Overview of the Library Services and Construction Act- Title I

Jules Mersel
Morton H. Friedman
Emory H. Holmes
John F. Knudson
Eugene R. Streich

R. R. BOWKER COMPANY, NEW YORK, LONDON, 1969

Published by R. R. Bowker Company, (A XEROX COMPANY)
1180 Ave. of the Americas, New York, N.Y. 10036
Standard Book Number: 8352-0274-7
Library of Congress Catalog Card Number: 71-87065
Manufactured in the United States of America

This report was prepared by the System Development Corp., 2500 Colorado Ave., Santa Monica, Calif. 90406, as report TM-4053/001/00, pursuant to contract number OEC-0-8-089027-4475(095) with the U.S. Department of Health, Education, and Welfare, Office of Education, Bureau of Research, Division of Information Technology and Dissemination, Library and Information Sciences Branch, March 20, 1969.

Introduction

"The program of tomorrow is a fascinating topic for speculation, but a clear-eyed critical view of today is our first requirement. In many places and in many respects, we have only one foot in the twentieth century—and we seem at times to have got that far only by accident." This rather graphic statement was made in stressing the value of review and evaluation during the 1961 Allerton Park Institute on the impact of the Library Services Act by Ralph Blasingame, Jr., who was at that time the State Librarian of the Pennsylvania State Library.

We do know *why* the Library Services Act (the predecessor of the present Library Services and Construction Act) was passed by Congress and signed by President Eisenhower in 1956. Investigations at that time showed that some 27 million children and adults were living in areas without public library services, and 53 million more had only inadequate services available to them. The intent of this early legislation was, quoting the Act, "to promote the further extension by the several States of public library services to rural areas without such services or with inadequate services."

Although Congress greatly expanded this legislation in subsequent years (the Library Services and Construction Act now consists of five distinct programs), the backbone of the LSA/LSCA legislation from the beginning to now has been Title I (Public Library Services) which represents the expansion of the rural Library Services Act to urban areas, with increased funding. Under this title, funds may be used for salaries and wages, books and other library materials, library equipment, and general operating expenses. As demonstrated in the following study, a wide range of library activities can be supported under Title I funds—activities that are as urgent and as complex as any in the entire field of librarianship.

This report describes the impact of Federal funding on public library services and measures the effectiveness of State programs under Title I. There would be a concern with funding, personnel, standards, and methodology. It was seen as a "methodological foray" that would help to develop a model for future data gathering and program analysis.

An evaluation of the management of the Library Services and Construction Act was part of the project as well as full identification of problem areas. It was thought that the finished report—through its bibliographies and other aspects of the survey—could serve as a strong base for future reviews and evaluations of the Act. Certainly this publication should be judged by the reader as research which should lead to still further analysis and evaluation. There is value in reading this report in conjunction with the recently issued study of Nelson Associates, *Public Library Systems in the United States* (Chicago: American Library Association, 1969). Many systems analyzed in this publication received strong grant support under LSA/LSCA.

The System Development Corporation established an LSCA Impact Project in its Library and Documentation Systems Department in Santa Monica, Califronia, to conduct the study. The case study method of research was used, with focus on the period July, 1964 to June, 1968. To fully consider all levels of government participation in LSCA, stress was placed on field studies and interviews.

The Office of Education, based on the advice of appropriate staff and outside library administrators familiar with the LSCA program, selected eleven States for the study. In connection with library services, each State was unique in having its own problems and situations. Since only a portion of the States could be studied in depth because of available funds and time, it was believed that a truer picture of the overall program could be obtained from an analysis of States with contrasting characteristics.

Selection of the States was made on a number of factors which included position of the State library agency in the State structure, stages of statewide development and systems concept, presence of different population groups within the State, variety of public library service, and lack or presence of State aid. As part of the "mix", it was considered important that there be at least one State in each of the Department of Health, Education, and Welfare regions. Since direct administration of the Library Services and Construction Act is now carried out in these regional offices, the report can be said to reflect, in part, the activities and ideas of the nine Library Services Program Officers.

This is some of the background of this study which—taken at its minimum value—tells us where we are in eleven specific States. It is, I hope, telling us much more than this. As one example, it points up the need for better ways to measure the effectiveness of programs and activities, an outstanding example being measurement of the effectiveness of library programs for the disadvantaged. (As an historical note, this is the first review of programs for the disadvantaged funded under LSCA.) To my own mind, we are also being told of the increasing necessity for a new, up-to-date, and comprehensive inventory of national library needs.

What the report says about funding and management will be carefully considered by the Office of Education. Needless-to-say, this is an independent report, and all of the statements and their implications require review and appraisal.

This project was funded under the library research and demonstration portion of Title II-B of the Higher Education Act of 1965. All of us in the Office of Education who are concerned with the administration of the Library Services and Construction Act are grateful for the cooperation and understanding of F. Kurt Cylke, the acting chief of the Library and Information Sciences Research Branch, Bureau of Research, and other staff of the Office of Education who helped in planning the original concept for the study.

RAY M. FRY, DIRECTOR
DIVISION OF LIBRARY PROGRAMS,
BUREAU OF ADULT, VOCATIONAL, AND LIBRARY PROGRAMS
U.S. OFFICE OF EDUCATION

FINAL REPORT

Contract No. OEC-0-8-089027-4475(095)

OVERVIEW OF LIBRARY SERVICES AND
CONSTRUCTION ACT - TITLE I

Jules Mersel*
Morton H. Friedman
Emory H. Holmes
John F. Knudson
Eugene R. Streich

System Development Corporation
2500 Colorado Avenue
Santa Monica, California 90406

March 1969

The Survey reported herein was performed pursuant to a contract with the Office of Education, U.S. Department of Health, Education and Welfare. Contractors undertaking such projects under Government sponsorship are encouraged to express freely their professional judgment in the conduct of the project. Points of view or opinions stated do not, therefore, necessarily represent official Office of Education position or policy.

Submitted to:

U.S. Department of Health, Education, and Welfare
Office of Education, Bureau of Research

*Principal Investigator

ABSTRACT

This document reports the results of the first comprehensive analysis of the effects of Federal funds on public library services in the United States. Under a contract with the U.S. Office of Education (USOE), Bureau of Research, Division of Information Technology and Dissemination, Library and Information Sciences Branch, a System Development Corporation team studied Federally funded public-library projects in 11 States: Massachusetts, New York, North Carolina, South Carolina, Ohio, Wisconsin, Kansas, Arkansas, Utah, California, and Washington. The study focused on projects supported by the Library Services and Construction Act (LSCA), Title I--Services, of 1964 (as amended), and also considered the effects of the predecessor to LSCA, the Library Services Act (LSA) of 1956. Using a case-study approach, the team spent two weeks interviewing State library agency and local public library personnel in each State. This report concentrates primarily on the results of these visits.

The purpose of LSCA Title I is to extend public library services to those who have been without such services or who have had inadequate services. The Act is explicit in reserving to the responsible State library agencies the power of determining, within the intent of the Act, how Federal funds shall be spent in each State. The study team concluded tnat the State agencies have been successful in accomplishing this, particularly in the ways in which they have been sensitive to both the needs and the economic, geographic, and political environments of their States. The magnitude of the effect of Federal funds has, however, varied according to the level of public-library development that each State had achieved in the years before Federal funds became available. The study also revealed that the quality of public library services in general is a function of three principal factors--total funding, the number of trained personnel, and membership in library systems or networks. Future studies of the effects of Federal funding should concentrate on analyzing available statistics on how Federal funds have affected these factors.

Although no specific attention was paid, in the study, to USOE's Division of Library Services and Educational Facilities, which is the agency responsible for administering and monitoring LSCA at the Federal level, an examination of LSCA documents in State and Federal files indicated that the Division has been effective in ensuring that the States use LSCA funds in accordance with the intent of the Act.

The results of the study have two implications for Federal library-services policy: (1) that the formula by which LSCA funds are allocated to the States should be revised to more realistically reflect State and local attitudes toward public library service, and (2) that USOE should assume national leadership in the development of research, professional-training, and interlibrary coordination programs.

ACKNOWLEDGMENTS

The project members wish to express their deep appreciation to the librarians, government administrators, library trustees, and other individuals who so freely gave of their time and knowledge in helping us to understand how the Library Services and Construction Act (LSCA), Title I (Public Library Services) affected the public libraries of their individual States. The nine Regional Library Services Program Officers enabled us to obtain an awareness of library development in each of their regions. The State Librarians (or State Library Agency Directors) received us with sincere welcomes, genuine cooperation, and plentiful data relating to the activity, on all levels and in all areas of their States, that would affect an evaluation of LSCA Title I. We also wish to thank F. Kurt Cylke, the Acting Chief, Library and Information Sciences Research Branch, who provided the support that enabled this research to be performed. Our gratitude is extended to personnel of the Division of Library Services and Educational Facilities of the U.S. Office of Education who made their Library Services Act and LSCA Title I files available for our use. We also wish to acknowledge the extremely useful criticism of Carlos Cuadra; any faults that the report contains are, of course, due to the authors. Lastly, we wish to acknowledge the conscientious assistance of our secretaries, Harriet Edgerton and Susan Rodarte, and the many contributions of our editors, John Luke and Louise Wilhelm.

TABLE OF CONTENTS

TABLE OF CONTENTS
(Continued)

TABLE OF CONTENTS
(Continued)

TABLE OF CONTENTS
(Continued)

List of Figures

TABLE OF CONTENTS
(Continued)

List of Figures

TABLE OF CONTENTS
(Continued)

List of Tables

TABLE OF CONTENTS
(Continued)

List of Tables

CHAPTER I
INTRODUCTION

PURPOSE OF THE STUDY

The purpose of the study, as established by the U.S. Office of Education (USOE), was to conduct the first comprehensive analysis of the impact of Federal funding on public library services. The study was restricted to the Library Services and Construction Act (LSCA), Title I, Public Library Services.

The main focus of the study was on the development and expansion of public library service during the period July 1964 to June 1968, with some attention given to the impact that the Library Services Act (LSA) had on State library administrative agencies, statewide library development, and library services in rural areas in 11 selected States from 1957 to 1964.

The 11 States, selected by USOE, are:

Arkansas	Ohio
California	South Carolina
Kansas	Utah
Massachusetts	Washington
New York	Wisconsin
North Carolina	

DESCRIPTION OF THE REPORT

This report has three logically distinct parts and five appendixes. The first part, Chapters I-IV, reports on background information; the second part, Chapters V-XV, reports on the 11 States studied during the course of the survey. The third part, Chapter XVI, states the general findings of the study.

Chapter I, Introduction, states the purpose of the study and describes the report. The Summary, Chapter II, is divided into three sections, the first summarizing the background information, the second containing summaries of each of the individual State chapters, and the third summarizing the general findings. The third chapter, Background and Objectives of the Study, reports on the legislative history of LSCA, the need for improved planning information, and specific objectives of the study. The fourth chapter describes the methodology of the study.

Chapters V-XV describe the findings in the 11 States, presented in the order of the numbering of HEW Regions (alphabetically within each region). Although the States are treated as 11 separate studies, the following general format is used for all:

     I.   Sources of Information
    II.   Background for LSCA Operations
  III.   LSCA Program
   IV.   Description of Representative Uses of LSCA Funds
    V.   Evaluation
   VI.   Bibliography

The final chapter, Chapter XVI, states the general findings of the study. These findings include statements of goals and objectives of the State programs, the methods of planning State programs, the financial resources for the State programs, the use of matching funds by the States, the assignment of responsibilities, LSCA program successes and problems, the administration of LSCA by USOE, the implications of the dependency of the States on Federal funding, the implications for Federal and State planning, and the implications for the methodology of future appraisals.

Appendix A contains the Library Services and Construction Act as amended by the "Library Services and Construction Act Amendments of 1966," Public Law 89-511, approved July 19, 1966, and by Public Law 90-154, approved November 24, 1967. Appendix B presents the Federal Allotments and Required Matching Expenditures from State and Local Sources for Title I, Public Library Services, for Fiscal Year 1968. Appendix C contains the checklists used by SDC for interviews in the States. Appendix D contains a list of persons visited in connection with our examination of USOE's administration of LSCA. Appendix E contains a general bibliography.

CHAPTER II
SUMMARY

INTRODUCTION

This chapter summarizes the contents of this report. Like the report, it
is divided into three general sections--the first summarizing the background
and method of the study, the second summarizing the study findings for each
of the 11 States surveyed, and the third summarizing the general findings
of the study.

BACKGROUND

The Library Services and Construction Act (LSCA), passed in 1964, is a
successor to the Library Services Act (LSA) of 1956. LSA was an act to
promote the further development of public library service in rural areas.
It did not include incorporated or unincorporated towns having a population
of more than 10,000 persons. Title I of LSCA retains the purpose of extending public library services to those without such services or with inadequate
services; the population restriction, however, is removed. The appropriation
for Title I was $25 million in Fiscal Year 1965 and has increased to $35
million for Fiscal Year 1969. (The authorization for Fiscal Year 1969 was
$55 million.)

The specific objective of this study was to provide an intensive analysis
of the effect of LSCA Title I that would take into consideration the planning
and implementation by the States, the original intent of the legislation, the
level of success achieved, and the kinds of problems and barriers encountered.
The study utilized a case-study approach. Eleven States were selected by
the U.S. Office of Education for the study: Arkansas, California, Kansas,
Massachusetts, New York, North Carolina, Ohio, South Carolina, Utah,
Washington, and Wisconsin.

In performing the study, the SDC study team first conducted interviews with
Federal program personnel. The study team then made a comprehensive review
of relevant documentation. The major part of the study was devoted to field
visits. Initial contacts were made with the Library Service Program Officer
at the HEW Regional offices. Next, personnel of the State library administrative agencies were interviewed. Discussions were then held with library
staff personnel at local libraries. After all visits to all States were
completed, systematic analyses were made of the interview and other data
collected for each State.

SUMMARY OF STATE SURVEYS

MASSACHUSETTS

The Massachusetts Board of Library Commissioners is the agency designated to receive and disburse State aid funds as well as funds allocated under LSCA. Because Massachusetts has long had public libraries, extending, strengthening, and enriching public library service in the State are far different processes than they are in States that do not have widespread public library bases.

The Massachusetts Bureau of Library Extension recognized the need for library systems at least as early as 1936. Since the passage of State aid legislation in 1960, and with the availability of LSA/LSCA funds, the Bureau has concentrated its efforts on combining the development and administration of the State plans for the expenditure of State aid, LSCA, and other Federal funds, and on further encouraging the development of systems.

There are now three regional systems, divided into subregions, which cover the entire State. The services provided by the regional library systems are:

- Interlibrary Loan
- Bookmobile Service
- Film Service
- "Recommended Reading" Lists
- Workshops

The effect of LSA and LSCA funds on public library development in Massachusetts has been to arouse additional support for, and encourage the passage of, legislation for State aid to libraries.

NEW YORK

The Division of Library Development (DLD), within the State Department of Education, administers LSCA in New York. New York, like several other States, relies heavily on library systems to ensure that satisfactory library services are provided for the maximum number of citizens. New York provides the matching funds required for LSCA entirely from State aid money appropriated by the legislature; State aid funds are far greater than the funding from the Federal Government, while local monies far surpass the total of State and Federal funds.

New York uses its LSCA Title I funds, and its matching funds, for the following 10 projects:

1. EXTENSION--To extend public library service to those without convenient access to a library outlet.

2. REFERENCE SERVICE--To improve the informational and reference services of public library systems.

3. DISADVANTAGED--To promote outreach of the public library to the disadvantaged, the deprived, minority groups.

4. INTERSYSTEM EXPERIMENTAL PROGRAMS AND PLANNING TO MEET READER NEEDS--To encourage planning, studies and intersystem experimentation which will assist in the development and evaluation of library service programs in relation to reader needs.

5. COOPERATION TO MEET STUDENT NEEDS--To promote the coordination of all types of libraries, with the particular objective of meeting the needs of students of all ages through programs of cooperative action.

6. PERSONNEL, LEADERSHIP, EDUCATION--To assist in the development of adequate personnel for library service and leadership, including professional and non-professional staff and trustees.

7. AUDIOVISUAL RESOURCES--To promote the provision of programs utilizing non-book resources and the newer educational media as a part of total library services.

8. TECHNICAL SERVICES--To assist and promote the establishment of a statewide acquisition and cataloging center and relating processing centers to serve public library systems, by contract with the Association of New York Libraries for Technical Services.

9. STATE LIBRARY AND EXTENSION AGENCY--To strengthen the State Library's general reference and consultant services so that the agency may more adequately backstop the public library systems and assist in statewide library development.

10. PUBLIC LIBRARY SYSTEMS--To strengthen public library services by State grants-in-aid under Education Law 272-273 to public library systems. (This is the existing matching project which qualifies N. Y. for federal funds by the expenditure of State funds.)

Very little LSCA money--approximately 2 to 5 percent--goes into augmenting the holdings of the State Library. The largest amount of money is for grants. Projects for the disadvantaged have the highest priority of system-initiated projects. DLD determines which projects will be funded by

considering proposals submitted by the State's 22 systems, following guidelines laid out in the State plan. DLD manages local projects with information gathered through annual reports from all recipients of LSCA monies and
from field workers' reports evaluating the projects.

Because of the 1971 terminal date of LSCA, DLD has felt it prudent to avoid
projects whose goals could be reached only by long-range programs.

The impact of LSCA Title I in New York has been small compared to the impact
of the large amount of funds provided by State and local tax sources; however,
the projects for the disadvantaged and for DLD's extension work would suffer
greatly if LSCA funding were discontinued.

NORTH CAROLINA

The North Carolina State Library is responsible for administering LSCA in
the State. The State Library has used LSA and LSCA funds to continue and
augment a policy of State aid that began in 1941. Even with LSCA support,
however, the libraries of North Carolina are woefully underfinanced.

The policy of the State Library is to strengthen the county libraries
through cash grants, whose size depends upon the amount of effort the
counties have expended toward strengthening their own libraries, and to
offer--on a statewide basis--resources or services that individual county
libraries could not supply to themselves. The State, in its management of
LSCA, has established requirements that the county libraries must meet if
they are to receive grants of Federal and State monies. These requirements
are concerned with library management, funding, and the availability of
library service to all persons, without discrimination.

The State's aid to libraries program comprises six project categories:

- State Services to Public Libraries
- Library Systems Grants
- Processing Center
- Education and Training
- Institutes and Workshops
- Development Plan

In general, the State Library's management has created a working relationship
with the county libraries that has benefited the libraries of the State without causing the counties to feel that they are manipulated by the State. The
State plan's concentration on support of the county libraries does, however,
prohibit the flexibility that would allow the State to support municipal
libraries directly.

SOUTH CAROLINA

The agency designated to administer LSCA Title I funds in South Carolina is the State Library Board, which, in addition to being responsible for extending and approving library services in the State, is charged with setting standards for public library service, with certifying librarians, and with maintaining a Reference and Interlibrary Loan collection to supplement collections held locally throughout the State. The first annual State grant-in-aid program was initiated in 1943; in 1967, the General Assembly passed a new program of State aid, which provides $.20 per capita to each county.

At the time LSA was initiated, public libraries in South Carolina (with one or two exceptions) were very inadequate. Because the State Library Board assessed its primary task as that of strengthening a whole range of library capabilities within the State, it chose to allocate support through specific program elements, or projects, primarily implemented by itself. In Fiscal Year 1957 (the first year LSA support was available), the per capita library expenditures in South Carolina's 46 counties ranged from a low of $.02 to a high of $.69. Ten years later, in 1967, per capita support ranged from $.09 to $2.21, averaging $.95 per capita expenditure. Local financial support and State grant-in-aid funds provide the basic support to South Carolina public libraries. LSCA Title I funds augment this basic support by funding the projects listed below:

- Book Collection Improvement Project
- Periodicals Project
- Library Interpretation Project
- Personnel Project
- Small Libraries Project
- County Library Project
- Regional Library Project

Strong incentives are present in the State Library Board's management of the LSCA program. The allocation of both State aid and LSCA funds is contingent upon recipients' meeting quite detailed minimum library standards and/or having prescribed levels of local financial support.

Among the LSCA program strengths is the availability of State-aid funds to supplement Title I funds and the skillful use of "incentive" program management. Among the problem areas are the low economic level throughout most of the State and the lack of enough trained personnel. Despite these problems, however, Federal funds have had a marked effect on the improvement of library services in South Carolina.

OHIO

The State Library Board is the agency responsible for receiving, and approving the allocation of, LSCA Title I funds in Ohio. The Board appoints a State Librarian, who acts as the executive officer of the State Library and secretary to the Board.

Until recently, library-development planning in Ohio has been accomplished without a formal State master plan outlining long-range goals and programs. Under the present State Librarian, Joseph Shubert, LSCA Title I funds were used to conduct the first comprehensive study of library services at State and local levels. This study has provided the basis for the current development of a formal master plan.

The State Library's budget was used to match Ohio's allotment under LSA. A combination of State and local funds is used to match LSCA funds.

The State Library has assumed the primary responsibility for planning and administering LSA and LSCA projects. To monitor expenditures of LSCA projects administered locally, the State Library Board requires that a certified semiannual report of expenditures be submitted to the State Library LSCA Office. Local library and State Library LSCA expenditures are audited by State examiners. The State Library also maintains contacts with local projects through periodic visits, conferences, telephone communications, and final reports.

Although in the past a heavy percentage of Ohio's LSA and LSCA funds has been concentrated in State Library-administered programs, two new directions of administration, being emphasized by the State Librarian, may presage a different emphasis in future expenditures. One is the assumption by the State Library of a stronger leadership and consulting role; the other is the recent increase in the number of locally administered projects.

The formulation of a State master plan has increased the likelihood that the State legislature will properly fund the State Library. If this support is obtained, LSCA funds could be released to be spent on more innovative special projects.

WISCONSIN

The agency designated to receive and disburse LSCA Title I funds in Wisconsin is the Division for Library Services of the Wisconsin State Department of Public Instruction.

The LSCA program in Wisconsin has two major emphases:

> Extension services, provided by the Division staff and funded in part by LSCA monies and in part by State appropriations for Division operating expenses.

• Specific library-development projects conducted at the local level (though coordinated by the Division staff) and supported by LSCA and local funds.

Periodic institutes on public library management provide an opportunity for city officials, library trustees, and librarians to come together to discuss library problems of mutual concern. This activity is partially funded under Title I. Title I grants have also been provided for postgraduate study, primarily in library systems at the State University School of Library Science.

The Division for Library Services has a significant role in the planning of new library projects throughout the State. Not only are requests for State and Federal funds forwarded to the Division for review and approval, but, in a more pervasive sense, there is little in the way of library planning activity that it does not become involved in, either directly, on its own initiative, or indirectly, through influence.

Wisconsin provides an example of a well-managed State library program. Its strengths include linkages with other educational systems in the Department of Public Instruction and a wide range of extension services such as consultant assistance, interloan and reference capability and personnel scholarship and training programs. The regional library system configuration and network linkages with the State agency and system resource libraries have created an effective operational statewide system.

The major problem areas in Wisconsin are shared by most of the other states-- inadequate funding and a shortage of personnel. The unique problems of partially inadequate State library legislation and a needed State grant-in- aid program have long been recognized and corrective action is being initiated.

KANSAS

The Kansas State Library is the agency responsible for administering LSCA in the State.

The major theme of LSCA in Kansas is library systems. This theme has been responsible for the State devoting effort to the creating regional library systems and a statewide information network.

In 1965, the Kansas legislature enacted the Regional System of Cooperating Libraries Law which created the present arrangement of seven library systems and also provided the impetus for the establishing of the Kansas Information Circuit.

With the acceleration of Federal assistance to public libraries under the 1964 Library Services and Construction Act, a reorganization was effected in the State Library to make maximum use of the available Federal funds.

Previous to this Kansas was only able to claim a little more than 60 percent of the funds actually allocated to it. In essence, a shift was made from an emphasis on direct State use of the Federal funds to the utilization of regional library systems. Originally, the State Library used LSA funds for direct aid, usually in the form of bookmobile demonstrations.

LSA and LSCA have been very successful in Kansas in creating seven regional library systems and the Kansas Information Circuit. Local support has been increased and has led to the strengthening of local library service.

ARKANSAS

The Arkansas Library Commission is responsible for receiving and allocating LSCA Title I funds and State grant-in-aid appropriations in Arkansas. The Commission serves primarily as a service agency for county and regional (multicounty) libraries. At present, the Commission is focusing its activities on encouraging individual county libraries to either form new regional library systems or affiliate with existing systems.

Under the present legal restrictions, which contain a 1-mill ceiling on local library support, counties or communities that have an increasing population and a rapidly expanding industrial complex are unable to vote additional millage for library services to meet the expanding needs of their population and local industries. In order to bypass the 1-mill restriction, some communities have instituted an additional, voluntary 1-mill assessment for library services.

LSCA funds are used to support and supplement traditional library activities, such as the purchase of new books and materials. Because Federal funding is small (only $391,716 for FY 1968), and because of other economic factors, the Arkansas Library Commission has continued the same program as that initiated under LSA. Since the main need has been to upgrade basic library services, the Commission has not allocated LSCA monies for the development of special or innovative projects for urban or rural areas.

The funds retained by the Commission for its own operations ($61,870/$148,229 in Fiscal Year 1967) are used to support and supplement the increased staff, books, equipment, and operating expenses required for the centralized processing that serves public libraries throughout the State. Funds are also spent on workshops and in-service training courses that are conducted for local libraries.

LSCA funds have been allocated to local multicounty libraries to supplement State and local resources and provide for additional staff, equipment, and supplies.

Federal funds have supported and encouraged the development and expansion of regional library systems and have provided bookmobile service to areas that have previously been unserved or that have not voted the 1-mill county library tax.

UTAH

The Utah State Library Commission is the agency responsible for administering LSCA in the State. Before the Library Services Act was passed in 1956, Utah had no State Library. Not until LSA money became available was Utah able to create a Library Commission and a State Library. Federal (LSCA) monies appropriated to Utah in Fiscal Year 1968 amounted to $245,448; this amount was more than matched by State aid funds, which amounted to nearly $200,000.

Because most of Utah's population unserved by libraries is thinly dispersed over a large area, it was clear that the only way to provide library services to that population would be through bookmobiles. Accordingly, the Library has channeled 98 percent of its allocated LSCA funds into bookmobile demonstrations; the remaining 2 percent is used to provide a central reference collection maintained at the State Library for use by bookmobiles and local libraries. The State now has 13 bookmobiles in operation, beside the 1 now being operated by San Juan County.

The success of the bookmobiles--and hence of LSCA in Utah--may be measured in two ways: (1) the adoption of the State's bookmobile service on a permanent locally supported basis by every county in which a demonstration was conducted; and (2) the increase in tax support for existing local libraries and for the State Library as a direct result of the public interest aroused by bookmobiles.

CALIFORNIA

The California State Library is the agency responsible for administering LSCA funds in California.

The Federal support of public libraries began in 1957-58 with LSA and the funds were used for special demonstration projects designed to initiate new forms of library service and organization. Most of those early demonstrations are now established systems, with local funds having supplanted Federal funds.

The central idea embodied in the California State plan regarding the use of State aid and Federal funds for library services is that those funds should in one way or another support the development and maintenance of library systems.

The State Librarian and the Assistant State Librarian determine whether a project is in accord with the California Master Plan for library service and with the California State Plan submitted to USOE. The State Library allocates State aid and LSCA funds to five classes of projects:

1. BOOKMOBILES--There are several bookmobile programs in operation in California.

2. ENRICHMENT--Inherent in most of the LSCA projects that are funded in California is the expectation that each program will enrich the service provided to patrons.

3. CENTRAL PROCESSING--At the State level, the State Library operates a Central Processing Center for 28 subscribing libraries.

4. MECHANIZATION--A project has been initiated to establish computer processes in the California State Library.

5. THE DISADVANTAGED--One important theme in the California plan is extension of service to the disadvantaged.

If the LSCA program in California were to be discontinued, aid to local libraries would be diminished, and the development of regional library systems would be slowed. The overall library program, however, would continue as a result of wide public support.

WASHINGTON

The Washington State Library Commission is responsible for administering LSCA funds in Washington. The State Library Commission appoints the State Librarian, who serves as secretary to the Commission and operates the State Library. The Commission is chartered to provide book services to areas where no libraries exist, and (through the State Library) to act as a supplementary book source for, and focal point of, an interlibrary loan system among the libraries of the State. Washington uses its State grant-in-aid funds, as matching funds to qualify under LSCA.

After a study made in 1948, the Washington State Library Commission adopted a long-range regional plan for library development in the State. The State was divided into 12 regions, each of which was to receive standard library service. When Federal funds became available, the State Library Commission decided to use those funds to further implement the regional plan. The 12 library regions receive, in addition to LSCA Title I allocations, State grants as well as support in the form of local tax monies. Three types of grants are supported: two-year demonstration grants, operational grants to libraries that are members of library systems, and grants made for studies designed to advance the development of library service in the State.

It has taken the State Library 26 years to succeed in establishing two regional library systems. At that rate, using the demonstration approach, many years will pass before library service will be provided to all of the State.

FINDINGS

GOALS AND OBJECTIVES OF STATE PROGRAMS

The States, in fulfilling the purpose of the law (LSCA) to extend public library services to areas that do not have such services or have inadequate services, have adopted the following strategies, which reflect the library and political environment of the States:

- Forming library systems.
- Attracting professional librarians.
- Holding institutes.
- Conducting surveys.
- Increasing holdings and reference services.
- Funding "disadvantaged" projects.
- Cooperating with schools.
- Carrying out public-relations activities.
- Providing consultant services.
- Providing central processing.
- Maintaining central holding.
- Forming networks.

ADMINISTRATION OF STATE PROGRAMS

Each of the State Library administrative agencies has chosen a different procedure for implementing the LSCA program in its State. Some States already had plans for the use of State monies and have chosen to use Federal funds to augment the existing funds for these plans; other States, which also had existing plans for the use of State monies, have chosen to have still another set of programs for the use of Federal funds. Some States have chosen to dispense funds by having local libraries propose projects for consideration by the State library administrative agencies. Other States disburse funds according to formula. One State, Utah, made the State Library, in effect, the local library for most of the State.

Though all of the States may not have been aware of it at the times they first chose their LSA and LSCA programs, a major decision, which was made through the choice of each State's different program, was whether they would consider Federal funding as continued funding or funding with a terminal date. These States either used money for a noncontinuing effort or chose to fund demonstration projects--that is, projects that would be continued with local monies after LSCA money from the State had been discontinued.

With the enactment of LSCA, the requirement that program funds be spent only in rural areas has been removed. As a consequence, each State is able to show that the State and local funds spent on library service in the State are more than sufficient to meet the amount of matching funds from the State that the law requires. Thus, the matching fund requirement no longer affects the amounts of Federal funds that are actually distributed to each State; the current distribution of funds varies only according to the population figures for each State.

Although the responsibility for managing LSCA programs in the States rests formally with the heads of the State library administrative agencies, the actual responsibilities are shared by State agencies and the local library organizations that receive grants from the State agency.

LSCA PROGRAM SUCCESSES AND PROBLEMS

The major LSCA programs successes are:

- Increased financial support for existing libraries.

- Establishment of experimental library projects to serve the "disadvantaged."

- Extension of library services to rural areas.

- Centralized processing for public libraries.

- Creation of library systems.

- Development of a comprehensive State plan for library development (Ohio).

- Creation of information networks.

- Establishment of a State Library (Utah).

The major problems are:

- Insufficient funds.

- Insufficient numbers of personnel.

- A lack of interface with non-public libraries.

- A lack of understanding of how to provide service to those who do not presently use libraries.

- A lack of understanding on the part of the public of services that libraries already offer.

- A lack of ability on the part of the public libraries to react quickly to demands for large increases in services.

- A lack of criteria with which to measure library performance.

ADMINISTRATION OF LSCA BY USOE

The U.S. Office of Education has little authority in directing the expenditure of LSCA Title I funds. The act is explicit in reserving almost all privileges to the States and their local subdivisions. If any State is dissatisfied with the Commissioner's final action with respect to the approval of its State plan, the State may appeal to the U.S. Court of Appeals. The judgment of that court is subject to review only by the U.S. Supreme Court. USOE has, therefore, restricted its activities to being informed about what the States are doing and to offering consulting services to them.

Within USOE, the Division of Library Services and Educational Facilities (DLSEF) administers LSCA. DLSEF is within the Bureau of Adult, Vocational, and Library Programs, and is separated organizationally from many of the other USOE organizations that have responsibilities for library programs. The primary contacts with the State librarians are the nine Regional Library Services Program Officers. Library Services Program Officers are not employees of DLSEF. DLSEF reports to the Office of the Commissioner through Adult, Vocational and Library Programs; the Regional\Library Services Program Officers report to the Office of the Commissioner through Field Services.

IMPLICATIONS OF THE FINDINGS OF THE STUDY

The States have adopted different attitudes about becoming dependent upon Federal funding for library support. While some States have disbursed LSCA Title I funds in such a manner that a discontinuance of this funding would not seriously impair library successes achieved with the use of the funds, other States would have their present library service strongly affected by the loss of further LSCA support.

There are two implications of the study for Federal policy. One implication is that a revised measure should be used to determine the level of Federal support. The increase in Federal support for the sum of the several States should equal the increased amount of local and State support summed over all of the States. The distribution of these additional funds should be made according to the population and matching requirements of the present law. The other implication is that USOE should assume a more prominent national role, rather than become involved in the State-level administration that has already been performed well by the State agencies. This national role should include additional research, support of new technology, encouragement of librarian recruitment, training and education, the creation of interstate communication channels, and the fostering of intrastate library coordination among public and non-public libraries. To provide this leadership, the present dispersal of library programs among different Bureaus of USOE should be replaced with a single Bureau headed by an Associate Commissioner of Education for Libraries.

The implications of the report for State planning are that the State agencies should seek more flexibility in funding than is presently the case, that they provide far more publicity about the services that are available from libraries, and that they foster increased coordination between the public and non-public libraries of the States.

The findings of this study indicate that future studies of the impact of Federal funding on public library service should choose a different methodology. The present study showed that the adequacy and availability of library services are so strongly influenced by total funding, number of trained personnel, and membership in regions or networks that a future study might concentrate on statistics that could correlate the effect that Federal funding has had on these things. Such a study would concentrate less on field trips and more on the analysis of already available data.

CHAPTER III
BACKGROUND AND OBJECTIVES OF STUDY

BACKGROUND

LEGISLATIVE HISTORY OF LSCA

The Library Services and Construction Act, passed in 1964, represented a modification and extension of the Library Services Act of 1956, which was the result of more than 10 years of cooperative effort on the part of the library community and several members of Congress.

As early as the spring of 1945, considerable groundwork for supportive library legislation had been done by Paul Howard, then Chairman of the American Library Association's Federal Relations Committee. Mr. Howard had consulted with officials of the Library Services Division of the Office of Education, with the National Education Association, and with members of Congressional committees, concerning the desirability of a bill to provide for demonstration of library services in rural areas. In preparing such a bill for Congressional support, he was assisted by the Legislative Reference Service of the Library of Congress. Subsequently, in March 1946, the proposed legislation (the Public Library Demonstration Bill) was introduced in both houses of Congress by Congresswoman Emily Taft Douglas of Illinois and Senator Lister Hill of Alabama.

During the next 10 years the bill, redrafted and entitled the Library Services Bill, was reintroduced in every succeeding Congress. Support for the measure grew with each year, and it was cosponsored by 18 Senators and 27 Representatives when the 84th Congress convened in January 1955. It was this Congress that passed the Library Services Act, which was signed as Public Law 597 by President Eisenhower on June 19, 1956, to become effective immediately and run for a period of 4 years.

The declaration of policy in the Library Services Act (LSA) states: "It is the purpose of this Act to promote the further extension by the several States of public library services to rural areas without such services or with inadequate services." (The language of the Act provides this definition: "The term 'rural area' does not include an incorporated or unincorporated town having a population of more than 10,000 persons.")

LSA authorized a total of $30,000,000--$7,500,000 for each of the 4 years-- to be expended among the 52 States. (For purposes of the Act, Alaska, Hawaii, Puerto Rico, and the Virgin Islands were defined as States.) Actually, a lesser amount was appropriated: in Fiscal Year 1957, $2,050,000; in fiscal 1958, $5,000,000; in 1959, $6,000,000; and in 1960, $7,500,000. The Act provided for cost-sharing between the Federal government and States as follows: "For the purpose of this section the 'Federal share for any State shall be a 100 per centum less the State percentage and the State percentage shall be that percentage which bears the same ratio to 50 per centum as the per capita income of such State bears to the per capita income of the continental United States (including Alaska), except that (1) the Federal share shall in no case be more than 66 per centum or less than 33 per centum,..."

Though the title no longer contained the word "demonstration," the LSA was still considered by the Eisenhower administration to be a demonstration act that would terminate in a few years' time. (In fact, the word "demonstration" appeared only in one sentence: "The Commissioner is also authorized to make such studies, investigations, and reports that may be necessary or appropriate to carry out the purposes of this Act, including periodic reports for public distribution as to the values, methods, and results of various State demonstrations of public library services in rural areas undertaken under this Act.")

The Eisenhower administration continued to think of LSA as being a demonstration act that would terminate at the end of the 5-year period. When the Act came up for a 5-year extension (for a total of 9 years) in 1960, testimony before the House Committee was exceedingly laudatory and enthusiastic. Dr. Lawrence G. Derthick, then U.S. Commissioner of Education, stated: "Because of the success of this program we are recommending an extension. We do feel, however, that this is an area where the Federal government should endeavor to stimulate additional activity at the State level and that when this additional activity has been stimulated, Federal participation should be terminated. We hope, therefore, that the Congress will make it clear as a matter of legislative intent that at the end of the 5-year period provided for in this legislation, the Federal participation will cease and that the States will be expected to assume the full load. One way, of course, of underlining this conviction would be for the Congress to arrange for a tapering off of the Federal share."

At the time of considering the extension of the Library Services Act, the House Committee had before it more than 40 very similar bills. Provisions in some of these bills would have made benefits available to more than the "rural areas" (not including towns of 10,000) defined in the original Act. The bill that was eventually passed did not in fact modify the 10,000 population restriction; it did, however, extend the $7.5 million annual authorization until June 30, 1966, a total of 10 years from the effective date of the original Act.

In 1962 the House Committee on Education and Labor heard testimony on further modification of the Library Services Act. A number of bills had been introduced with various provisions for (1) a 5-year program extension, (2) removal of the 10,000 population limitation, (3) increase of the annual appropriation from $7.5 million to $20 million, (4) library services to public elementary and secondary schools, (5) matching grants to colleges and universities for the acquisition of books, and (6) authorizations allowing $10 million to be spent annually at colleges and universities to operate short-term or regular-session institutes to improve the qualifications of librarians and of students preparing to engage in library work.

The changing attitude of the Executive branch towards library assistance was reflected in the testimony of Wilbur J. Cohen, then Assistant Secretary for Legislation, Department of Health, Education, and Welfare. During the 1962 hearings, Mr. Cohen stated: "It is clear that additional Federal assistance for library programs is necessary." However, in the course of the April 1963 hearings of the Subcommittee of the House Education and Labor Committee, Francis J. Keppel, then Commissioner of Education, requested funds that were far less than what Congress wished to appropriate. The administration none-theless threw its support behind the passage of the Library Services and Construction Act of 1964.

The 1964 Library Services and Construction Act (LSCA) removed the restriction that services be tendered only to rural areas. The authorization for appro-priation was changed to $25 million for Fiscal Year 1964, and "such sums as the Congress may determine" for Fiscal Years 1965 and 1966. The other major change to the Library Services Act was the authorization of funds for public library construction; this provision was embodied as Title II of the LSCA and, of course, necessitated the renaming of the Act.

Further hearings in 1966 resulted in two additional titles being appended to the Act. One title was specific about interlibrary cooperation; the other was for specialized State Library services (i.e., State institutional library services and library services for the physically handicapped). At this time, a large number of proposed authorizations for the expanded LSCA were placed before both the House and the Senate. Of these, the Senate considered three bills: One, sponsored by a majority (53 Senators), urged the authorization of $35 million for Title I for Fiscal Year 1967; the other two recommended an amount of $60 million. Harold Howe, II, then Commissioner of Education, indicated in his testimony that the Executive branch was not ready to consider as large an amount as Congress was willing to authorize. Commissioner Howe supported the Administration request for $27.5 for Title I in Fiscal Year 1967. The bill eventually passed authorized $35 million for that year. Actual appropriations for Fiscal Years 1965-1969 have been as follows:

FY 65	$25,000,000
FY 66	$25,000,000
FY 67	$35,000,000
FY 68	$35,000,000
FY 69	$35,000,000

These last two appropriations of $35 million are less than the amounts authorized by the act--$45 million for Fiscal Year 1968 and $55 million for Fiscal Year 1969.

Appendix A contains the Library Services and Construction Act.

Appendix B shows for each State the Federal allotment and the required matching expenditure for Fiscal Year 1969.

THE NEED FOR IMPROVED PLANNING INFORMATION

In order to plan realistically for the continuing administration of LSCA, the U.S. Office of Education required information addressed to at least four basic questions:

1. What action, if any, should USOE undertake in obtaining further categorization of Title I?

2. What data should USOE gather in order to present a complete report to the Congress when the extension of LSCA becomes a matter for legislative action?

3. What facts should USOE gather in order to advise the Bureau of the Budget as to the amount of appropriation that the administration should request of the Congress during the remaining years of the Library Services and Construction Act and what authorization should USOE suggest to the Congress for any legislative extension of LSCA Title I?

4. What change, if any, is needed to allow the Commissioner of Education to continue to administer LSCA?

It was the intent of the survey to derive the needed information, primarily by analysis of data to be obtained from the selected States. LSCA had provided the States with many new ways of extending library services to those previously without such services or with inadequate services. Between 1965 (when LSCA funding first became available) and 1968 (when the SDC study was commissioned) the States had the opportunity to discover and explore these new ways. It was expected that the methods used by the States would disclose unexpected benefits as well as shortcomings, in both the law and the methods of implementation; and it was anticipated that a knowledge of these disclosures would help both the USOE and the States in planning their future actions with respect to LSCA.

On the State level, it was anticipated that the information reported in this Overview might enable the State library administrative agencies to improve the administration, or supervision of the administration, of the plan for the further extension of public library services in their respective States. The 11 States about which chapters are written were believed to represent sufficient diversity, with regard to methods of extending public library services, to provide a wealth of suggested alternatives to any State for future modifications of its plan.

SPECIFIC OBJECTIVES OF THE SDC STUDY

The specific study objectives were to provide an intensive analysis that would consider the original intent of the legislation, the planning and implementation approach taken by the States, the level of success achieved, and the kinds of problems encountered. The output of the analysis would be a comprehensive report intended to be of immediate use to the States and to the U.S. Office of Education in providing direction and support for more effective public library service.

Some of the considerations of the analysis are stated below:

The analysis would take into consideration the original intent of the legislation, the level of success in each of the selected States, and it will indicate weaknesses and strengths in existing LSCA programs which will be useful both to the U.S. Office of Education and to the States in fulfilling their leadership roles in providing effective public library service....

The following questions are given as examples of the kinds of considerations that were included in the study; however, they are in no way exhaustive:

1. Has the State formulated and adopted clearly and measurably stated goals, objectives, and standards for public library development? Can such measures be applied in a practical way to picture the existing status of public library development in the State? Can such measures be applied in a practical way to estimate resources (Federal, State, local) required over a 5-year time span to achieve the formulated and adopted goals, objectives, and standards for public library development in the State?

2. In terms of the above, can the State develop a meaningful 3- to 5-year plan for library development? If a plan exists, how was it developed? If not, what staff and resource capability or other factors would be required by the State Library Agency to do so?

3. Where State plans for library development have been implemented, has this implementation been effective and what measures have been developed for determining this effectiveness?

4. What has been the response to Federal legislation in terms of State legislation and what has been the effect of Federal appropriations on State appropriations for programs related to LSCA?

5. Where specific local programs have been established, are these programs really successful, is success being measured by a built-in success factor, or are there alternative approaches that would have proven more successful?

CHAPTER IV
METHODOLOGY OF THE STUDY

BASIC APPROACH

It seemed highly probable that the 11 States would implement the LSCA program differently because of varying social, economic, and political considerations. Thus a too-rigorous attempt to make comparisons and generalizations across States might involve the sacrifice of valuable data. Each State, therefore, was intended to represent an individual case study; however, comparative analyses were to be undertaken in those cases where uniform data bases were available or where similarities in program administration existed.

An overview of survey tasks suggested three main elements of work: (1) preliminary planning and information gathering, (2) field visits, (3) data analysis and interpretation. Each of these work elements is described in detail in the following paragraphs.

PRELIMINARY PLANNING AND INFORMATION GATHERING

ANALYSIS OF OBJECTIVES AND CONSTRAINTS

The basic objectives of the study were outlined by USOE. To translate these objectives into a study rationale and specific work tasks, it was necessary to take account of a number of methodological and practical constraints. For example, in evaluating the total LSCA program impact in a given State, it was not possible to distinguish between those factors directly related to Federal support and those indirectly connected with, or independent of, such support. One might have been able to do this, in part, if for each State or program there had been some kind of "control" situation, where Federal funding was not involved. No such control situation was found in any of the 11 States; thus, the separation of effects of Federal funding from other factors was necessarily a matter of subjective judgment based on less-than-ideal information.

Another major constraint was the existence of relatively little "hard" data (i.e., quantified or readily quantifiable information) on the impact of various State programs; therefore, some aspects of the analysis of necessity relied on qualitative data and narrative/descriptive information. Also, the available data were not, in some instances, equivalent or uniform throughout the sample of selected States.

SPECIFICATION OF INFORMATION TO BE OBTAINED

Limitations in time and funding did not permit examination, in exhaustive detail, of all aspects of each State's program. Some selectivity was therefore mandatory, and it was decided to emphasize collection of data related to the following:

- State goals and standards;
- Methods to measure effectiveness;
- Effectiveness of State planning;
- Effectiveness of programs within and across States;
- Resources required for existing or planned program;
- Long-range State plans;
- Federal and State legislation;
- Federal versus State and local appropriations.

COMPREHENSIVE REVIEW OF RELEVANT DOCUMENTATION

The initial phase of the survey began with a review of relevant documentation, provided by USOE and/or solicited by the project. This documentation included:

- Federal legislation,
- USOE directives and planning guides,
- State legislation,
- State program plans, directives and reports,
- Supplementary documentation from local agencies,
- Other information, such as published technical reports or news stories.

In this review, SDC personnel identified State goals, objectives, and standards in terms of operationally measurable program elements. (Some aspects of this review extended throughout the project. For example, although documents on the program of each State were examined at the outset of the project, they were analyzed in considerably more detail prior to the field visits to that State.)

CONDUCT OF INITIAL INTERVIEW WITH FEDERAL PROGRAM PERSONNEL

After initial analysis of the basic legislation and program documentation and prior to field visits to the selected States, SDC considered it desirable for project personnel to meet with selected Federal personnel, at national and regional levels, to insure that our initial assumptions about the broad objectives and operation of the program were consonant with the facts. These initial interviews it was expected, would enable the research team to validate or improve some of the procedural aspects of the survey, as well as to identify other potentially valuable information sources.

IDENTIFYING AND EFFECTING LIAISON WITH INFORMATION SOURCES

On completion of the four activities described above, the study team was able to identify other important information sources, aside from documentation. These sources included: (1) Federal and State employees associated with the State programs; (2) State legislators and municipal officials; (3) civic leaders and library trustee groups; and (4) users of some of the library services resulting from LSCA programs.

SDC anticipated that, in some instances, it would be desirable for personnel at USOE's headquarters and at its various regional offices to assist in making initial high-level contacts in particular States.

DEVELOPMENT OF TOOLS AND PROCEDURES

Since interviews were to play a major role in data collection efforts, and since each project member was to be involved in individual State interviews, SDC developed and pretested interview guides, not only to provide reasonably uniform data but also to assure reasonably uniform inquiry. It was expected, however, that these initial interview categories would be incomplete and would be further expanded and refined in the pretesting phase early in the data gathering. Further, it was recognized that all categories of information might not be applicable to each State's particular program configuration.

Based upon initial interviews in California (the first State visited), four interview checklists for the remaining States were created. One checklist was developed for each of the following categories of persons interviewed:

  · Regional library services program officer,

  · State Library personnel,

  · Local library personnel,

  · State Finance Officer.

The intent of these lists was to provide for comprehensiveness and standardization of interview data and yet to allow for the diversity anticipated in State and local programs. Because of the extreme diversity encountered in the first four States investigated after California a number of items were considered inapplicable for those States and other items were consequently substituted. The four checklists are attached as Appendix C.

FIELD VISITS

The acquisition of information on library services in the selected States, in general, focused upon two types of data: documented materials and information obtained from interviews with various agency and library personnel.

On initiation of the study contract, arrangements were made with USOE to obtain copies of State plans, annual reports, and other relevant LSA and LSCA program information for each of the 11 selected States. In addition, the project staff, working through SDC's reference librarian, sought out relevant background articles in the professional journals of both national and State library organizations. These materials provided much information-- on the organization of library services, the funding patterns, and the types and locations of demonstration projects--that was helpful both in the planning stages (prior to visiting the various States) and in actual interviews with State and local library personnel.

Another class of data was obtained on site: copies of planning reports, surveys, special studies, and other documented materials were obtained for later analysis. However, it was recognized that the formal reports provided by the States might not always contain detailed information on some potentially important aspects of the programs involved. In particular, some information that would help to indicate strengths or weaknesses in the planning and implementation of the LSCA programs might not be in such reports. Thus, it was necessary to supplement and support documented information with accounts of personal reactions, unreported experience, and so forth, obtained in the course of field interviews.

Field visits were conducted as follows:

- Initial contact was with the Library Services Program Officer at the Regional Office. At this level, discussion centered on the broader aspects of program administration and served as an introduction to the accomplishments, problems, and other issues concerning library programs in the particular State(s) involved.

- Next, discussions were held with personnel of the State library agency responsible for administration of the LSCA program. These discussions were extensive, covering the history and organization of the agency, the nature of the State library service, its relationship to related services, and pertinent background of Title I projects.

- At the local project level, discussions with library staff personnel were, in many instances, augmented by interviews with local government officials, library board members, or representatives of interested civic groups.

All visits were documented in informal field notes dictated onto tape by the interviewers immediately after each visit. At the time these memoranda were dicated, no attempt was made to resolve inconsistencies in content. The memoranda were intended to capture the thoughts and reactions of the interviewer before his impressions were affected by later interviews. They varied with the style of the interviewer, the nature of the site, and the amount of time available to the interviewer for committing his thoughts to tape before making his next visit. The memoranda, together with documented materials, formed the raw data for the extensive analysis that was conducted during the last 7 weeks of the contract.

DATA ANALYSIS AND INTERPRETATION

After the visits to each State, a cursory appraisal was made of that State's program and tentative "conclusions" drawn. Available information on comparable programs in other States was next reviewed to provide the interviewer/analyst with a broader perspective on the State being studied. The third and most rigorous step was a systematic analysis of the interview data and other material collected in the State. On the basis of these data, the analyst attempted to discover and develop information in qualitative form. Statistical analysis was performed in those instances where the data were amenable to statistical techniques.

The program and activities in each State were analyzed not only in relation to avowed objectives but in relation to the possibilities offered by current technology. In the absence of such comparative analysis, one might be misled to consider a program adequate if it were in accordance with its objectives, even though it failed to take good advantage of the state of the art.

The complete appraisal of a particular program in a State was helped by careful review of comparable programs in other States; thus, the "final" conclusions regarding each State's program were not made until the full range of comparative and contextual information was available.

REGION I:

Connecticut
Maine
MASSACHUSETTS
New Hampshire
Rhode Island
Vermont

Arlene Hope, Library Services
   Program Officer, AVLP
John F. Kennedy Federal Building
   Government Center
   Boston, Mass. 02203

CHAPTER V
MASSACHUSETTS

I. SOURCES OF INFORMATION

The following organizations and persons were visited to obtain information for this study (see Figure M-1 for a map of the State):

Date	Place Visited	Persons Visited
9/16/68	USOE Regional Office Boston, Massachusetts Region I	Arlene Hope, Library Services Program Officer
9/17/68	Massachusetts Division of Library Extension Boston	Mrs. V. Genevieve Galick, Director Mary Burgarella, Senior Supervisor of Public Library Development
9/19/68	Fitchburg City Library Fitchburg	Arthur S. Kissner, Librarian
9/20/68	Taunton Public Library Taunton	Ruth Synan, Librarian
9/20/68	Wellesley Free Library Wellesley	Margaret J. Arnold, Librarian
9/24/68	Suffolk University Library Boston	Richard J. Sullivan, Chairman, Massachusetts Board of Library Commissioners
9/24/68	Boston Public Library Boston	Philip J. McNiff, Director
9/25/68	Worcester Public Library Worcester	Jack W. Bryant, Director
9/25/68	Forbes Library Northampton	Oliver R. Hayes, Librarian
9/26/68	Springfield City Library Springfield	Francis P. Keough, Librarian
9/27/68	State Regional Library Center North Reading	Mrs. Rachel M. Sullivan, Librarian Mrs. Marjorie E. Hazelton, Bookmobile Librarian
9/26/68	Berkshire Athenaeum Pittsfield	Robert G. Newman, Librarian

Much valuable information was also obtained from the publications listed in the Bibliography in Section VI of this chapter.

II.   BACKGROUND FOR LSCA OPERATIONS

THE STATE AGENCY

The Massachusetts Board of Library Commissioners is the agency designated by Massachusetts State law to receive and disburse State grants-in-aid as well as funds allocated under LSA and, later, LSCA. The five-member board, appointed by the Governor, delegates the responsibility for administering and supervising these funds to the Bureau of Library Extension, which operates under the general jurisdiction of the Department of Education (see Figure M-2). The Director of the Bureau (presently Mrs. V. Genevieve Galick) is selected by the Board of Library Commissioners, with the approval of the Board of Education, and is the executive officer responsible to the Commissioners for actual administration. The Director is assisted by a Senior Supervisor of Public Library Development (presently Miss Mary Burgarella) and a staff of specialists.

DEVELOPMENT OF LIBRARY SERVICES IN MASSACHUSETTS

The State has long had public libraries; indeed, many of the nation's developments in public library service were pioneered in Massachusetts. Two factors have been particularly important in the State's history of library development: the tradition of early Massachusetts scholars who established and supported many local public libraries and, even more important, the predominance of the small governmental unit--the township-- which brought government to the citizens on almost a neighborhood basis. As a result of the tradition of scholarship and generous endowment, almost every town had a public library; some small towns have more than one. And the reliance on township, rather than county, government has made for strong autonomy; the control of local matters is a closely guarded preroga- tive. Thus many a town with small population and inadequate tax base has attempted the entire support of a local library, or even more than one. In 1966, the State's 351 cities and towns supported 389 public libraries.

To extend, strengthen, and enrich public library service in Massachusetts, then, is a far different process than in a State that does not have a wide- spread public library base. Though many of the libraries in Massachusetts are small and in need of additional local support, the foundation for that support already exists and, for the most part, development of library service has been a matter of building on the existing structure. Yet the Bureau of Library Extension must be very careful in implementing and administering its programs, so that local authorities will not resent Bureau influence. Keeping local librarians and authorities well informed regarding goals and plans is an important means of gaining their acceptance for the Bureau's programs.

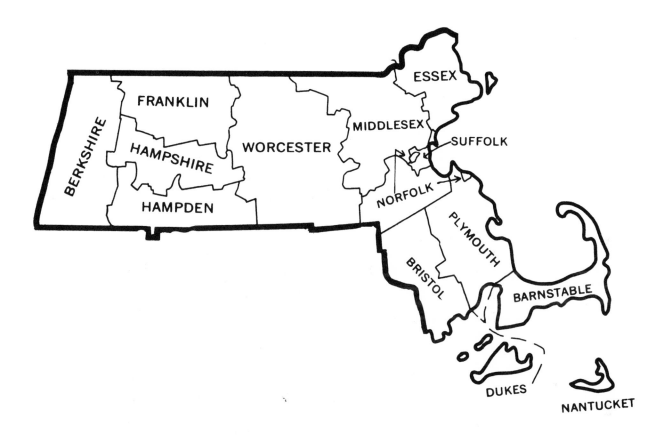

Figure M-1. Map of the State of Massachusetts

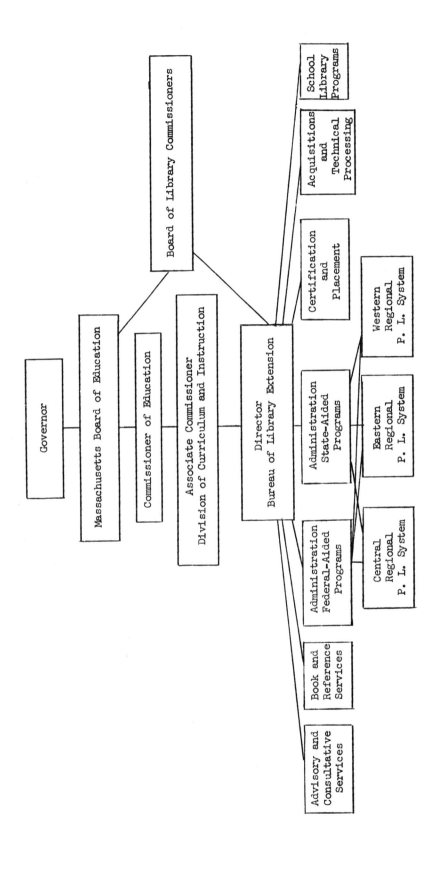

Figure M-2. Organization Chart of Massachusetts Board of
Education Showing Bureau of Library Extension

REGIONAL SYSTEMS

The need for regional library systems was recognized at least as early as 1936, when a recommended regional library plan was introduced as a joint effort of the Board of Library Commissioners, the Bureau of Library Extension, and the State's library community. Two difficulties at first hindered the implementation of such a plan: lack of funds (Massachusetts then had no State aid to libraries) and the initial hesitancy of local authorities to relinquish control. As a result of Works Progress Administration funding, it became possible to experiment with the plan and to prove its feasibility and in 1940 three regional projects began operation with the support of Federal funds. These regions were later supported by State appropriation when Federal funds terminated and eventually incorporated into the State-aided regional systems.

Since the passage of State-aid legislation in 1960 (see section on LIBRARY FUNDING, below), and with the availability of LSA/LSCA funds, the development of regional systems received fresh impetus. Three major regional public library systems have now evolved. It was not until 1966, however, when the Boston Public Library began operations (in two capacities: as the head-quarters of the Eastern Regional System and as library of last resort for the entire State) that Massachusetts had a truly statewide library system.

The three regional systems are divided into subregions which cover the entire State. The Eastern Region, with headquarters at the Boston Public Library, serves 205 libraries in 180 cities and towns. Subregional centers are located at the public libraries of Andover, Falmouth, Lowell, New Bedford, Quincy, Taunton, and Wellesley. The Central Region, with headquarters at the Worcester Free Public Library, serves 70 libraries in 70 cities and towns. There is only one subregional center, located at Fitchburg. The Western Region, with head-quarters at the Springfield Library, serves 107 libraries in 101 cities and towns. Subregional centers are located at the Forbes Library in Northampton, the Berkshire Athenaeum in Pittsfield, with intermediate reference centers in the public libraries of Greenfield and North Adams.

The services provided by the regional library systems are the same for each region, though they may vary depending on local need. They are as follows:

- Interlibrary Loan and Reference Service. Local library requests for service go to the nearest subregional library. If the request cannot be filled at that level, it is forwarded to the regional headquarters. For difficult-to-get or out-of-print materials it may be necessary to contact another regional headquarters through the electronic teletype system. Finally, if none of the three regional headquarters (including the Boston Public Library) can comply, the request is handled by the Boston Public Library in its capacity as library of last resort for the State. In this role, the Boston Public Library utilizes the full extent of its considerable resources, often communicating with other libraries outside the State.

- Advisory and Consultative Service on Public Library Organization, Administration and Use. All three regions provide this service through its own consultants or through consultants requested from the Bureau of Library Extension.

- Bookmobile Service. To supplement the collections of local libraries, regions supply book deposits via bookmobile to towns with a population of less than 25,000. Bookmobiles providing this service to the Eastern Region operate out of Boston, Fall River, and North Reading, with a similar service planned for Cape Cod; to the Central Region, out of Worcester; and to the Western Region, out of Greenfield, Pittsfield, and Springfield.

- Film Service. All three regions make films available to libraries and community organizations without charge. Titles cover a wide range of subjects for all age groups.

- Publications, Newsletters and Reading Lists. These are supplied to all libraries for patrons of all age groups, suggesting good books on a variety of subjects.

- Workshops. The three regional headquarters hold a number of workshops in different parts of their regions throughout the year, as part of an extensive and well-received program of continuing education for librarians.

LIBRARY FUNDING

The Board of Library Commissioners, the Bureau of Library Extension, and library leaders throughout the State worked for many years to get a State Aid to Public Libraries law. With LSA as a catalyst, a law was enacted by the General Court in 1960 (and amended in 1963) authorizing a maximum of $1,287,459 annually for the establishment of a comprehensive statewide program of regional public library service, and $1,250,000 annually for direct grants to municipalities whose libraries meet certain minimum standards. Massachusetts uses its State-aid money as matching funds to qualify for LSCA allocations. Thus, the State-aid money, supplemented by LSCA funds, supports two major efforts in helping public libraries. Table M-1 shows the appropriations for State aid to regional public library systems and for direct grants to cities and towns during fiscal years 1965-1968.

Table M-2 shows the allocations of LSCA funds for the State for fiscal years 1965-1968. These funds continue to serve as a stimulus for State support of public libraries.

Table M-1. State Aid for Public Libraries*

Fiscal Year	State Aid Appropriation for Regional Public Library Systems	Direct Aid Grants to Cities and Towns for Public Library Services	Totals
1965	$ 612,857	$1,270,029	$1,882,886
1966	370,449**	1,276,641	1,647,090
1967	792,546	1,286,662	2,079,208
1968	1,287,458	1,295,272	2,582,730

*Source: Bureau of Library Extension, Massachusetts State Department of Education.

**The State Aid for Regional Public Library Systems is a fixed 25¢ per capita per annum. The reduced amount in 1966 would simply indicate that there was a carryover of excess funds from the 1965 year. The figure for 1968 would represent the first year of full funding for all three regional public library systems.

Table M-2. LSCA Title I Allotment for Massachusetts*

Fiscal Year	LSCA Allocations
1965	$658,637
1966	658,637
1967	940,815
1968	940,815

*Source: Regional Office, Region I, USOE.

When the 1960 public library support law was enacted, the source of funding was the State income tax. Revenue from this source constituted an illusory State aid for public libraries since local municipalities were not obligated to appropriate the funds locally for public library services. In 1963, the State Aid to Libraries Act of 1960 was amended so that the source of funds for the State grants to local cities and towns came from the general fund which monies the local municipalities were obligated to appropriate for public library services. Under this arrangement, Massachusetts had a true State aid to libraries law and State-appropriated funds were available to fully earn the LSA allocations. (It should be noted that the Board of Library Commissioners, the Director of the Bureau of Library Extension and her staff, and library leaders throughout the State had all recognized early the need for this amendment. It was not until the 1963 session of the General Court that their efforts were successful in effecting its passage.)

State grants-in-aid are given to libraries upon application and certification that the libraries meet certain minimum standards. Occasionally a library may receive a grant conditionally after filing a statement that one or more of the minimum standards will be reached within a specified period of time. Thus the Board and the Director of the Bureau are flexible and pragmatic in granting funds, for they are concerned with assisting local libraries in every way to meet standards and to extend services to the public. As a result of this adaptive approach, a number of libraries have increased the hours of service and raised professional standards for personnel.

III.   LSCA PROGRAM

OVERVIEW

In addition to being responsible for administration of Federal funds, the Bureau is required by law to take a leadership role in the development of programs to improve library services throughout the State. In conformance with its charter, the Bureau has:

- Developed and administered the State plan covering the standards and regulations for the program of State aid to public libraries, including direct grant payments to municipalities for local library service and reimbursement payments to the central and subregional libraries of the State's regional library systems.

- Developed and administered the State plan for the disbursement and expenditure of LSCA and other Federal funds allotted to Massachusetts.

- Administered legislation that provides for the certification of librarians.

- Provided supervision over a communication network between regional library systems.

- Maintained a placement referral service with an active registration file of both open positions and persons interested in library employment.

In administering the State grant-in-aid program and the several Federal library-support programs--including LSCA--the Bureau has defined project categories for allocation of the funds at its disposal. The project categories for the current (1969) fiscal year are as follows:

- Strengthening the Bureau of Library Extension

- Supervision and Support of Regional Public Library Systems

- Coordination of Statewide Program of Interlibrary Loan and Reference Service

- Education and Training of Library Personnel

- Special-Purpose Grants to Local Public Libraries

For activities and projects falling under these categories, each of the regions receives LSCA funds on the basis of expressed need, after submitting formal written requests or proposals to the Bureau.

IV.   DESCRIPTION OF REPRESENTATIVE USES OF LSCA FUNDS

The use of LSCA funds in Fiscal Year 1966 well illustrates the way in which the Bureau expends the Federal allotment in implementing the State plan.

On the statewide level, activities supported were as follows:

- Since the Boston Public Library has excellent resources and a competent staff, the Bureau has contracted, for several years past, to make these resources and personnel available to all of the State. In Fiscal Year 1966, an allotment of $125,000 was made to the Boston Public Library as reimbursement for expenses incurred in serving as the clearinghouse and library of last resort for interlibrary loans.

- An allotment of $130,186 was made to the Bureau so that the advisory and consultant services program could be strengthened. This has made it possible to add professional and supporting personnel to the Bureau staff. A portion of the allotment was also used to purchase needed materials and equipment; another portion to administer the State Plan for Construction under LSCA Title II; an allotment of $5,000 was made to begin an intersystem communication network between system headquarters libraries to expedite interlibrary loan requests; and a grant was made to Simmons College to cover the costs of planning, coordinating, and conducting a one-day institute on staffing the small library for library trustees.

On the regional level, the following activities were supported:

- An allotment of $185,449 was made to the Eastern Region to provide bookmobile service to rural towns in the northern area served by the State Regional Library Office at North Reading and in the southern area served by the State Regional Library Office at Fall River, and to provide money for book collection improvement to small towns serving less than 25,000 population, as well as to seven libraries planning to serve as regional reference or supplementary service centers. These grants were used primarily to strengthen reference collections in anticipation of the start of the Eastern Regional Public Library System service.

· An allotment of $114,000 was made to the Central Region to institute a new bookmobile service and to continue the already proven service by earmarking funds for personnel, books, materials, supplies, and equipment.

· An allotment of $105,000 was made to the Western Region to expand its established services. These funds were used for additional staffing; for book collection improvement grants to regional headquarters and subregional libraries; for purchase of equipment for the Greenfield subregional center; and for the renovation of, and purchase of equipment for, the regional bookmobile office at the Berkshire Athenaeum in Pittsfield.

V.   EVALUATION

PROGRAM STRENGTHS

The effect of LSA and LSCA funds on public library development in Massachusetts has been to arouse additional support and encourage passage of legislation for State aid to libraries. The 1960 law, together with the important amendments of 1963, was a direct result of the infusion of LSA funds; and since the enactment of LSCA in 1964, there have been notable increases in State and local support for public libraries. For example, many libraries have received substantial increases in local appropriations for book expenditures in recent years.

Under the present Director and with the present excellent staff support, the Bureau of Library Extension has done a very able job of implementing the State plan for extension of library services throughout the State. The Bureau has chosen to make LSCA allocations in such a way as to supplement existing efforts, rather than to launch new projects, undertake studies, or conduct pilot programs. In a State such as Massachusetts, which has a long history of public library service and a well-developed statewide library system, these allocations constitute an excellent usage of LSCA funds.

CONCLUSIONS

If the LSCA program in Massachusetts were to be discontinued, the State's public library program would undoubtedly suffer. That program would, however, continue with the support of State and local funds.

VI.   BIBLIOGRAPHY

Massachusetts State LSA and LSCA Title I annual plans, reports, and programs submitted to USOE during the period 1957-1968 (miscellaneous titles).

Arthur D. Little, Inc. Library Planning Study: Report to the Bureau of Library Extension, Department of Education, Commonwealth of Massachusetts. Cambridge, Mass., August 1967, 74 pp.

Beal, H. Marjorie; Fair, Ethel M.; and Merrill, Julia Wright. The Regional Library Experiment in Massachusetts in Relation to the Library Situation in the State. Report of a survey for the Massachusetts Board of Free Public Library Commissioners, Massachusetts Department of Education, Boston, Mass., 4-12 September 1944, 19 pp.

Commonwealth of Massachusetts, Department of Education. Annual Reports of the Board of Library Commissioners during the period June 30, 1956 - June 30, 1967, Mass.

Massachusetts Department of Education, Division of Library Extension. The Western Massachusetts Library Federation. 1954.

Verschoor, Irving A., and Bundy, Mary Lee. Regional Library Systems Development in Massachusetts: A Report of an Investigation With Recommendations. November 1963, 49 pp.

REGION II:

Delaware
New Jersey
NEW YORK
Pennsylvania

Eleanor T. Smith, Library
  Services Program Officer, AVLP
42 Broadway
New York, N.Y. 10004

CHAPTER VI
NEW YORK

I. SOURCES OF INFORMATION

The following organizations and persons were visited to obtain information for this study (see **Figure NY-1 for a map of the State**):

Date	Place Visited	Persons Visited
10/7/68	USOE Regional Office, Region II New York, New York	Mrs. Eleanor T. Smith, Library Services Program Officer Joseph Hendrick, Regional Assistant Commissioner
10/8/68	New York State Library Albany	Jean L. Connor, Director of the Division of Library Development
10/8/68		John Humphry, State Librarian and Assistant Commissioner for Libraries
10/8/68		Mason Tolman, **Director of the** State Library
10/9/68		Robert J. Flores, Chief, Bureau of Public Libraries Dorothy C. Smith, Associate, Bureau of Public Libraries
10/10/68	New York Public Library New York Countee Cullen Regional Branch	Edward G. Freehafer, Director Mrs. Jean O. Godfrey, Chief of Branch Libraries Wendell Wray, North Manhattan Project Virgil Broadbent, Regional Librarian
10/10/68	Queens **Borough** Public Library New York City	Elizabeth Campanis, Chief of Extension Services Harold W. Tucker, Director
10/10/68	Brooklyn Public Library New York City	John C. Frantz, Director Philip Adam, Executive Assistant to the Director

Date	Place Visited	Persons Visited
10/11/68	Pioneer Library System Rochester	Harold S. Hacker, Director, and Head of Monroe County Library System and Head of Rochester Public Library Mrs. Madelene Wenkert, In-Service Training Librarian Mrs. Kathryn Adams, Nonusers Program Librarian
10/21/68	Buffalo and Erie County Library Buffalo	Joseph B. Rounds, Director Winifred K. Harper, Deputy Director, Circulation Paul M. Rooney, Deputy Director, Reference William A. Miles, Coordinator, Inner City Project Mrs. Nina T. Cohen, RRR Coordinator
10/21/68	New York Public Library New York City Mott Haven Branch	Louise Lopez, Administrator, South Bronx Project Gerald Gold, Coordinator, Bronx Branch Libraries
10/21/68	Southern Adirondack Library System Saratoga Springs	Florence E. Harshe, Director
10/21/68	Upper Hudson Library System Albany	Edgar Tompkins, Director Robert Omer, Audiovisual Consultant
10/22/68	Brooklyn Public Library New York City	Mrs. Bessie Bullock, Bushwick Community Coordinator
10/22/68	Queens Borough Public Library New York City	John Solomita, Executive Director for Personnel and Management Analysis
10/22/68	Chautauqua-Cattaraugus Library System Jamestown	Maureen Curry, Assistant Director

Date	Place Visited	Persons Visited
10/22/68	Queens Borough Public Library New York City	Mrs. Elizabeth Merkelson, Head, Library-Go-Round Project Mildred L. Hennesey, Deputy Director
10/22/68	Mid-York Library System Utica	Alfred C. Hasemeir, Director
10/22/68	Mohawk Valley Library System Rotterdam	Juliette Bryson, Deputy Director
10/23/68	Nassau Library System Hempstead	Andrew Geddes, Director Mrs. Dinah Lindauer, Coordinator of Programs and Services
10/23/68	Chemung-Southern Tier Library System Chemung System Headquarters Corning	Herbert L. Leet, Director
10/23/68	Chemung-Southern Tier Library System Southern Tier Headquarters Elmira	Kenneth R. Fielding, Jr., Assistant Director Phyllis Morse, Catalog and Ordering
10/23/68	Finger Lakes Library System Ithaca	William T. Weitzel, Director Gertrude L. Laird, Assistant Director
10/23/68	New York City University School of Education New York City	Dr. Virgil Clift, Research Staff
10/23/68	North Country Library System Watertown	Ronald L. Roberts, Director Glenn S. Mallison, Head of Advisory Services
10/24/68	Four County Library System Binghamton	Marcus A. Wright, Director Raymond W. Smith, Assistant Director

Date

| 10/24/68 | Westchester Library System Mount Vernon | Loretta M. Winkler, Assistant Director |
| 10/25/68 | Ramapo-Catskill Library System Middletown | Mrs. Eleanor C. Harris, Director |

Much valuable information was also obtained from the publications listed in the Bibliography, Section VI of this chapter.

II.   BACKGROUND FOR LSCA OPERATIONS

THE STATE AGENCY

The State agency responsible for administering LSCA funds in New York is the State Education Department, headed by James E. Allen, Jr., Commissioner of Education and President of the University of the State of New York; actual administration of LSCA has been delegated to Jean L. Connor, Director, the Division of Library Development (DLD). Figure NY-2 shows the organizational placement of Miss Connor's office. John A. Humphry, the Assistant Commissioner for Libraries and Miss Connor's immediate supervisor, maintains a close awareness of LSCA disbursements, but his responsibilities go beyond LSCA.

Management of LSCA funds and projects is one of Miss Connor's several responsibilities as Director of the DLD. In this task, she and her staff are guided by an LSCA Advisory Committee, which includes an Advisory Committee to the Board of Regents as a subgroup. On the LSCA Advisory Committee are some of the State's most prominent librarians, as well as lay representatives.

HISTORY OF STATE AID TO NEW YORK LIBRARIES

In New York State, as in a number of other States, there is a heavy reliance on library systems to ensure satisfactory library services for the maximum number of citizens. The first important legislation in this direction was the State Aid and Systems Law of 1950, which provided some incentives for the formation of library systems. The incentives, however, proved insufficient to attract the larger libraries, without which the systems had little real strength. The law further proved to be an obstacle for rural areas in that it required any county system to be approved by the County Supervisors as well as by almost all of the county libraries. Agreement of so many individuals upon a single course of action proved difficult to obtain, particularly where multicounty systems were needed.

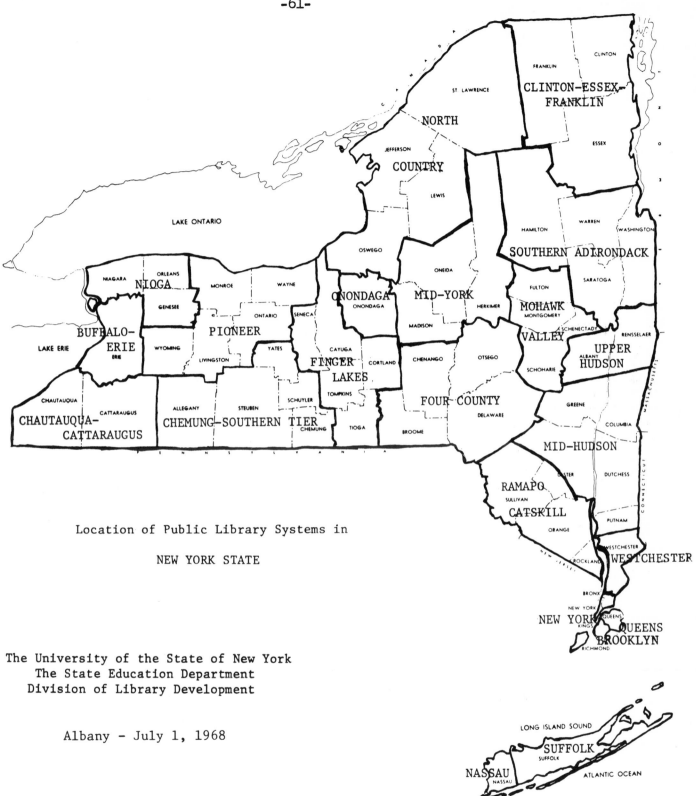

Location of Public Library Systems in

NEW YORK STATE

The University of the State of New York
The State Education Department
Division of Library Development

Albany - July 1, 1968

Figure NY-1.   Location of Public Library
Systems in New York State

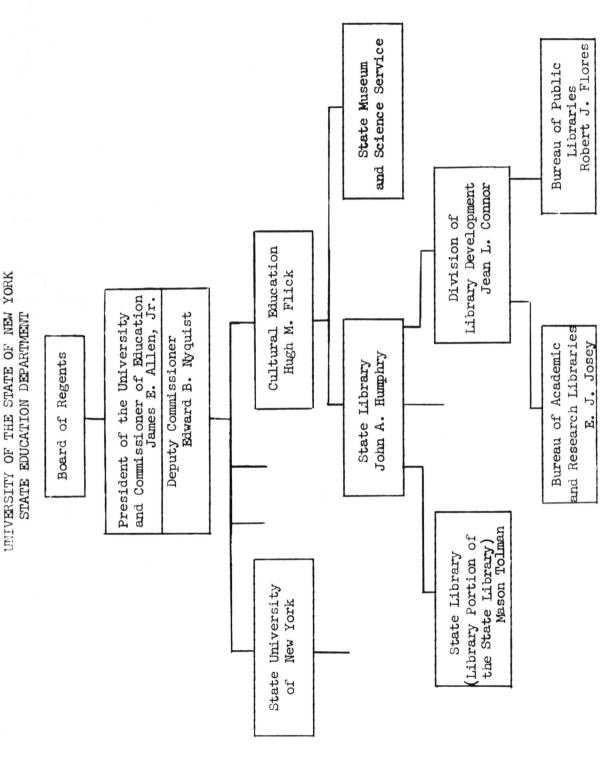

Figure NY-2. Partial Organization Chart, New York State Education Department

Subsequent legislation in 1958 was aimed at attracting large libraries into the systems and facilitating the formation of systems that would benefit rural areas. Three types of library systems were defined as qualifying for State Aid: the consolidated system (found in large cities which had an existing central library with branches, controlled by a single administrator and a single library board), the federated system (established on a county basis by action of a county board of supervisors), and the cooperative system (established by direct action of independent local libraries). Appropriations have been impressive in comparison with funding in the other States visited: In Fiscal Year 1967, grants-in-aid (exclusive of Federal funds) totalled $13,325,000[1]; in Fiscal Year 1968 they amounted to $14,200,000. The appropriation for Fiscal Year 1969 is expected to reach $15,000,000.

RELATIONSHIP OF STATE AGENCY TO OTHER ORGANIZATIONS

New York Library Association

The New York Library Association, a statewide professional society, has played an important role in library development. Working with the State Education Department's State Library personnel, they have sought to influence decisions affecting libraries. Another active body has been the Library Trustee Foundation. The large amount of support that the public libraries in New York State receive from the State government is partially due to these parallel efforts.

LIBRARY FUNDING

New York State provides the matching funds required for LSCA entirely from the State-aid money appropriated by the legislature; none of the local monies used for library support are identified to USOE as matching funds. As indicated by Table NY-1, the State-aid funds are far greater than the funding from the Federal government, while local monies far surpass the total of State and Federal funds.

---

[1]See Table NY-1.

Table NY-1. Comparison of Income from Various Governmental
Sources for Public Library Services, 1964-1967

LOCAL TAX MONIES[a]

1964	$53,591,992[b]
1965	46,888,123
1966	49,770,295

STATE-AID APPROPRIATION

1964-65	$10,200,000
1965-66	10,200,000
1966-67	13,325,000

LSCA APPROPRIATION, TITLE I

1964-65	$1,942,725[c]
1965-66	1,932,585[c]
1966-67	2,840,719

[a]Part of these monies may be transferred into capital fund
for capital expenditures; it is not possible to determine
specific amounts from printed statistics.

[b]This figure includes approximately $11,000,000 for construction
of Buffalo and Erie County Public Library.

[c]Originally an equal amount was allotted for the two fiscal
years. However, the amount of reallotment for 1965-66 was
less than for 1964-65.

III.   LSCA PROGRAM

OVERVIEW OF ACTIVITIES

Current New York State aid to libraries covers most of the conventional
library services, and indeed many of the activities that in less wealthy
states are funded from LSCA monies. New York State has established ten
well-defined sets of objectives for the LSCA program. All the work done
in furtherance of a single set of these objectives is referred to by the
DLD as a project. A small percentage of the monies is used for augmenting
The State's audiovisual services, a somewhat larger amount for program
administration and for providing consulting services to local libraries;
but the bulk of LSCA money is used for grants to library systems for
conducting a variety of projects. Having a wide range of such projects
among which to choose, the library systems are better enabled to meet the
widely differing_ needs of urban and rural, affluent and disadvantaged
communities.

The New York State Plan, describing these projects, is prepared in advance
for each fiscal year by the Division of Library Development and submitted
to all library system headquarters in the State as a guide in preparing
their own proposals for LSCA grants. The plan also contains information
about duration of funding and about which projects are acceptable only in
the event sufficient LSCA monies are received by the State. For example,
the New York State Plan, 1967-68, summarized below, lists 10 projects.
The first eight are funded entirely by LSCA; libraries may choose among
these in requesting LSCA funds. Project IX derives most of its support
from State funds. Project X is the State's own grant-in-aid program.

    PROJECT OBJECTIVES, SUMMARIZED[2]

    I.   EXTENSION

          To extend public library service to those without convenient
          access to a library outlet.

    II.   REFERENCE SERVICE

          To improve the informational and reference services of public
          library systems.

    III. DISADVANTAGED

          To promote outreach of the public library to the disadvantaged,
          the deprived, minority groups.

---

[2]New York State Plan under the Services Title, Federal Library Services and
Construction Act for 1967-1968. Library Development Division of the New York
State Library. Albany, 1966, pp. 6-7.

IV.   INTERSYSTEM EXPERIMENTAL PROGRAMS AND PLANNING TO MEET READER NEEDS

To encourage planning, studies and intersystem experimentation which will assist in the development and evaluation of library service programs in relation to reader needs.

V.   COOPERATION TO MEET STUDENT NEEDS

To promote the coordination of all types of libraries, with the particular objective of meeting the needs of students of all ages through programs of cooperative action.

VI.   PERSONNEL, LEADERSHIP, EDUCATION

To assist in the development of adequate personnel for library service and leadership, including professional and non-professional staff and trustees.

VII.   AUDIOVISUAL RESOURCES

To promote the provision of programs utilizing non-book resources and the newer educational media as a part of total library services.

VIII.   TECHNICAL SERVICES

To assist and promote the establishment of a statewide acquisition and cataloging center and relating processing centers to serve public library systems, by contract with the Association of New York Libraries for Technical Services.

IX.   STATE LIBRARY AND EXTENSION AGENCY

To strengthen the State Library's general reference and consultant services so that the agency may more adequately backstop the public library systems and assist in statewide library development.

(State aid)

X.   PUBLIC LIBRARY SYSTEMS

To strengthen public library services by State grants-in-aid under Education Law 272-273 to public library systems. (This is the existing matching project which will qualify N.Y. for federal funds by the expenditure of State funds at the 13 million dollar level.)

These summary statements are amplified in the New York State Plan to aid the systems in understanding what proposals the State will entertain and what is beyond the State's interpretation of the summary. The following pages, from the same source, provide the amplification of Project I (Extension).

Project I - __EXTENSION__[3]

To extend public library service to those without convenient access to a library outlet.

1. __Specific Grants and Services__ - Offered to systems.

1.1 __Bookmobiles - Initiation of Service Grants__

If a system wishes to establish bookmobile service for the first time in an area, or to extend coverage substantially in an area now served by a bookmobile, it may apply for a bookmobile service grant not to exceed $40,000. The vehicle purchased must be an addition to existing equipment and services; it cannot be a replacement of an existing vehicle. If the system already has bookmobile service, the system must show how the grant will expand such service by showing existing and proposed schedules. Professional staffing is required.

First preference will be given to systems which have not had a bookmobile demonstration grant.

Intersystem planning is encouraged in utilization of book-mobiles.

1.2 __New Libraries or Reorganization of Libraries - Establishment Grants for Books__

1.2.1 Establishment grants to encourage the organization, where needed, of new public libraries in communities of sufficient population to support a local public library. Require minimum population (5000), minimum level of tax support and library system membership. On a matching basis.

1.2.2 Establishment grants to encourage the reorganization, where desirable, of existing libraries. Require minimum population, minimum level of tax support and library system membership. On a matching basis.

---

[3]Op. cit., p. 8-9.

1.3 <u>Libraries in New or Enlarged Quarters - Improvement Grants for Books</u>

Grants for purchase of books to expand and strengthen book collections in libraries that have substantially improved their physical facilities. Maximum population served 15,000. Require library system membership and minimum standards of local support, hours of service, personnel and building.

2. <u>System Projects</u> - Systems may initiate plans and budget requests for projects such as:

2.1 <u>Studies</u>

2.1.1 Grants for studies relating to costs and adequacy in extension of service from a library to an unserved area by contract.

2.1.2 Grants for studies, on a systemwide or intersystem basis, to determine area needs for additional library outlets, to analyze alternatives in organizing for such service, method of finance, etc.

2.2 <u>Other</u>

Applications by systems for grants for other projects which fit the major objective of Project I will be considered.

Since the State's continuing aid to library systems provides long-term support that the system libraries can depend upon, New York originally chose to limit the duration of any specific LSCA project in a given library or system. These projects aim either to accomplish something almost immediately or to demonstrate programs for the purpose of finding local support. The original guidelines allowed for a possible second year's extension. By now, third-year extensions are possible, but they are limited in number. Severe restrictions are placed upon fourth-year and fifth-year extensions.

New York's original goal in limiting the duration of projects was twofold:

• Since Federal money was available under an act that had a terminal date, the State agency wished to avoid having any library become dependent upon this support.

• Since only limited monies are available, the State agency hoped to reserve funds for initiation of new projects.

ALLOCATION OF LSCA TITLE I FUNDS

Division of Library Development allocations for Projects I through VIII
are entirely from LSCA Title I money; for Project IX, State and Federal
funds are mingled; and Project X allocations are entirely from State
monies. The systems are called upon in some types of projects to match
some part of the Federal funding. This matching may either be explicit,
in the form of an equal amount of money spent, or it may be implicit, as
in the case of a large-print project, where LSCA funds might pay for the
books but not for the personnel.

As can be seen from Table NY-2, very little LSCA money--approximately 2 to
5 percent--goes into augmenting the holdings of the State Library, and all
of this is for the provision of audiovisual resources available to the
public library systems. A larger amount of money is retained by the State
for purposes of either administering LSCA monies or for strengthening State
services such as consultant services that are outward oriented. The second
category also includes projects performed by outside groups as an aid to
the State in managing LSCA funds. The largest amount of money is for grants.

Table NY-3 shows the expenditure of money by project in Fiscal Years 1965,
1966, 1967. Projects for the disadvantaged have the highest priority of
system-initiated projects. The large amount of money shown for the State
Library Extension Agency is mainly supplied out of State money rather than
LSCA money. The major change in priority is shown by a decrease in the
money for Project V, Cooperation to Meet Student Needs. Other projects
maintain roughly the same relative priority.

Table NY-2. Allocation of LSCA Funds

Category of Allocation	Year	Percent
1. Strengthening the State's Own Collection	1964 - 65	5%
	1965 - 66	2%
	1966 - 67	4%
2. State Consultant Services and State Administration of LSCA Title I	1964 - 65	26%
	1965 - 66	19%
	1966 - 67	18%
3. Grants to Library Systems	1964 - 65	69%
	1965 - 66	79%
	1966 - 67	78%

Table NY-3. Expenditure by Project for Fiscal
Years 1965, 1966, and 1967

Project (Number of Title)	Fiscal Year 1965 Total Funds	Fiscal Year 1966 Total Funds	Fiscal Year 1967 Total Funds
I. Extension	139,071	145,600	219,379
II.A Reference Service	138,950	247,488	244,469
II.B Advance Reference	78,500	119,000	116,530
III. Disadvantaged	582,493	586,791	790,775
IV. Meeting Reader Needs	252,370	329,805	233,875
V. Co-op. to Meet Student Needs	277,898	105,500	63,832
VI. Personnel Leadership Education	163,033	194,260	144,067
VII. Audiovisual Resources	176,845	296,062	303,175
VIII. Administration of Constr.[a]	37,200	35,920	3,075
IX. State Library & Extension[b] Agency	1,230,989	1,775,205	1,036,268
X. Public Library Systems (State Aid)	10,200,000	10,200,000	13,325,000
TOTALS	13,277,349	14,035,591	16,443,135
1. State	11,356,426*	12,103,006	14,171,813
2. Local[c]	None	None	None
3. Federal	1,920,923	1,932,585	2,271,322
TOTAL	13,277,349*	14,035,591	16,443,135

*Includes $176,137 earned and received in Fiscal Year 1965.

[a]The title of Project VIII was changed to Technical Services in Fiscal Year 1968. (Change in definition of construction administration in 1967 meant these costs are now largely borne from Title II monies.

[b]$74,563 was Federal money in Fiscal Year 1965, $145,600 in Fiscal Year 1966, and $149,455 in Fiscal Year 1967, if one assumes that the difference between State aid and State money goes into Category IX.

[c]No local money is shown on New York State summary forms, though it is often shown on individual reports, thus local contributions out of State aid cannot be reported twice.

Selection of Projects for LSCA Funding

Initial determination of projects for funding is made by the State agency entirely on the basis of proposals submitted by the 22 systems, following the guidelines laid out in the State plan. These proposals are evaluated by the Division of Library Development with the assistance of both technical specialists who are knowledgeable about the proposed activities and consultants who are familiar with the various regions. If a project appears worthwhile but the proposal itself does not meet the State's standards, the agency will aid the system staff in preparing an acceptable submission.

In evaluating requests for renewals or extensions of grants, the agency considers not only the proposal but also the system's progress reports to the Division, as well as the agency field worker's reports.

Of the library systems visited by the study team, most have had all, or nearly all, of their proposals approved by the State agency, although the agency often grants a smaller amount of money than requested. Occasionally the agency will stipulate that the system contribute a portion of the proposed funding. The Division of Library Development also reserves the power not to renew the funding of a project if it appears to have lost its value.

REPORTING AND EVALUATION PROCEDURES OF STATE AGENCY

The agency requires semiannual progress reports from all recipients of State aid and LSCA monies. Some of these are brief--for example, reports on the administration of small grants for projects requiring little investigative work. Other reports, such as those on the cadet programs or the programs for disadvantaged, are much longer and more detailed. The systems headquarters visited also kept detailed logs on many of their projects. Some activities involve as the final task, a written summary report to the State. These interim and final reports are used by the agency as aids in the management of LSCA projects and funds.

Field workers' reports are also important in the administration and evaluation of LSCA projects. In addition the State agency uses outside consultants to help in assessing the programs; for example, Bank Street College was retained to evaluate and report on the projects for the disadvantaged in the three New York City systems. A group at New York University has been given a similar assignment for the disadvantaged projects upstate. Other consultants are employed to advise the State about such topics as mechanization of libraries and the implementation of the State's audiovisual program.

IV.   DESCRIPTION OF REPRESENTATIVE USES OF LSCA FUNDS

Figure NY-1 (p.61) shows a map of the New York State Library Systems. SDC
personnel visited 17 of the 22 systems. The systems that were not visited
are: Clinton-Essex-Franklin, Onandaga, Nioga, Mid-Hudson, and Suffolk. As
a result of these visits, and with the documentation provided by the Division
of Library Development, the study team was able to get a picture of how
money is spent in each of the eight categories now available for LSCA
funding.

PROJECT I: EXTENSION

Five different types of projects have been granted to individual library
systems under this heading. One type is bookmobile demonstration. Grants
for this purpose have been made to a number of systems to take care of some
of the areas surrounding the communities having established libraries. Of
those visited, Nassau Library System, North Country Library System and
Chautauqua-Cattaraugus System were recipients of such demonstrations. It
is expected that support from the counties will enable the systems to carry
on this service at the termination of the demonstration period.

A second type of grant has been for a book trailer. Such a grant was made
to the Chemung-Southern Tier System where two communities (Big Flats and
Prattsburg) had outgrown the services of small stations or bookmobiles,
but were not able yet to support chartered libraries.

A third category is the establishment grant. These grants, which require
local matching funds, are for books for newly chartered libraries. They
accomplish the dual purpose of providing capital funds for rapid book
collection and acquisition, and encouraging the establishment of new
libraries where acceptable State standards can be met by the community.
Such grants have been made to Island Trees, Mount Pleasant, Mechanicville,
and Port Jefferson Station-Terryville Public Library. Island Trees had
previously had a bookmobile demonstration--the one mentioned for Nassau
County.

A fourth Extension project is an outright grant for the purchase of a bookmobile for continuing regional service, as distinguished from a bookmobile
demonstration. Such grants have been made to the Chemung-Southern Tier,
Mid-York, Chautauqua-Cattaraugus, and Onandaga Systems.

The last item under Extension is surveys. One survey was performed by
Nassau County to discover the effects of saturation library service when
tendered to adults. Another was performed at Nioga to determine what
emphasis should be placed on extension services rendered by bookmobile
reference services.

PROJECT II: REFERENCE SERVICE

In the past, two types of reference project are listed by the New York State
Plan. Project II-A, Reference Services, has as its purpose to improve
regional reference and information services in public library systems.

These projects are designed to assist the rapid development of resources and personnel. Since 1965, grants have been made for the provision of adequate professional and supporting clerical staff for reference service in the central libraries. Grants have also been made for the acquisition of reference materials. Surveys of use patterns have also been conducted both by the Queens Borough Public Library and by the Ramapo-Catskill Public Library.

Project II-B is Cooperative Programs for Advanced Reference Services. The purpose of this project is to plan, promote and provide for advanced reference and information resources through cooperative programs involving all types of libraries to meet user needs which cannot be fully met through the existing public library system network. In Fiscal Year 1968, 16 systems and their central libraries were benefiting under this program. All 21 systems outside the city of Albany have TWX connections. Project II-B funds are intended to ensure the coordination of the public library advanced reference services with projects under the New York State's Reference and Research Library Resources (3-R) Program. Under the 3-R programs, nine Reference and Research Library Resource Systems have been formed; these are superimposed upon the 22 library systems. The LSCA teletype service is supplemented by a statewide experiment in coordinated, reimbursed, inter-library loans, with the New York State Library serving as a clearinghouse and referral center. This interlibrary loan system (NYSIIL) is financed through State funds. The State Library has entered into contract with three large public libraries and eight major research libraries to lend support to a program of compensated interlibrary loan. The heaviest users of this loan network are the State's public library systems. All of the 22 library systems are involved in the statewide interlibrary loan program.

PROJECT III: DISADVANTAGED

This project has as its purpose the promotion of "outreach of the public library to the disadvantaged, the deprived minority groups." It has received the single greatest amount of Federal money of any of the eight projects for which New York State makes LSCA grants.

· Brooklyn

   Brooklyn's Community Coordinator Project, a pilot project in the Bedford-Stuyvesant community, was started in March of 1961 under the direction of Hardy Franklin. This experimental program works with Federal projects, State and city programs, community and social service organizations to inform the population of library resources. Under LSCA, Brooklyn has been able to expand the program so that there is now a community coordinator for each of four Brooklyn areas with comparable problems: they have a considerable number of high school dropouts, cultural illiteracy is prevalent, and earning power is limited.

The study team was taken through the Bushwick area by one of the community coordinators, Mrs. Bessie Bullock. Mrs. Bullock, like all of the community coordinators, is from the Brooklyn Public Library professional staff. Though she has an office at the library and is aided by two assistants, she spends her time working with the different groups in the community, "hawking" the library. In addition, the staff is experimenting with a "3-B" program (bars, beauty shops, barber shops) in an attempt to place some of the library paperback holdings in such places, advertising the library to people who are not reached by service agencies.

The project has conducted experiments with the attractiveness of large-print books to those not confident of their literacy. In general, however, this program, like many of the other disadvantaged programs, is reaching out to those who are not functionally but culturally illiterate.

In addition to its Community Coordinator Project, Brooklyn has a program for disadvantaged preschool children that is designed to present specially designed programs in day-care centers, pre-kindergartens, and branch libraries. The programs are intended to acquaint the children with books and reading for their own pleasure and enrichment, and to assist them in becoming socially prepared for a formal learning experience in school.

· Queens

Queens has a project entitled Operation Head Start. (The Queens Borough Public Library chose that name long before the more famous Operation Head Start began.) Queen's Head Start project was attempted some years ago, but funding could not be obtained; implementation had to wait until LSCA monies were available.

Operation Head Start is a program for preschoolers that is under way in 10 branches in the economically more disadvantaged areas. Aimed at three-to-five year-olds from bookless homes, the program is dependent upon the parents' having enough interest to bring children to the library (where a concurrent parent program is held).

In order to extend the reach of the library to children whose parents are either not around or not motivated to bring to the library, a parallel program, the Library-Go-Round, has been initiated. The Library-Go-Round travels to different areas, where stories are told to children in a library-owned van.

- Chemung Southern Tier Library System

In Elmira, where the Steele Memorial Library is located, a small program for the disadvantaged was started in 1967. Known as the Eastside project, it was funded in the amount of $14,655 and resulted in an experimental expansion of bookmobile service to include evening and Saturday special bookmobile runs and stops within three Negro wards in the older section of the community. Project Eastside marked the first attempt of any library within this five-county area to reach this type of audience.

- Westchester

The Westchester Library System Project has concentrated on assisting member libraries in cooperating with local Community Action and other antipoverty programs and on stimulating and encouraging libraries to initiate library-sponsored programs for the culturally deprived. Grants to libraries enable them to purchase library materials to deposit in Community Action centers.

- Pioneer Library System

The project in the Pioneer Library System, now completed, was concerned with effecting changes in the attitude of the regular library personnel towards what is now considered a regular and normal part of the library's clientele. The project staff investigated the needs of the disadvantaged and worked to design programs to meet these needs. Some of the library activities carried on were the selection, acquisition, and promotion of high-interest, easy-to-read books, the development of collections for use in community agencies, additional story hours and film programs in inner-city branches, and special projects for minority ethnic groups. Branch and town libraries developed outreach programs in their service areas.

- New York Public Library: North Manhattan Project

The North Manhattan Project is intended to demonstrate the value of intensive library service to all age groups in the northern third of Manhattan, with particular attention to Harlem. Project headquarters are at the Countee Cullen Branch on 136th Street in Harlem; the director is Wendell Wray, a professional librarian

who was formerly in charge of the Schomburg Collection at Countee
Cullen. During the 1930's this branch library was the site of a
program conducted with WPA funds. This earlier effort was far
more extensive than the present project: At its peak there were
over 50 WPA workers, while the North Manhattan program has had a
maximum staffing of 16. The WPA project, directed toward a
population that used the library of its own accord, was so
successful that the same location was chosen for the present
program when LSCA funds became available.

The North Manhattan Project works to expand services for regular
users and to develop and utilize techniques to attract nonusers.
Community liaison personnel are used to reach the neighborhood
audience and draw them to the library for guided tours. In the
year before the project was initiated there were 6,000 such visitors;
during the first year of the demonstration there were 16,000 and in
the second year 32,000.

- New York Public Library: Schomburg Collection

At the Countee Cullen Library, the site of the North Manhattan
Project, a Carnegie building is used to house the Schomburg
Collection, donated by a Puerto Rican Negro named Schomburg.
Schomburg had been told that there were no books on Negro history.
He discovered and acquired books on this subject and at his death
left a collection of 4,000 volumes to the New York Public Library.
The collection now has 40,000 volumes in it. Although LSCA money
has been granted to augment this collection as part of the Disadvantaged project, the collection itself can hardly be considered a
collection for the disadvantaged. It is, rather, a fine research
collection of materials and exhibits, fostering pride in the
cultural heritage of the Negro. The collection has been enriched
by the acquisition of 2,822 books, 103 phonograph records, 184
tapes, 2,000 photographs, and 216 boxes of archival papers
purchased with LSCA funds.

- New York Public Library: South Bronx Project

The New York Public Library has a project in the South Bronx that
is directed towards the predominantly Spanish-speaking community in
that area. The South Bronx Project provides Spanish-English-
speaking staffs for eight branch libraries. The design of the
Spanish-language project was aided by experience gained from the
North Manhattan Project, which highlighted the necessity of
acquainting people with library services and attracting users.
Spanish-language books and simple books in English have been
purchased, group activities have been conducted, and the project
staff has established contact with community organizations.

There has been a great deal of difficulty in obtaining Spanish-language books written at an appropriate level. The most important aspects of the project, however, have centered around community liaison. The community liaison person typically goes into the community, from house to house, introducing himself as a representative of the public library, explaining (in Spanish or English) what the libraries offer--what equipment is available, what kinds of services can be requested and obtained. He encourages the people to register (to receive library service information), to visit the libraries, to request, read and take out books.

- Buffalo and Erie County

The major Federally funded activity for the disadvantaged is Project LEAP, in Buffalo, coordinated by William A. Miles. Begun in 1965 as a one-year pilot project, LEAP was conceived as an inner-city program with some features that extended out into the county. It is being continued at present as a full-fledged inner-city project which employs a variety of approaches to provide meaningful service to this community. In an attempt to reach various age groups including preschool children, training programs have been initiated for young people on probation or parole, mothers of young children, and civil service applicants. A program of Black history has been undertaken. A small staff of "detached librarians" using an audiovisual-equipped van circulates on a "go-where-the-action-is" basis. They have also utilized the 3-B noncirculating paperback reference concept.

- Nassau

The Disadvantaged project of the Nassau Library System (now completed) attempted to secure adequate data on who are the disadvantaged in Nassau County, what agencies provide what types of programs for these people, what are the possible relationships between the library and other agencies' activities, and what implications there are for libraries in legislation enacted or proposed on all levels of government. The project has worked in four selected areas in Nassau County. A small permanent library was created to stock the materials requested most frequently for the disadvantaged. All librarians in the county were given in-service training for working with the disadvantaged.

- Additional Disadvantaged Projects

In addition to the projects mentioned above, the SDC team learned of the proposed Queens Borough Public Library projects for disadvantaged persons in the Corona-Elmhurst section. We also encountered frequent referral to the Bank Street College Study performed to evaluate the Disadvantaged projects in the New York City area. In addition, we visited the project at New York University that will attempt an evaluation of the Disadvantaged projects upstate.

PROJECT IV: INTERSYSTEM EXPERIMENTAL PROGRAMS AND PLANNING TO MEET
READER NEEDS

This project's purpose is to encourage planning, studies, and intersystem
experimentation which will assist in the development and evaluation of
library service programs in their relation to users' needs.

The New York Public Library has had a project to test and evaluate the
needs for, interest in, and use of large-print books (in 18-point type)
for readers with severe sight limitations. The LSCA portion of this
project has been completed. Circulation of large-print books continues
to increase. Major bibliographies have been published and there is a
growing number of large-print books available.

A private-line intracity teletype network (connecting the Brooklyn and
Queens systems and the New York Public Library) was funded to improve
interlibrary loan service in New York City, and to make the resources of
the three city systems more readily accessible to the statewide exchange
service network.

Three library systems (Four-County, Finger Lakes, and Chemung-Southern
Tier) have had a joint public relations program. The so-called
Metropolitan Systems (Westchester, Brooklyn, Nassau, New York, and Queens)
have also had a public relations program, now expanded to include all of
New York State. This program has made extensive use of spot announcements
on radio and television. Both the Four-County and the Chemung-Southern
Tier Systems have taken advantage of this project to conduct studies of
use patterns in an attempt to provide improved services.

A number of other small grants have been made under Project IV: Suffolk
County received funding for mechanization of technical processes in the
early years of LSCA before the new Project VIII was available. The Ramapo-
Catskill System received a grant to contract with Suffolk County for centralized processing. Nassau County has received monies to prepare book lists for
young adults. Both the Upper Hudson and the Mid-York Systems have had
surveys of service programs and other central library programs, conducted
by R. St. John.

The Division of Library Development has made LSCA grants available to
smaller libraries to hire qualified consultants.

The federated Chemung-Southern Tier Library System has had some unresolved
organizational problems, including questions about the role of the central
library, the structure of system administration, and the location of
Southern Tier's headquarters. To obtain an objective appraisal, and to help
project the central library's building needs, Hoyt Galvin and Frank Sessa
were commissioned to conduct a study of the five-county complex and make
recommendations.

PROJECT V: COOPERATION TO MEET STUDENT NEEDS

This project aims to promote the coordination of all types of libraries,
with the particular objective of meeting the needs of students of all
ages through programs of cooperative action. Several public library
systems have received grants under this project title.

- Nassau

  The Nassau Library System had a three-year project to plan and
  test coordinated programs and to expand and make available
  selected system services directly to school libraries and
  school library personnel.

- Nioga

  The Nioga Library System had a four-year project to increase use by
  students and teachers of public library services. Planning for
  coordination of LSCA and ESEA funds was stressed.

- Onondaga

  The purpose of the Onondaga Library System Project was to upgrade
  the quality of the Young Adult book collections in Onondaga County.

- Westchester

  The Westchester Library System extended its paperback project to
  provide duplicate titles in the subject areas most in demand for
  student research purposes and to introduce more libraries to the
  use of paperbacks.

- Mid-York

  Just as Project III has seen interaction with other Federal programs,
  such as those under OEO, Project V has seen cooperation between LSCA
  programs and ESEA (Elementary and Secondary Education Act), Title II
  programs.

  Funds were granted to the Mid-York Library System to hire a school-
  public library coordinator to do advanced planning aimed at developing
  into a plan which could be worked out with school personnel participation in the hope of involving ESEA funds.

PROJECT VI: PERSONNEL, LEADERSHIP, EDUCATION

This project offers assistance in the development of personnel, library
service, and leadership--professional, nonprofessional, and trustee.
Among the different types of projects sponsored under Project VI have been
conferences, studies, training grants, in-service training, and recruitment.

We will not attempt in this report to describe the many projects funded under Project VI. Three projects, however, conducted in the Pioneer Library System, are worth particular mention. The first is a Cadet Program, which takes college juniors and brings them into the library for the summer as cadets. They are exposed to various professional aspects of librarianship, with the hope that when they return to school they will choose librarianship as their fifth-year program. The program has met with sufficient success thus far to justify continuation.

Another Pioneer System project is a second-career program, which had the distinct purpose of bringing women into the library who feel that they have completed their full-time functions at home.

The third project at Pioneer is an in-service training program. This has as its purpose the creation of courses that will allow the many libraries in the system to continue to keep their professional and non-professional staffs trained in modern methods of librarianship.

PROJECT VII: AUDIOVISUAL RESOURCES

The purpose of this project is to promote programs utilizing nonbook resources. The project is concerned with the modern media that will become part of the holdings of libraries. The auxiliary Services Section in the Division of Library Development continues to acquire and supply films, phonograph records, slides and film strips. As this resource increases, use increases. The State audiovisual consultant presents workshops for the different library systems throughout the State.

The Division of Library Development provides scholarships for the audiovisual staff of the individual systems. Grants have been given to at least 15 different systems within the State for the development of central film resources, for renovation of present film resources, or for additional projectors.

PROJECT VIII: TECHNICAL SERVICES

In 1966, the Division of Library Development commissioned a survey by Nelson Associates, Inc.,[4] which recommended the establishment of one centralized acquisition and cataloging center to serve the public libraries of New York State, and the centralization of processing facilities. Discussion stemming from these recommendations led to the chartering of a new educational corporation, the Association of New York Libraries for Technical Services (ANYLTS). To assist with this, a new project was written into New York's Title I plan in Fiscal Year 1968. During that year, the trustees received and reviewed a further study.[5] All ANYLTS activity had been coordinated with the automation program of the State Library and the New York Public Library research facilities.

[4]Centralized Processing for the Public Libraries of New York State. Nelson Associates, Inc. New York, 1966, 156 pp.

[5]Implementing Centralized Processing for the Public Libraries of New York State. New York, November 1967, 35 pp.

V.   EVALUATION

PROGRAM STRENGTHS

The New York State Library has chosen a policy for the management of
LSCA Title I funds that takes account of past progress in obtaining
financial support for public libraries in the State.   The citizens
of the State have provided:

1. A State-aid program that began 14 years before the passage of
   LSCA and that anticipated the LSCA goals of extending public
   library services to areas without such services or with
   inadequate services.

2. Local tax support and endowments for the libraries of the
   major cities, permitting these libraries to become some of
   the best public libraries in the world.

3. Local and State tax support that is very large compared to the
   amount of LSCA Title I funds allotted to the State.

The State Library's policy for the management of LSCA Title I funds thus
contains the following three desirable features:

1. Projects that strengthen the libraries of those rural areas
   where the service has been weakest.

2. Projects to fund the studies and planning that enable non-
   metropolitan library systems to improve the library services
   they provide.

3. Projects providing the funds to metropolitan library systems
   for use in experimental programs for the disadvantaged.

The State Library's management of LSCA Title I funds is such that the
State's many diverse library needs receive attention.

The organizational location of the Division of Library Development deep
within the large and important State Education Department has a distinct
advantage when the vote of the State legislature is sought for State aid
for libraries.   When the Division seeks money for State aid, it must work
with, and convince, the State Education Department hierarchy above the
Division.   Once that is done, the request is supported by the prestigious
Board of Regents of the University of the State of New York.   Furthermore,
the request for libraries is only a small part of the budget that the
State Education Department submits to the State legislature.   For these
reasons, it achieves passage more readily than it would if it were
submitted as a separate item from an independent library department.

There are other consequences of the Division of Library Development's organizational location. As a part of the State Education Department, the Division is forced to remain aware of allied and related programs within the Department. The Division is also informed of other activities in which local libraries should participate or to which these libraries should adjust their programs. Since the Division has no organizational responsibility for the library portion of the State Library, it has no reason to be biased in favor of using LSCA funds to strengthen the State Library holdings.

Since the LSCA Advisory Committee includes professional librarians, it keeps the Division aware of the needs of the State's library community. Those members of the Committee who are part of the Board of Regents Advisory Committee can advise the Regents when, and if, there is a deterioration in the excellent management of LSCA by the State Library.

As to the proposals submitted by the systems, those examined by SDC were carefully prepared, reflecting a thorough understanding of both the needs and the required techniques.

The reports submitted to USOE by the Division of Library Development provided very fine documentation of LSCA Title I activity. The reports submitted by the systems to the Division ranged from adequate to excellent. The system reports which were the products of studies were timely as well as being of good quality.

PROBLEM AREAS

The Division of Library Development has not been able to maintain its two-year limit for providing LSCA Title I funds to any one project. When the State Library wished to terminate its support of the first projects for the disadvantaged in New York City, the New York City government refused to accept the financial burden of continuing these projects. The protests from citizens in the areas served by these projects forced the State Library to continue providing the necessary funds. As a result the Division has not been able to initiate as many new disadvantaged projects as anticipated.

Because of the terminal date of the Library and Services Construction Act, the Division of Library Development has felt it is prudent to avoid projects whose goals could only be reached by long-range programs. This self-imposed restriction has limited its range of operations.

The uncertainty as to the actual amount of each year's LSCA Title I appropriation has caused difficulty for the Division in planning; further-more, the fact that Federal appropriations are not made until months after the start of the fiscal year has caused difficulty for the library systems in planning staff support for LSCA projects.

Personnel

The study group was impressed with the large number of competent professional librarians in New York. Though there were vacancies that had not been filled, the number of professional librarians already available was generous compared to what had been viewed in other parts of the country. There were, however, two distinguishable problems: There is a shortage in some rural areas, where both lower salaries and the lack of attractions offered by the urban centers discourage many professionals. And within New York City there existed the problem caused by the distance between the top of the system and the lowest level of professional librarian. This to some extent has caused unions to form in New York City.

In an attempt to keep the supply of professional librarians coming from the library schools, systems have provided LSCA programs such as the Cadet Program described earlier. Both the Cadet Program and the very similar Library Futures Program are aimed at aiding the library profession as a whole, rather than just the individual library system.

CONCLUSIONS

The LSCA program in New York State has been tailored to meet the differing needs of the State's library systems, and the management of LSCA projects and funds has been careful and competent. The impact of LSCA Title I has been masked by the large amount of funds provided by State and local tax sources; however, the projects for the disadvantaged and the extension work of the Division of Library Development would suffer greatly if LSCA funding were discontinued.

VI.   BIBLIOGRAPHY

New York State LSA and LSCA Title I annual plans, reports, and programs submitted to USOE during the period 1957-1968 (miscellaneous titles).

Miscellaneous

Pioneer Library System. Second Career: Internship Manual 1968: Pilot Project. Rochester, N.Y., 1968, 13 pp.

Prentiss, S. Gilbert. The Evolution of the Library System (New York). 33rd Annual Conference of the Graduate Library School, Chicago, Ill., 29-31 July 1968, 23 pp.

Westchester Library System, Young Adult Services. Teenagers Speak in Book Talk. N.Y., N.Y., 1968, 28 pp.

Nassau and Suffolk Counties

Geddes, Andrew, Director. Library Services & Construction Act Projects. Report of the Nassau Library System. Hempstead, N.Y., February 27, 1967, 4 pp. (memo).

Nelson Associates, Inc. Basic Problems and Possibilities for a Reference and Research Library Resources System. N.Y., N.Y., 9 April 1965, 44 pp.

Turiel, David and Glick, Edgar. Reference Service in the Nassau Library System. Nassau County, N.Y., May 1967, 25 pp.

New York State Library

Blasingame, Ralph and Associates. A Report of a Study of Rockland County Libraries. East Brunswick, N.J., August 1968, 50 pp.

Eisner, Joseph and Crane, Stanley. Ramapo-Catskill Library System Reference Survey. Catskill, N.Y., 31 July 1965, 49 pp.

Galvin, Hoyt R. and Sessa, Frank B. The Chemung-Southern Tier Library System. Public Library Consultants, Charlotte, N.C., 1968, 82 pp.

Goldstein, Harold Professor, Dean. The Continuing Role of the New York State Library in Statewide Audiovisual Activities. Florida State University, Tallahassee, Fla., November 1967, 34 pp.

Moshier, L. Marion, Wickersham, Lucille, and Shepherd, G. F., Jr. System Wide Reference Services. Albany, N.Y., 26 June 1965, 39 pp.

Nelson Associates, Inc. Centralized Processing for the Public Libraries of New York State. N.Y., N.Y., 1966, 156 pp.

Nelson Associates, Inc. Implementing Centralized Processing for the Public Libraries of New York State. N.Y., N.Y., November 1967, 35 pp.

New York Public Library. Puerto Rico: Branch Library Book News. N.Y., N.Y., October 1968, 11 pp.

Reichmann, Felix. Library Resources in the Mid-Hudson Valley. Poughkeepsie, N.Y., 1965, 511 pp.

University of the State of New York. A Directory of New York State Public Library Systems. Albany, N.Y., July 1968, 71 pp.

University of the State of New York. Emerging Library Systems: The 1963-66 Evaluation of the New York State Public Library System. Albany, N.Y., February 1967, 291 pp.

University of the State of New York. New York State Annual Program Statement, 1968-1969: Title I - Services, Library Services and Construction Act. Albany, N.Y., 21 July 1968, 24 pp.

University of the State of New York. Public and Association Libraries: Statistics/1966. Albany, N.Y., 1967, 156 pp.

University of the State of New York. Report of the New York State Plan Under the Federal Library Services and Construction Act. Albany, N.Y., September 1968, 23 pp.

University of the State of New York. Summary of the Status of Approved Projects. Albany, N.Y., 1 March 1965, 12 pp.

Winsor, Charolette B. A Study of Four Library Programs for Disadvantaged Persons. Bank Street College of Education, N.Y., N.Y., July 1967, Part 1, Part 2A, and Part 2B.

Queens Borough Public Library

Merkelson, Elizabeth. Teenmobile Project - Library-in-Action. N.Y., N.Y., 1 October 1968, 9 pp. (report).

Mironchik, L. and Steinfeld, M. Tell-A-Tale Trailer. N.Y., N.Y., 1 October 1968, 8 pp. (project report).

Nelson Associates, Inc. A Study of Current Use and Project Demands. N.Y., N.Y., August 1968, 95 pp.

Nelson Associates, Inc. A Study of the Needs of Flushing Branch Reference Patrons for Improved Access to the Central Library's Collections. N.Y., N.Y., December 1967, 30 pp.

Queens Borough Public Library's Operation Head Start: Picture Book Program. Queens Borough Public Library, N.Y., N.Y., 1967-68. Contents:

Aboard the Library-Go-Round. 22 pp.

A Manual on Programs for Parents of Pre-School Children Participating in the Queens Borough Public Library's Operation Head Start. 45 pp.

Library-Go-Round - Human Interest Stories. 13 pp.

On-the-Job Training Program for Library Aides Working in Queens Borough Public Library. 28 pp.

Operation Head Start--A Parent Study. 6 pp.

Operation Head Start Picture Book Program for 3-5 Year Olds. 16 pp.

Queens Borough Public Library Operation Head Start. 25 pp.

Queens Borough Public Library Program for Bookless Homes. 34 pp.

REGION III:

District of Columbia
Kentucky
Maryland
NORTH CAROLINA
Virginia
West Virginia
Puerto Rico
Virgin Islands

Evelyn D. Mullen, Library
  Services Program Officer, AVLP
  220 7th St., N.E.
  Charlottesville, Va. 22901

CHAPTER VII
NORTH CAROLINA

I.   SOURCES OF INFORMATION

The following organizations and persons were visited to obtain information
for this study (see Figure NC-1 for a map of the State):

Date	Place Visited	Persons Visited
8/12/68	USOE Regional Office Charlottesville, Va. Region III	George Wallace, Director, AVLP Evelyn D. Mullen, Library Services Program Officer Carl Seifert, Regional Asst. Commissioner
8/13/68	North Carolina State Library Raleigh	Philip S. Ogilvie, State Librarian Elaine von Oesen, Asst. State Librarian Francis D. Gish, Extension Librarian Mrs. Marion Johnson, Processing Center George Hellen, Processing Center
8/14/68	Cumberland County Library Fayetteville	Mrs. Dorothy E. Shue, Librarian
8/14/68	Sandhill Regional Library System Carthage	Vince Anderson, Director
8/15/68	Randolph County Library Asheboro	Charlesanna L. Fox, Librarian
8/15/68	Scotland County Memorial Library Laurinburg	Helen H. Thompson, Librarian
8/16/68	Mecklenberg County Library Charlotte	Hoyt R. Galvin, Director
8/16/68	Gaston-Lincoln Regional Library Gastonia	Mrs. Barbara E. Heafner, Director Mrs. Alice B. McKelvie, Asst. Librarian Mrs. Isbill, Branch Librarian
8/20/68	Legislative Commission to Study Library Support Phone Call	David Stick, Chairman

Date	Place Visited	Persons Visited
9/16/68	East Albermarle Regional Library Headquarters Elizabeth City, N.C.	Mrs. A. V. Irvin, Acting Director
9/16/68	Roanoke Rapids City Library Roanoke Rapids	Mrs. A. M. Davis, Librarian L. Taylor Oakes, Head, Library Board
9/17/68	Institute for Government University of North Carolina Chapel Hill	Robert Phay, Staff
9/17/68	University of North Carolina Library	Jerrold Orne, Librarian, and Member of the Library Board for the State Library
9/18/68	High Point Municipal Library High Point	Neil Austin, Librarian
9/19/68	Morganton-Burke Library Morganton	Mrs. Douglas Barnett, Librarian
9/19/68	Ashville Public Library Ashville	Kenneth Brown, Librarian
9/20/68	State Administration Building Raleigh	G. Andrew Jones, State Budget Officer

Much valuable information was also obtained from the publications listed in the Bibliography in Section VI of this chapter.

II.   BACKGROUND FOR LSCA OPERATIONS

THE STATE AGENCY

The legal name of the State Library administrative agency that has sole responsibility for administering LSCA in North Carolina is the North Carolina State Library. The officers authorized to submit plans are the State Librarian, Philip S. Ogilvie, and the Assistant State Librarian, Miss Elaine von Oesen. Mr. Ogilvie has overall responsibility for LSCA and is specifically responsible for Titles IVA and IVB. Miss von Oesen is responsible for Title I, II, and III. Her work with LSA-LSCA extends back over several years. She was acting State

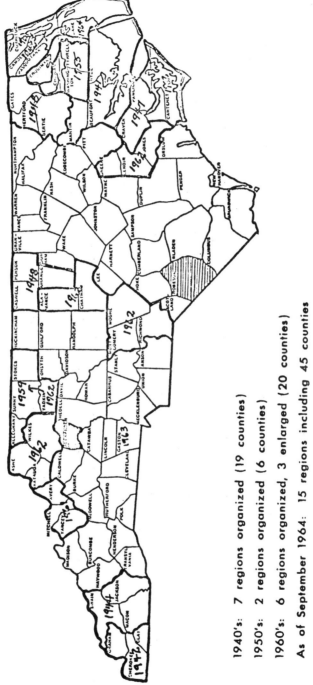

Figure NC-1. North Carolina Regional Libraries

Librarian in the interim between the period when that position was held by Elizabeth Hughey and the time of Mr. Ogilvie's appointment; and during much of Mrs. Hughey's administration she was the Extension Services Librarian.

Figure NC-2, which shows a partial diagram of the State Library organization, emphasizes the agency function of the Library. Above Mr. Ogilvie and Miss von Oesen is the State Library Board of Trustees. The Board consists of six members chosen by the Governor, and two ex officio members. (The Governor is not eligible for re-election, and he possesses no veto power. Thus, his influence is felt mainly through his prestige and his power to appoint members to the Board.) By statute, one member must be a librarian. The Board tends to act on the advice of the State Library. Its chief function is to represent the opinions of nonlibrary personnel. The State Library feels confident of its understanding of library problems. It needs, and seeks, the advice of the Board of Trustees to make sure that it is properly reacting to the needs of the State as seen by nonlibrary personnel.

Miss von Oesen is in charge of the Library Development Division. She is assisted by Miss Frances Gish, the Chief Consultant. This division is responsible for most of the services that are proffered under Title I. It maintains an Extension responsibility, a State aid responsibility, and contains the important audiovisual section, whose services are described in more detail later in this chapter. The Processing Center is headed by Mrs. Marion Johnson. It performs its activities for many of the public libraries in the State and is one of the major LSCA contributions made by the State under LSCA Title I.

HISTORY OF STATE AID TO NORTH CAROLINA LIBRARIES

LSA and LSCA in North Carolina are continuations of a deliberate policy of State aid that began in 1941. The original effort started with Dr. Frank Graham.

The original State aid plan gave $100,000 of State money to the 100 counties in the State. (The county is the predominant political unit in North Carolina.) When State aid first started, the rural counties insisted that equal aid be given to each county. With LSA, the grant policy was changed to offer a large grant to a county that was part of a library system. Thus there was a cash incentive for a library to become a member of a system. There was also an incentive for a strong library to take on a weak library. The next variation in the use of LSA money was an effort grant; money was given on the basis of the amount of money a county contributed towards its library. The tax money was based on the amount appropriated in relation to the wealth of the county as determined by State income tax returns. The next form of grant offered by the State Library was a personnel grant. This took the form of additional money that was to be spent on hiring professional personnel. Eventually, special money was offered for items of statewide significance. There are

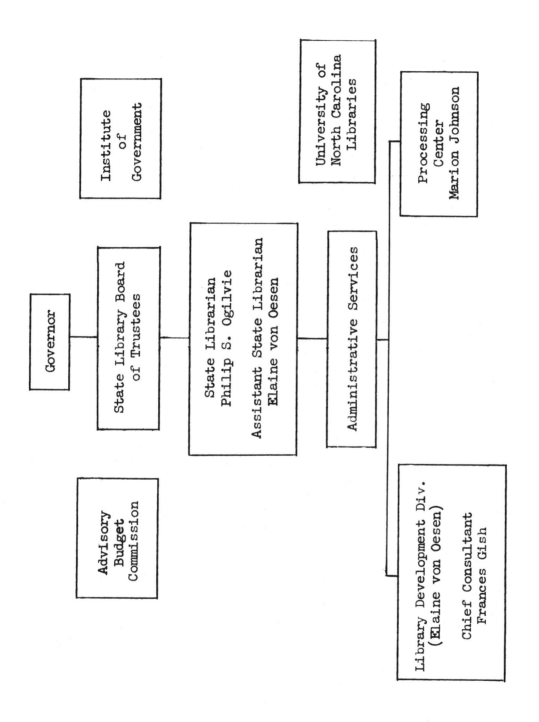

Figure NC-2. North Carolina State Library Organization

special research collections at strategically placed libraries in the State, a statewide processing service is offered, and statewide audiovisual collections are available.

The philosophy of the State Library is to strengthen the county libraries of the State through cash grants whose size depends on the amount of effort the counties have expended towards strengthening their own libraries. County library federations are encouraged as a further means of strengthening the individual county libraries. Innovative projects that would put counties in competition with one another are not part of the North Carolina philosophy for extending financial aid to the individual library. The only projects that exist are those that offer--on a statewide basis--resources or services that individual county libraries could not supply to themselves. Grant monies are still offered only to county libraries. Municipal libraries share in this aid indirectly by being able to obtain service through the county libraries.

RELATIONSHIP OF STATE AGENCY TO OTHER ORGANIZATIONS

Four different levels of intergovernmental relations should be noted.

The first and most important level is that of the Advisory Budget Commission. The Advisory Budget Commission, which has no organizational connection to the State Library, is the single most important group in the State in determining what portion of public funds goes to each of the State functions. The defense of the library budget is made by the State Librarian to the Advisory Budget Commission.

The second level of intergovernmental relationship is between the State Library and the Library Program Officer for USOE Region III, Miss Evelyn Mullen. Miss Mullen had been at the State Library. She had worked with North Carolina from USOE for many years before USOE regionalization. The State plan submitted to USOE is a controlling factor in what the State does. Therefore, the State Library uses Miss Mullen as a consultant rather than as a director, and as someone who gets the work done for them in interacting with Washington, D.C. They think of Miss Mullen as being a very strong consultant. They were worried, when regionalization started, that the lack of backup caused by the splintering of the consulting group at USOE would hurt them. However, Miss Mullen has either been available or they have known when she would be available after making a visit to one of her other States. Miss Mullen's leadership turns out to be leadership performed by carrying news gained from her wider view of what is going on outside North Carolina. One sees a rather nice balance between her role and the control and leadership influenced by the local people. Miss Mullen never visits any of the local libraries without being accompanied by someone from the State Library or having received the State's permission to visit a local group. There is no feeling that USOE, as it is represented by Miss Mullen, is a burden to the State.

Rather, the burden that the State complains about is the reporting that it is required to do. The State feels that the reporting procedures are unrealistic, and that the reporting forms are built for States with local projects, whereas North Carolina does not have local projects. The statistics that they create as to how LSCA money is spent by each title are arbitrarily decided upon. North Carolina favors an additional title that would give a certain amount of money to the State Library for administration and leave the rest of the money to be used for nonadministrative functions or for grants directly to the county libraries. For them, this would merely be an accounting simplification.

The third level of intergovernmental relationship is that which exists between the State Library and the county libraries. The State Library looks upon the Library Program Officer as a consultant; many of the county libraries lean even more heavily on the State Library for consulting services.

The fourth intergovernmental relationship is that between the State Library and the University of North Carolina. One of the ex officio members of the State Library Board is Dr. Jerrold Orne, Head of the Library at the University of North Carolina. Dr. Orne's position as a trustee allows for an inter-action between the public system and the library system of the State's University.

INWATS (see Section IV) and the interlibrary loan (see Figure NC-3) are examples of the beneficial working relationship that exists between the State Library and the University of North Carolina. This relationship has been partially fostered by Dr. Orne's being an ex officio member of the State Library Board of Trustees. The two main librarians of the State--the State Librarian and the University Librarian--work together. They are planning Title III work. The University has the Union Catalog for the State. The University Librarian eliminated the Extension Division that the University had set up because it was in competition with the Extension Division of the State Library.

The Institute of Government was formed as a place where State and local officials could be trained. It is located at the University of North Carolina at Chapel Hill, and is now part of the University. Twenty members are on the faculty of the University. Most of the members of the Institute are lawyers. The training program for librarians originated under George Esser and is now under Mr. Robert Phay. Mr. Phay held a training program in May 1968. Another one will be held in 1969, and training programs will probably be held each year. The purpose of the training programs is to teach the trustees that libraries are more than just book depositories. Staff from the State Library lecture in conjunction with the Institute staff. The institute teaches the trustees the legal aspects of being library trustees. They have printed a guidebook for the trustees of the North Carolina libraries. Though quite good, it was printed in 1959, and the Institute is now considering turning out an improved and more up-to-date book.

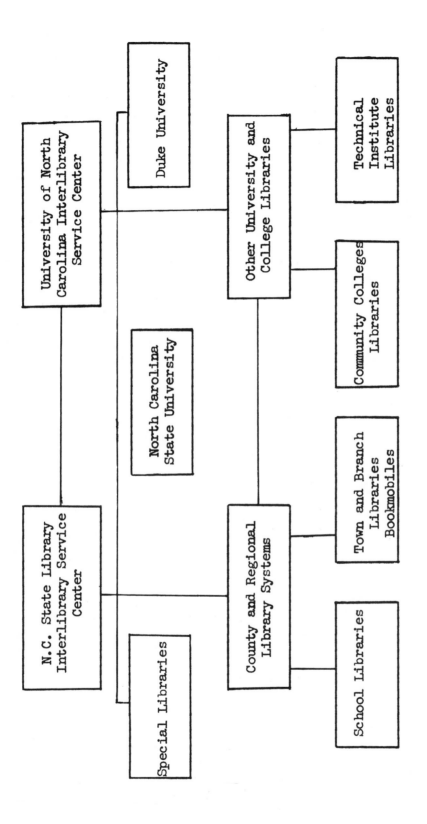

Figure NC-3. North Carolina Interlibrary Service

LIBRARY FUNDING

Table NC-1 shows the amounts of public library income in North Carolina.[1] The total per capita support, from all sources, is $1.41. This low level of per capita support has moved the State Library, in its use of Federal and State monies, to stimulate additional local support for public libraries. The money that has come to North Carolina under LSA and LSCA has been used to augment the State's already existing plan of aid to the county libraries. Thus, conceptually, there has been a mingling of funds both on the part of the State and on the part of the county libraries or regions that have received the money. This conceptual mingling is broken down for accounting purposes when the State submits reports to the Federal government or the counties submit reports to the State, but the separation of funds occurs only on paper.

This mingling has not caused difficulties under LSCA. Under LSA, however, Federal funds could be used only for rural areas. Under the 1960 census, 70 percent of the population of North Carolina was considered rural under LSA. Before 1960, an even greater percentage of the State fit the rural classification. Therefore, to meet the requirements of the law, North Carolina would distinguish between projects that were completely for rural areas and projects that were statewide. It would claim 100 percent reimbursement for the rural projects and 70 percent reimbursement (after the 1960 census) for statewide projects. In fact, it could have claimed more than the 70 percent, since it has given a heavier emphasis on service to the rural areas. All of this prorating, however, is accounting legerdemain to satisfy the requirements of the law. North Carolina has always claimed all of its Federal allotment; it has usually met its matching requirement; it has used the money both from its own State Treasury and from the Federal Treasury for the benefit of the libraries and has satisfied the bookkeeping requirements demanded of it by law.

Table NC-2 was supplied by the State Library. It shows the record of State aid and Federal aid. (The State aid for Fiscal Year 1942, which is not shown, was $100,000;[2] the Federal aid for Fiscal Year 1957, which also is not shown, was $40,000.)[3] Examining the figures, one can see the dramatic increase in support of libraries by county governments over the 26-year period. This support is primarily due to the stimulation provided by the State's plan.

---

[1]Report of the Legislative Commission to Study Library Support in the State of North Carolina, August 1968. Chairman, David Stick, Kitty Hawk.

[2]There was no State aid in FY 1941; in 1942 it was $96,501; the difference between the latter and $100,000 was used for administration.

[3]Actual Federal-aid allotments to county and regional libraries in FY 1957 was $14,031.

Table NC-1. North Carolina Public Library Income, 1966-1967

Municipal Libraries	Local Government	Gifts, etc.	Total	Per Capita
Ahoskie	$ 3,500.00	$ 352.65	$ 3,852.65	.84
Black Mountain	4,300.00	324.63	4,624.63	.35
Canton	10,200.00	2,761.79	12,961.79	2.55
Chapel Hill	16,500.00	6,861.11	23,361.11	1.85
Dunn	4,150.00	1,009.97	5,159.97	.68
Farmville	10,562.00	1,722.58	12,284.58	3.07
Granite Falls	7,053.94	200.00	7,253.94	2.74
Hamlet	11,597.37	1,866.59	13,463.96	3.01
Hickory	63,282.75	5,505.72	68,788.47	3.43
High Point	180,010.00	---	180,010.00	2.81
Kings Mountain	7,246.00	2,733.43	9,979.43	1.24
Lumberton	8,080.00	2,091.17	10,171.17	.66
Mooresville	10,585.26	3,320.80	13,906.06	2.01
Red Springs	3,000.00	1,961.88	4,961.88	1.79
Rowland	---	438.67	438.67	.31
Southern Pines	17,320.00	2,129.24	19,449.24	3.74
Washington	12,400.00	5,358.94	17,758.94	1.78
Weaverville	3,051.00	217.38	3,268.38	3.13
Whiteville	7,162.56	980.96	8,143.52	1.73
	$380,000.88	$39,837.51	$419,838.39	2.32 Av.

Table NC-1. (Continued)

Region	Local Government	State Aid	Federal Aid	Gifts, etc.	Total	Per Capita
Albemarle	$ 24,099.66	$ 14,836.00	$ 9,400.00	$ 735.89	$ 49,071.55	.87
Appalachian	38,000.00	16,984.00	21,872.00	1,035.92	77,891.92	.94
Avery-Mitchell-Yancey	12,255.00	14,567.00	6,614.00	6,518.92	39,954.92	1.00
Beaufort-Hyde-Martin	23,344.26	14,760.00	6,000.00	5,439.65	49,543.91	.71
Central North Carolina	88,300.00	16,760.00	22,000.00	18,121.92	145,181.92	1.29
Craven-Pamlico-Carteret	39,446.46	16,005.00	15,405.00	2,605.86	73,462.32	.73
East Albemarle	40,935.42	20,949.00	21,291.00	3,377.95	86,553.37	1.97
Fontana	13,143.00	14,450.00	8,502.00	2,912.79	39,007.79	.94
Gaston-Lincoln	219,937.96	27,928.00	27,951.00	9,516.08	285,333.04	1.83
Hyconeechee	32,313.00	15,758.00	20,650.00	1,156.88	69,877.88	.78
Nantahala	20,430.50	14,244.00	10,639.75	1,499.97	46,814.22	1.65
Neuse	73,650.00	21,991.00	31,008.75	6,251.06	132,900.81	1.60
Northwestern	40,704.38	20,126.00	23,233.00	4,078.90	88,142.28	.87
Pettigrew	22,724.83	14,389.00	14,247.00	438.43	51,849.26	1.74
Sandhill	50,990.08	17,767.00	28,500.00	24,971.50	122,228.58	1.29
	$740,274.55	$261,514.00	$267,313.50	$88,711.72	$1,357,813.77	1.20 Ave.

Table NC-1. (Continued)

Counties	Local Government	State Aid	Federal Aid	Gifts, etc.	Total	Per Capita
Anson	$ 14,000.00	$ 5,735.00	$ 1,161.00	$ 210.57	$ 21,106.57	.84
Bladen	5,000.00	4,580.00	752.00	40.70	10,372.70	.35
Brunswick	8,068.75	5,452.00	319.50	534.36	14,374.61	.70
Buncombe	246,753.41	25,236.00	3,000.00	59.71	275,049.12	2.11
Burke	28,600.00	7,860.00	5,000.00	13,016.88	54,476.88	1.03
Cabarrus	38,240.87	8,187.00	3,034.00	8,833.91	58,295.78	.85
Caldwell	51,563.40	9,177.00	5,396.00	---	66,136.40	1.33
Catawba	41,500.00	5,542.50	8,585.50	3,191.48	58,819.48	.80
Cleveland	20,191.00	5,342.00	4,342.00	3,911.70	33,786.70	.51
Columbus	12,128.18	---	---	---	12,128.18	.24
Cumberland	126,320.02	9,518.50	12,018.50	6,136.89	153,993.91	1.03
Davidson	99,035.00	7,840.50	10,840.50	---	117,716.00	1.48
Davie	22,500.00	5,464.50	2,561.50	6,663.19	37,189.19	2.22
Duplin	6,164.15	4,406.00	---	48.45	10,618.60	.263
Durham	195,839.82	11,508.00	10,008.00	5,644.29	223,000.11	1.99
Edgecombe	32,075.00	6,213.00	7,727.25	3,711.56	49,726.81	1.26
Forsyth	359,718.44	17,803.50	16,303.50	55,982.00	449,807.44	2.37
Franklin	9,300.04	4,570.50	570.50	548.66	14,989.70	.52
Granville	31,454.21	9,070.00	---	1,033.31	41,557.52	1.255

Table NC-1. (Continued)

Counties	Local Government	State Aid	Federal Aid	Gifts, etc.	Total	Per Capita
Guilford	363,555.06	20,976.00	18,976.00	19,586.76	423,093.82	1.716
Halifax	30,560.35	5,192.00	3,444.00	4,463.48	43,659.83	.74
Harnett	11,600.00	4,489.50	1,530.50	175.69	17,795.69	.36
Haywood	20,600.00	6,447.00	1,657.00	5,011.92	33,715.92	.84
Henderson	32,893.98	5,707.00	3,520.00	1,459.45	43,580.43	1.20
Hoke	7,500.00	4,675.50	1,399.50	1,158.66	14,733.66	.90
Iredell	68,993.20	4,647.00	1,001.00	3,035.82	77,677.02	1.24
Johnston	57,568.00	4,944.50	4,936.00	6,989.46	74,437.96	1.13
Lee	34,200.00	5,666.50	5,234.50	1,964.32	47,965.32	1.77
McDowell	29,671.28	5,772.50	1,772.50	257.30	37,473.58	1.40
Madison	6,973.64	---	---	413.85	7,387.49	.42
Mecklenburg	512,023.64	28,818.00	26,918.00	149,916.96	717,676.60	2.63
Nash	37,306.04	6,784.50	2,784.50	15,949.20	61,924.24	.81
New Hanover	78,462.57	7,740.50	6,740.50	6,642.07	99,585.64	1.33
Northampton	12,674.43	4,934.50	934.50	---	18,543.43	.69
Onslow	29,606.30	5,314.00	4,630.00	966.71	40,517.01	.48
Pender	14,966.04	5,310.00	1,310.00	1,055.85	22,641.89	1.22
Perquimans	3,750.00	4,320.50	320.50	864.85	9,255.85	1.00
Pitt	106,179.11	10,630.00	8,430.00	4,487.72	129,726.83	1.85
Polk	8,880.46	4,630.50	802.00	44.51	14,357.47	1.25

Table NC-1. (Continued)

Counties	Local Government	State Aid	Federal Aid	Gifts, etc	Total	Per Capita
Randolph	65,515.83	8,665.00	10,246.75	15,633.93	100,061.51	1.62
Rockingham	126,400.00	16,136.00	5,667.00	9,223.99	157,426.99	2.26
Rowan	77,592.82	7,912.50	6,412.50	7,728.77	99,646.59	1.20
Rutherford	30,687.00	4,905.50	2,700.50	6,147.12	44,440.12	.98
Sampson	28,301.64	5,444.00	2,065.00	5,761.66	41,572.30	.83
Scotland	22,867.75	5,509.50	2,495.50	1,652.16	32,524.91	1.29
Stanly	38,858.00	6,111.50	3,464.25	4,911.52	52,445.27	1.28
Transylvania	5,000.00	4,337.50	663.50	1,899.02	11,900.02	.72
Union	43,340.87	6,983.50	2,983.50	9,183.40	62,491.27	1.398
Vance	15,671.20	4,968.00	2,574.00	744.29	23,957.49	.74
Wake	183,795.32	13,675.50	17,417.50	19,721.57	234,609.89	1.38
Warren	6,955.00	4,477.50	1,119.00	1,110.08	13,661.58	.69
Wayne	41,734.00	6,166.00	5,166.00	2,464.40	55,530.40	.67
Wilson	68,309.20	8,938.00	7,438.00	3,644.40	83,329.60	1.53
	$3,571,495.02	$404,735.00	$258,373.75	$422,038.55	$4,656,643.32	1.40 Av.
Grand Total	$4,691,770.45	$666,250.00	$525,687.25	$550,587.78	$6,434,295.18	1.41 Av.

Table NC-2. Statistics of North Carolina Public Libraries FY'41 - FY'67

	1940-41 134	1945-46	1950-51 260	1955-56 266	1960-61 317	1965-66 332	1966-67 332
No. of Public Libraries							
Support(Income)							
Municipal Govt.	166,759.30	$253,524.67	$ 461,394.49	$ 755,604.34	$1,165,933.31	$1,486,528.59	$1,649,781.00
County Govt.	140,997.03	311,409.21	560,985.48	918,662.40	1,564,831.90	2,880,057.84	3,041,989.00
State Aid	none	167,190.00	335,027.00	390,000.00	424,272.00	621,250.00	666,250.00
Federal Aid	none	——	——	——	179,371.00	473,035.00	525,687.00
Other (gifts, fines, etc.)	no record	229,488.56	154,706.95	252,470.62	322,373.19	496,311.33	550,587.00
TOTAL		$961,612.44	$1,512,113.92	$2,316,737.36	$3,656,781.40	$5,957,182.76	$6,434,294.00
Per Capita	.10	.26	.37	.57	.80	1.31	1.41
Expenditures							
Personnel	no record	no record	802,192.46	1,285,414.60	1,998,956.06	3,469,101.47	3,850,289.00
Books & Materials	no record	no record	383,723.15	518,297.76	804,211.09	1,257,094.42	1,362,577.00
Other Operating	no record	no record	248,497.40	442,900.60	729,320.23	805,097.00	896,560.00
TOTAL			$1,434,413.01	$2,246,612.96	$3,532,487.38	$5,531,292.89	$6,109,426.00
Volumes							
Total	1,090,301	1,454,939	2,150,096	2,987,978	3,932,500	4,857,430	5,346,572
Added		no record	214,856	248,129	305,289	349,830	347,708
Circulation							
Total	6,856,556	6,148,933	9,665,406	10,416,462	13,698,903	14,765,321	13,971,160
Bookmobile	——	——	4,654,328	no record	5,193,649	4,735,038	4,218,045

NCSL-7/26/67

A legislative commission, chaired by David Stick of Dare County and appointed to study library support in the State, concluded that the great majority of North Carolinians still are not receiving adequate modern library services of the type already being made available to the citizens of other States, and that under the present system of financing public libraries, North Carolinians can never expect the quality of library services they need and to which they are entitled. Therefore, it recommended, among other things, that:

> The State of North Carolina should gradually assume equal responsibility with local government for public library support. To insure maximum results this should be accomplished over a period of several years with annual increases in State grants to public libraries amounting to the equivalent of $0.20 per capita allocated according to a formula adopted by the State Library Board. This would call for increased appropriations for State aid to public libraries of approximately one million dollars each year on the basis of present population figures. Thus it is the specific recommendation of this commission that the 1969 General Assembly increase appropriations for State aid to public libraries to the equivalent of approximately $0.35 per capita in the first year of the biennium and $0.55 in the second year of the biennium. [4]

As can be seen by looking at Table NC-2, the Stick plan, if adopted, would eventually see the State of North Carolina providing aid that would reach the amount of $5 million.

The Stick plan has been submitted to the powerful Budget Advisory Commission where it received a cordial hearing. It is not yet possible to tell whether the request for money for libraries will survive the competition with all the other requests the Budget Advisory Commission must entertain. The need for such support is highlighted by statistics in the Stick Report, which show four counties receiving less than $0.40 per capita support for their libraries, while the most prosperous county, Mecklenburg, was able to support its library only to the extent of $2.63 per capita, an amount far below ALA minimum standards.

----

[4] Report of the Legislative Commission to Study Library Support in the State of North Carolina, August 1968. Chairman, David Stick, Kitty Hawk.

The main reason for the small local support of libraries is the low per capita income of North Carolina. In 1966, the State's per capita income was $2,235, compared to the United States average of $2,940. This ranked North Carolina 43rd among 50 states. Another reason is the State's tax law. A ruling of the State Supreme Court in the 19th century stated that libraries were not a necessary expense. The effect of this ruling was that libraries cannot be supported from ad valorem taxes without a local referendum. Local referenda have been held and passed in some communities, but many counties must depend totally on "non-tax" monies. Such monies can come from intangibles or the sale of liquor. We were not in North Carolina long enough to determine whether North Carolina's local option on liquor was such as to affect the consumption of liquor in a county, but we did determine that dry counties were not able to support their libraries in anywhere near the style that the wet counties were.

III.   LSCA PROGRAM

OVERVIEW OF ACTIVITIES

North Carolina merges its LSCA Title I program into its already existing State-aid program. Six projects constitute the State plan. The plan is managed in three ways. The first form of management is that in which the State Library is itself carrying out projects. This applies to Project A-- State Services to Public Libraries; Project C--Processing Center; and Project D--Education and Training.

The second type of management is that in which work is delegated to outside groups. There are two such projects: the one on institutes (Project E) and the one for the development plan (Project F).

The third type of management is that in which grants under Project B are carried out by the county libraries and regional library systems. Here the State Library puts restrictions on the behavior of the recipients of grants. It requires that the county library:

> Have its governing board establish a free public
> library, or, if the library is already in existence,
> that it have trustees duly appointed for it by
> governing officials, and that they be trustees who
> will accept the responsibility of developing policies
> with the certified librarian to provide more adequate
> library service.

• Employ a properly certified librarian as Director of Library Service.

• Provide county or regional headquarters in a centrally located place easily accessible to the public, and certify that the assurance of compliance with Title VI of the Civil Rights Act of 1964 is still in effect.

• Make library facilities available to all people within the county or region without discrimination.

• Secure funds to finance improved library service. If the library is in its first year, it must levy a tax to provide a minimum of $6,000 or 30¢ per capita, whichever is greater. If it is not the first year, the amount of the appropriation from both tax and non-tax revenues from each appropriating body must equal at least the amount appropriated for the previous year. In addition, State or Federal funds may not be used to replace local funds appropriated for public library service.

• Use funds already available for library purposes. A county or regional library with the balance of more than one sixth of its annual budget unencumbered will have the difference deducted from its basic allocation. It must arrange to have library financial records audited annually and a copy of the audit filed with the State Library Board.

• Submit the following to the State Library Board:

    • A 10-year plan adopted by the Board of Trustees or any revisions of a 10-year plan

    • Its current bylaws

    • The library budget as approved

    • A statement and assurance of compliance

    • An annual audit made by a certified public accountant including all funds expended by the library.

Beyond these administrative restrictions, the State Library requires that the combination of State aid and Federal funds may be used only for:

- The purchase and printing of books and periodicals, and the purchase of other printed and audiovisual materials for library collections.

- The salary and employer's share of the employees' benefits, such as social security, retirement, and hospitalization for a professionally trained library director and/or professionally trained assistant.

- The purchase, insurance, and maintenance of a bookmobile and other motor vehicles needed for library services.

- The bonding of the library treasurer.

- The library audit.

- Travel on library business.

- Telephone calls.

- Cost of trustee memberships in North Carolina, Southeastern, and American Library Associations.

ALLOCATION OF LSCA TITLE I FUNDS

Table NC-3 shows the relative priority for monies to be spent under the various categories. Since the figures are taken from the annual program submitted for Fiscal Year 1968, they represent intentions if the full appropriation were received rather than actual expenditures already made. The largest amount of money is expended for system grants. The next largest amount is for statewide services. This money includes not only the salaries of consultants and administrative staff but also the cost of a statewide audiovisual collection and of a reference and interlibrary service used by the libraries of the State. The Processing Center budget can either be considered as money kept completely at the State or money given completely to the libraries of the State with which to buy processing. Education and training had as its intent ten scholarships and three training grants. Both the Institutes and the development plan are of modest cost compared to the total budget for the State.

Table NC-3. Requested Expenditures for
Fiscal Year 1968

	PROJECT	FEDERAL	STATE	TOTAL
A.	Statewide Services	69,578	157,319	226,897
B.	Library System Grants	570,392	634,138	1,204,530
C.	Processing Center	141,216	-	141,216
D.	Education and Training	30,000	-	30,000
E.	Institutes and Workshops	9,000	-	9,000
F.	Development Plan	15,000	-	15,000
		835,186	791,457	1,626,643

REPORTING AND EVALUATION PROCEDURES OF THE STATE AGENCY

In managing the money expended by the libraries, so little option is given to
the State Library for monitoring day-to-day decisions that this management is
limited to seeing that its rules are followed and to performing an audit. In
giving money, the State Library has demanded that county libraries provide
10-year plans. These 10-year plans are less programs than they are statements of goals. To a large extent they have been unrealistic plans that have
been created to satisfy a demand on the part of the State Library; the plans
tend to be forgotten by the libraries soon after they are created, and the
State Library does not do a careful followup on them. Rather, after five
years, the State Library will point out that the 10-year plan is now five
years old and force the local library to review its plan and update it. The
goal is more to have the library have a set of goals than to demand a strict
management plan that must be followed. This lack of close followup by the
State Library on plans is in contrast to the very careful followup that the
State Library makes of the use of funds. The State Library demands that the
books be gone over by audit. This is to make sure that the local libraries
actually use the money to increase their operating costs, since it is operating cost that the State Library feels controls the level of service. The
State Library is also firm about the requirement for a certified librarian.
One library has lost its support because of failure to comply with this
requirement.

IV.   DESCRIPTION OF REPRESENTATIVE USES OF LSCA FUNDS

MAJOR PROJECT CATEGORIES

The State's aid to libraries program is divided into six project categories:

A. State Services to Public Libraries

B. Library Systems Grants

C. Processing Center

D. Education and Training

E. Institutes and Workshops

F. Development Plan

These projects are described below.

Project A.   State Services to Public Libraries

This project includes supplementary bibliographical and reference services
to public libraries. It also includes consultant services on administration,
building planning, and services to children, young people, and adults. Audiovisual services are also included. Information is given to local governments
and to the public regarding public library needs. Consultant service is
given both to library boards and to individual trustees. All of these services are given on request. This project includes all State Library services
to and about public libraries, including the administration of other LSCA
projects.

Project B.   Library Systems Grants

Grants are given to county and regional libraries that are inadequate. (The
State Library regards all public libraries in North Carolina as being inadequate.) Four types of grants are made. The first is the basic annual grant
that goes to each county in the State. Originally, in 1941, this annual
grant was $1,000 per county. In 1968, the annual basic grant was $4,000 per
county.

The second type of grant is a per capita grant based on an effort index score
determined by dividing the total personal income of a county into its county
library operational expenditures from local funds. Table NC-4 lists the
counties and library regions of North Carolina in decreasing order of the
amount of their support to libraries. Table NC-5 gives the per capita
payment available on the basis of the scores. This type of grant is
intended to provide an incentive to counties for supporting their libraries.

Table NC-4. Effort Index Scores 1967-68*
North Carolina Public Library Systems

Davie	10.15	Stanly	5.64	Wayne	3.47
Buncombe	9.03	Davidson	5.57	Madison	3.44
Granville	8.71	Nash	5.27	Vance	3.32
Mecklenburg	8.67	Pettigrew Region	5.27	Fontana Region	3.31
Pitt	8.33	Henderson	5.17	Albemarle Region	2.92
Union	8.13	Sampson	5.01	Warren	2.91
Wilson	8.03	Hoke	4.95	Rutherford	2.85
Rockingham	7.59	Wake	4.90	Franklin	2.83
Lee	7.44	Caldwell	4.81	Cabarrus	2.74
Pender	7.43	Edgecombe	4.75	Northwestern Region	2.68
Gaston-Lincoln Region	7.41	Cumberland	4.45	Robeson	2.55
Forsyth	7.36	A M Y Region	4.40	Transylvania	2.51
Durham	7.32	Rowan	4.40	Hyconeechee Region	2.49
McDowell	7.28	Perquimans	4.32	Catawba	2.47
Randolph	6.81	Burke	4.30	Halifax	2.39
Scotland	6.70	Central N. C. Region	4.21	Craven-Pamlico-Carteret Region	2.25
Neuse Region	6.50	Haywood	4.16	Cleveland	2.13
Alexander	6.49	Anson	3.94	B H M Region	1.94
Guilford	6.43	Nantahala Region	3.84	Bladen	1.77
East Albemarle Region	6.14	Appalachian Region	3.83	Onslow	1.70
New Hanover	6.04	Brunswick	3.78	Harnett	1.63
Iredell	5.94	Sandhill Region	3.56	Duplin	1.33
Johnston	5.89	Polk	3.53		

*Obtained by dividing the total personal income of counties into the total amount of local funds expended by county or regional libraries for operational costs, exclusive of capital outlay, in 1966-67.

NCSL - 12/21/67

Table NC-5. Per Capita Rate Sheet for 1967-1968

Effort Index Score	Rate for Jan. Payment
10.00 to 10.49	.095
9.50 to 9.99	.09
9.00 to 9.49	.085
8.50 to 8.99	.08
8.00 to 8.49	.075
7.50 to 7.99	.07
7.00 to 7.49	.065
6.50 to 6.99	.06
6.00 to 6.49	.055
5.50 to 5.99	.05
5.00 to 5.49	.045
4.50 to 4.99	.04
4.00 to 4.49	.035
3.50 to 3.99	.03
3.00 to 3.49	.025
2.50 to 2.99	.02
2.00 to 2.49	.015
1.50 to 1.99	.01
1.00 to 1.49	.005

NCSL - 12/21/67

The third type of grant, for personnel, encourages counties to pay professional librarians a salary that will be an incentive for their professionals to stay in, or come to, North Carolina. Personnel grants began in 1954. The present form of the personnel grant gives $6,000 to a county library serving a population of 50,000 or more, and $6,000 to a regional library that either serves 75,000 or more or contains six counties. (At present, there are no six-county regions.) Grants are awarded to libraries for employed, certified, full-time directors (and, in regions, for other professionals serving the entire region) when the salaries for these people meet or exceed the "Professional Librarian's Salary Scale" adopted by the State Personnel Department. Grants are not made to fill vacant positions.

The fourth type of grant is intended to encourage the creation of multi-county regions. Many of the 100 counties in North Carolina are too small to be able to sustain an adequate library by themselves. The State provides that, for regions composed of three or more counties and serving less than 75,000 people, each county qualifies for an additional allotment of $2,000 when the regional income from local government averages at least 30¢ per capita. As per capita receipts from local government increase, the regional grants are increased at the following rates:

50¢ per capita earns $3,000 per county

75¢ per capita earns $4,000 per county

$1 per capita earns $5,000 per county

The State would prefer that regions have at least 75,000 people. Recognizing that populous counties that join together in a region satisfy this goal, the State makes an even more attractive allotment available to counties that form more populous regions. Thus, for regions of two counties serving at least 100,000 people, and for regions of three or more counties serving at least 75,000 people, the allotment is $4,000 per county when the regional income from the local government averages at least 30¢ per capita. As the per capita receipts from local government are increased, the regional grant is increased at the following rate:

50¢ per capita earns $6,000 per county

75¢ per capita earns $8,000 per county

$1 per capita earns $10,000 per county

Project C. Processing Center

The Processing Center orders, classifies, catalogs, marks, and provides plastic jackets for books selected by participating libraries. Each book is supplied with a pocket, two book cards, and one or more sets of catalog cards

as requested. The purpose of the Center is to supply processing to libraries
that are too small to be able to provide efficient processing for themselves.
Processing is done for 55 libraries serving over 60 percent of the population
of North Carolina.

The processing is sold to the participating libraries at the price of $1 per
book. The cost is matched with money given to the libraries to be used to
purchase that amount of processing. The only real price required of the
participating libraries is the commitment to file the catalog cards. In the
early years, when the Processing Center first started, many of the small
libraries did not have the personnel to allow them to create a catalog; it
was hoped that the Processing Center could be used to start catalogs in
these libraries.

Project D. Education and Training

Under this project, scholarship grants are made to prospective public
librarians. The amount of each scholarship is $2,500. The grantee must be
accepted by an ALA-accredited library school. The recipient must promise to
spend at least two years after graduation working in North Carolina public
libraries. Training must be completed within 18 months from the time it
begins.

Employee study grants are also made under this project. The purpose of
employee study grants is to help qualified public library staff employees
who do not have professional certifications begin or continue ALA-accredited
library training when they are able to attend the library school one term or
semester at a time. The amount of the grant is $800 per employee for a
regular fall or spring semester, and $375 for a summer semester. The recipi-
ent must have been a full-time staff member of the library for at least one
year under the direction of a professional librarian.

Project E. Institutes and Workshops

This project provides funds for the training conducted at the Institute of
Government. This training has already been described under the heading
"Relationship of State Agency to Other Organizations."

Project F. Development Plan

As was noted earlier, the present State plan is a continuation of a plan that
has been in effect since 1941. The plan was designed to meet the needs of a
State with little library development; though it has been successful, the time
has come for the new State Librarian to re-examine the plan in light of present
needs. For this purpose, Arthur D. Little, Inc., has been engaged to perform
a study leading to a statewide library development plan that will promote
improved library service within the State of North Carolina. The study
attempts to answer a number of questions, among which are:

- How to provide financial support in such a way that the creation of regional systems will be enhanced and that larger regional systems will tend to evolve.

- What are the minimum and maximum sizes for regional systems, and how can the State Library relate State funding to parameters of this size?

- Should there be one type of regional system or may there be many?

- On what basis should State and Federal funds for library service be distributed?

- How much funding will be required to implement the recommended program?

- What is the relationship to the State Library to such a program?

V.   EVALUATION

PROGRAM STRENGTHS

Relations with Libraries of the State

The State Library manages itself economically and with a sensitivity for the needs of the member libraries. A measure of the library economy is given by the $1 cost to process a book. The sensitivity was indicated by the warm feelings displayed by all of those whom we interviewed about the services tendered by the State Library. In general, the management by the State has been such as to create a working relationship with the county libraries that has benefited the libraries of the State without causing a feeling of resentment at the county level because of manipulation by the State.

In 1957, when the first LSA program was formulated, the librarians of the State were brought in to help formulate this program. Under the present study a similar involvement of the librarians of the State exists. The librarians are being interviewed so that a representative sampling of the opinion of the library community is obtained.

Reactions to the State Library were favorable at the libraries we visited. The State Library, in turn, never thought of the county libraries as being run by the State, but, rather, as being run by local government and aided by State money provided under rather general restrictions. In forming the State plan, the State consulted with the county libraries when LSA first became available in 1957. In the current Arthur D. Little study, which may create a new plan, the State, through its contractor, is again consulting with the libraries of the State. Thus the State Library makes an effort not to be an arbitrary dispenser of money received either from North Carolina or through LSCA. A telling measure of its success in providing both statewide library services and effective consulting and extension services is that many of the weaker libraries, when asked how additional Federal money should be spent, reply that it should be spent to strengthen the State Library.

Both the vertical and the parallel intergovernmental relationships that the State agency has are excellent. Furthermore, the efforts of the Stick Committee indicate support for the State Library in a collateral branch of the State government.

Processing Center

The Processing Center is run very efficiently by Marion Johnson. She is a careful experimentalist who is willing to try new ideas in order to reduce the cost of providing good service; she is also willing to reject an idea that turns out not to work. The Center has as its goal a processing time of one week. Two weeks elapse from the time an order is sent out to a vendor to the time the books are sent to a library. The best time achieved by people in the public libraries in receiving books (from the time they submit an order) is three weeks. The slowest time that was reported to us is around two months.

The Processing Center is a model of high morale and efficient output. Its manual has been borrowed by many other libraries so that its procedures can be copied.

Institutes

The Institutes that have been held for years at the Institute of Government have been acclaimed throughout the southeast.

Scholarship Program

The scholarship program has worked well in North Carolina. There has been little buying out of contracted service in the State by the recipients of grants.

PROBLEM AREAS

Regionalization

Forty-seven of the 100 counties have joined in 15 regions. That a number of
the county libraries visited were unwilling to permanently encumber themselves with other counties indicates that the additional benefits offered by
the State Library in the form of grant money were not sufficient to induce
these libraries to join a region. This aversion to regionalization, however,
does not mean an unwillingness to entertain a less permanent relationship
with other counties. Cumberland County, for example, has a contract with
Hoke County for sharing personnel. It was our impression that, in strong
counties, the objection to regionalization usually came from the county
commissioners, who were afraid that they would be putting tax money into a
weak county. When the county was weak, the objection appeared to come from
the librarian who was afraid of being dominated by the librarian at the
stronger county library.

Public Libraries without Federal Support

The State plan's concentration on support for county libraries prohibits the
flexibility that would allow the State to support municipal libraries
directly. We visited two public libraries that do not get State support.
The first was that at Roanoke Rapids. Roanoke Rapids started its library on
its own because it felt the need for a library in the area. It was originally
a project of the Women's Club. The library was kept in a private home. Later,
the Junior Chamber of Commerce made a project of building a library on city-
donated land. Money was received from a foundation to help in creating the
library. The library has an operating budget of $8,786, which is inadequate:
it allows only $1,011 for books and $3,200 for the salaries of the two
librarians. The library serves a community of 26,000 people. More than
half of these people live within the city limits of Roanoke Rapids. The
others work in the city.

The difficulty stems from the political relationship between Roanoke Rapids,
the largest city in Halifax County, and Halifax, the county seat. The library
at the county seat is much too far from Roanoke Rapids to be of use to the
citizens of Roanoke Rapids.

Roanoke Rapids simply does not fit in with the State plan. The State plan is
built around county libraries. Roanoke Rapids does not have enough political
influence with the Halifax County Commissioners to ensure that it will have
the type of library, supported partially with county and Federal funds, that
it feels it needs.

The second library we visited was the one at High Point. High Point is in
the middle of a prosperous manufacturing section. The city chose not to
accept county support for two reasons. First, library support is so strong

in High Point that, if High Point did become part of the county library, it would have to divert more of its budget than it would receive back in the form of support. (High Point has four times as much local support as Greensboro, which is the county seat of Guilford County.) The second reason is that, in general, High Point has had poor experience with county service; it feels that the good service from the county usually is for the county seat. High Point had tried to affiliate in 1940 and wasn't wanted then. In 1952 it decided to proceed on its own. The city now has a collection of around 110,000 volumes housed in a fine building created in 1954. The library receives a per capita support of $3.60. The library has worked with OEO and Head Start. It has a fine collection of publications on furniture and a quarterly mailing on books that relate to some particular business aspect. The library does receive some aid from State services. It participates in film services and gets reference service and other interlibrary services. It does not get money support.

The important thing to observe here is that High Point, in contrast to Roanoke Rapids, is one of the finest libraries in the State. Many of the other fine libraries, such as the ones at Asheville and Charlotte, get only a small proportion of their support from Federal aid. Thus, the situation in North Carolina is that the richer areas are not dependent on Federal aid to have fine libraries.

A third library that is without Federal aid is the Columbus County Library at Whiteville. (This library was not visited.) It received State aid for a time under a waiver because it did not meet the requirement of having a qualified Director. Continued failure to comply with this requirement led to the withdrawal of the waiver by the State Library. Thus, in the case of the third library, failure to receive State funds was due to the insistence of the State Library that, after a reasonable amount of time, its requirements for State and Federal support be met by the local libraries. The Columbus Library's insistence on maintaining its own librarian despite certification was an expensive decision on its part. As can be seen from Table NC-1, Columbus has the poorest per capita support of any county library in the State. Receipt of Federal support would have meant a dramatic percentage improvement.

Disadvantaged Projects

The State has not had specific projects for the disadvantaged. The problem in North Carolina is different from that in the large northern cities, which have had large immigrations of rural workers. Though North Carolina has a large disadvantaged population, it is not a new population. The State's efforts have not been specifically aimed at the poor population of the State. Three types of efforts, however, can be noted.

One group of disadvantaged are the mountain people in the three-county region formed by Avery, Mitchell, and Yancey. These form a region called AMY. The work in this region was guided by Miss Dorothy Thomas, who had come from

New England and worked with the group at AMY for 25 years. She used money from the State to get films. The work was done with films because this group, like many of the other disadvantaged groups that have been noted, were more readily reached through the medium of films than through print.

The second disadvantaged effort to note is that in High Point. The library has been working with OEO and Head Start. They have a Community Services librarian whose function is to be part of the community groups and to operate with community groups who are concerned with helping the disadvantaged portion of the population. They do move a collection of books to the low-income portion of the city and to elderly people.

The third library whose disadvantaged project should be noted is the Mecklenburg County Library. The work there is not specifically supported by Federal funds. The availability of Federal funds for other library purposes has allowed the librarian to spend money to support projects for the culturally deprived. The work with the disadvantaged at that library involves the use of an adult-services community librarian and a children's-services community librarian aiding the library in its work with the disadvantaged with 10 full-time people from the Youth Corps. The library also works with a basic adult education center.

Shortage of Personnel

A March 1966 survey of professional needs reported that 181 professional librarians were needed in the public libraries of North Carolina, and that there were 30 vacancies. The survey estimated that 680 public library professional librarians would be required by 1973. The shortage of professional librarians is critical. The few professionals who are at work are very dependent upon the aid that they can receive from the State in the form of central services. The scholarship program provided by the State is of crucial importance. Fortunately for the purposes of the scholarship program, North Carolinians tend to stay in their State. Many of the professional librarians to whom the survey team spoke were professionals who had returned to North Carolina.

CONCLUSIONS

LSCA has had high impact on the libraries of the poorer parts of North Carolina. Ten of the 15 regional library systems obtain less than $50,000 per region from local tax support. For these 10 regions the combined State and Federal funds approach or surpass the local tax support.

No region other than Gaston-Lincoln receives more than $100,000 of local tax support. The combined State and Federal funds for the regions are $528,827; local tax support contributes $740,274. Only the Gaston-Lincoln Region (which receives $219,937 in local tax support) would not be seriously crippled by the removal of outside support.

The county library systems present a less one-sided picture of local support. Local tax support ranges from $3,750 for Perquimans County to $512,023 for Mecklenburg County, and per capita library income varies from $0.24 to $2.63. Local tax support for the counties is $4,691,770; combined State and Federal support is $1,191,937. Though the outside support is not as important for the counties as for the regions, the removal of this support would be a serious financial blow.

None of the counties or the regions had per capita income of more than $2.63, an amount of support that is small compared to ALA standards. Forty percent of North Carolina's counties provide less than $1 per capita support per year for their libraries. In short, even with LSCA support, the libraries of North Carolina are woefully underfinanced.

Matching monies supplied by North Carolina come from the State Treasury; they do not include local expenditures. It is difficult to say whether Federal money stimulated State spending. State spending was there before the Federal money was available. We received contradictory guesses as to whether Federal money inhibited further State expenditure or stimulated it. It would be our guess that State aid changed from a form of responding to the requests of the State Librarian to a form which was merely necessary to match the Federal monies.

The State Library has done an effective job of administering the responsibilities associated with LSA and LSCA monies.

VI. BIBLIOGRAPHY

North Carolina State LSA and LSCA Title I annual plans, reports, and programs submitted to USOE during the period 1958-1968 (miscellaneous titles).

Downs, Robert B., Dean. Governor's Commission on Library Resources: Resources of North Carolina Libraries. Raleigh, N.C., 1965, 236 pp.

Four-County Project Committee. Four-County Home Demonstration--Public Libraries Project in Reading 1961-1962 Report: Haywood, Onslow, Randolph and Stanley Counties, North Carolina. Asheboro, N.C., 1962, 17 pp.

Mace, Ruth L. Guidebook for Trustees of North Carolina Public Libraries. Institute of Government, University of North Carolina, Chapel Hill, N.C., April 1959, 88 pp.

North Carolina State Library. Statistics of North Carolina Public Libraries covering each year during the period 1 July 1955 - 30 June 1966.

North Carolina State Library Processing Center. North Carolina State Library Processing Center Development and Procedures: January 1, 1960 - June 30, 1961. Raleigh, N.C., 1961, 81 pp.

Stick, David. Report of the Legislative Commission to Study Library Support in the State of North Carolina (mimeograph). August 1968, 79 pp.

REGION IV:

Alabama
Florida
Mississippi
SOUTH CAROLINA
Tennessee

Shirley A. Brother, Library
  Services Program Officer, AVLP
  50 Seventh Street
  Atlanta, Georgia 30323

CHAPTER VIII
SOUTH CAROLINA

I.   SOURCES OF INFORMATION

The following organizations and persons were visited to obtain information
for this study (see Figure NC-1 for a map of the State):

Date	Place Visited	Persons Visited

9/23/68	USOE Regional Office
	Atlanta, Georgia
	Region IV
		Shirley A. Brother, Library
		  Services Program Officer
		B. E. Childers, Director, Adult,
		  Vocational, and Library Programs

9/24-25	State Library Board
	Columbia, South Carolina
		Estellene P. Walker, Director
		  South Carolina State Library
		  Board
		Betty E. Callaham, Director of
		  Field Services
		John H. Landrum, Reference Librarian

9/26/68	Greenville County Library Greenville	Charles E. Stow, Librarian H. Caldwell Harper, Chairman, Board of Trustees Romayne A. Barnes, Trustee Judy Bellamy, Trustee Jean A. Galloway, Trustee E. A. Burch, Trustee H. Z. Jones, Trustee
	Leslie Public Relations Greenville	Ronald L. Copsey, Representative
9/27/68	Laurens County Library Laurens County	Mrs. Phil D. Huff, Librarian
9/27/68	Abbeville-Greenwood Regional Library System Greenwood	Elizabeth L. Porcher, Director Dubose Stuckey, Children's Librarian
10/7/68	Florence County Library Florence	Marguerite G. Thompson, Chief Librarian Elizabeth Law, Extension Librarian Gale Campbell, Tech. Service Librarian Thomas Stork, Reference Librarian
10/7/68	Williamsburg County Library Kingstree	Mrs. Anita Burgess, Librarian
10/8/68	South Carolina State University Orangeburg	Maceo Nance, President Barbara J. Williams, Chief Librarian

Date	Place Visited	Persons Visited
10/8-9	Charleston County Library	Emily C. Sanders, Librarian Margaret D. Mosimann, Deputy Librarian Roberta O'H. Bonnoit, Dept. Head, Reference and Interlibrary Loan Rachel E. Ellis, Dept. Head, Extension Elizabeth L. Moran, Branch Librarian, Cooper River
10/10/68	Colleton County Memorial Library Walterboro	Mrs. Lila W. Morley, Librarian
10/10/68	Aiken-Bamberg-Barnwell- Edgefield Regional Library Aiken	Josephine Crouch, Director Carrie Gene Ashley, Coordinator, Adult Services Mrs. Thelma B. Murtha, Technical Processes Librarian Walter C. Plunkett, Jr., Chairman, Board of Trustees
10/11/68	Benedict College Library Columbia	Mrs. Mae S. Johnson, Librarian

Much valuable information was also obtained from the publications listed
in the Bibliography in Section VI of this chapter.

II. BACKGROUND FOR LSCA OPERATIONS

THE STATE AGENCY

The agency legally designated to administer LSCA Title I funds in South
Carolina is the South Carolina State Library Board, established in 1929 by
an act of the General Assembly and charged with the responsibility for
extending and improving public library service throughout the State. During
the 1967 session of the General Assembly, the original act was amended to
provide the Board with the broader powers of a State Library and enable it
to administer additional services, essentially corresponding to LSCA Titles
III, IV-A, and IV-B.

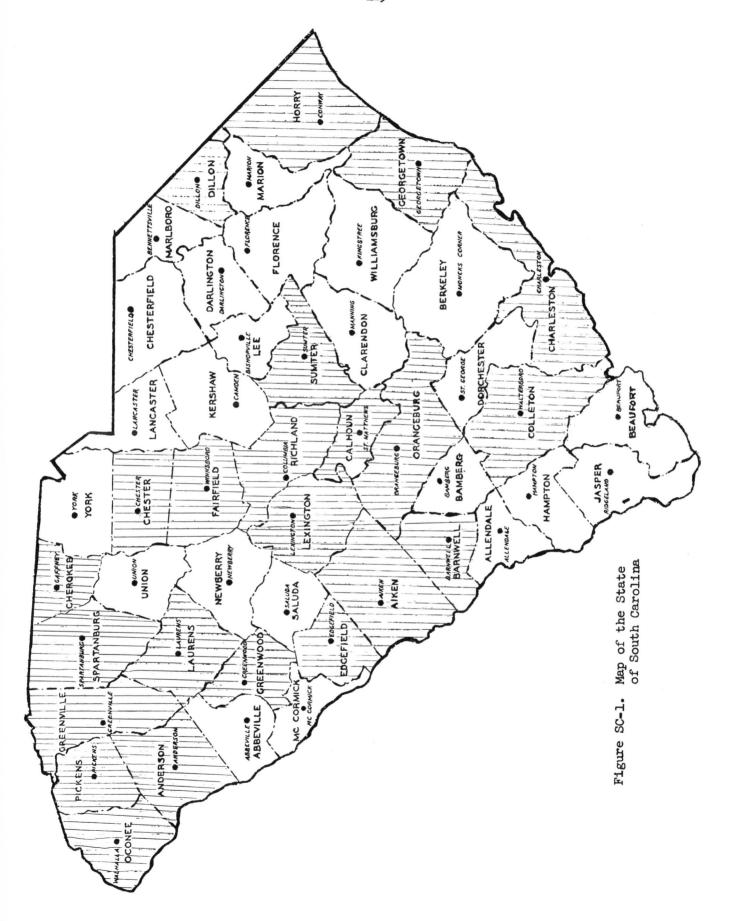

Figure SC-1. Map of the State of South Carolina

The State Library Board, which reports directly to the Governor, is composed of five members appointed by the Governor upon the recommendation of the Superintendent of Education and a staff (including secretaries) of 20 persons. The Board appoints a Director, who is the prime person responisble for LSCA program activities in the State. The present Director is Estellene P. Walker, who has been associated with the agency since 1946. She is assisted in her LSCA program activities by Betty E. Callaham, who is Director of Field Services. In addition, two full-time field-services librarians, or consultants, are involved in extension activities throughout the State. A reference consultant and a consultant on technical services are available to assist the local library in planning reference service and in dealing with problems of book acquisition and processing. Other professional staff librarians provide specialized assistance when needed. Figure SC-2 shows the organization of the State Library Board.

The Library Board, in addition to its responsibilities for extending and improving library services in the State, is charged with setting standards for public library service, with certifying librarians, and with maintaining a Reference and Interlibrary Loan collection to supplement collections held locally throughout the State. Aside from the Board's collection, there are four major State-operated libraries in Columbia, the State capitol: the State Library (a legislative reference library), the State Archives, the Supreme Court Library, and the South Caroliniana Library. These four libraries are organizationally distinct from the Board, but there is a strong possibility that the Board will be designated as the State Library when the new building is completed in late 1969.

HISTORY OF STATE AID TO SOUTH CAROLINA LIBRARIES

The first annual State grant-in-aid program, which provided grants of $200 per county, was initiated in 1943. This was increased to $1,500 per county in 1955. To qualify for State aid, a county library had to meet certain standards of service to ensure the wise use of library funds and the economical administration of the library. Prior to 1967, a cash allotment was generally made directly to libraries that were well established and that had a professionally trained librarian in charge. Smaller county libraries that did not have a professional in charge would receive the same amount ($1,500) to spend for books under State supervision. In 1967, after a campaign by librarians, public library trustees, and interested citizens, the General Assembly passed a new program of State aid, based upon $.20 per capita of the county population. This resulted in a substantial increase in the amounts available as State aid. This money may now be used for the purchase of books, materials, or equipment, and for the employment of qualified personnel, provided certain standards pertaining to library facilities and personnel are met.

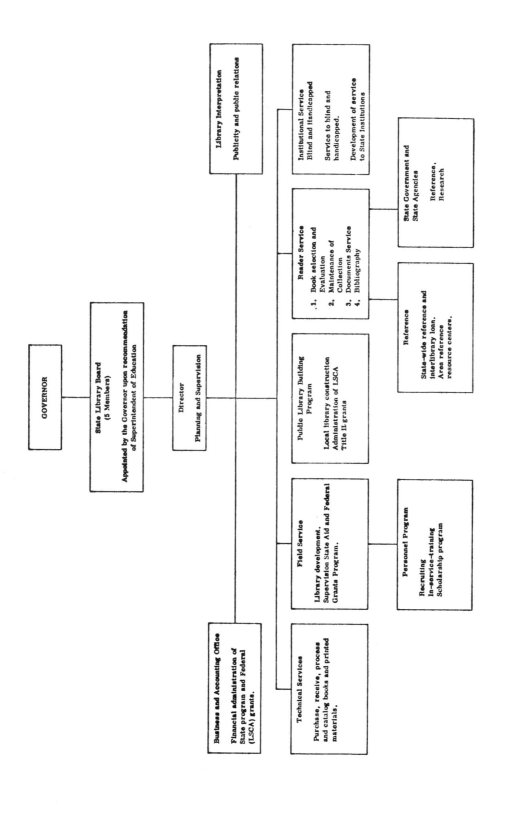

Figure SC-2. Organization of State Library Board

ROLE OF THE STATE AGENCY IN PUBLIC LIBRARY DEVELOPMENT

At the time of the initiation of LSA, legally established countywide library service was in operation in 39 of the State's 46 counties. In each of the seven counties without countywide service, at least one public library was in operation. In spite of its wide extent, all public library service was inadequate both in the basic book collection and in qualified personnel. Many counties had no library service whatsoever, and counties that either provided county service or had a municipal library in one of the larger communities suffered from an inadequate basic collection and a shortage of personnel. This condition strongly influenced the direction that library development took when LSA funding became available.

Library development in South Carolina has been characterized by the following:

- A strong leader. Because of the small size of the Board's staff, and because of her own administrative skill, Miss Walker has been primarily responsible for the lines of library development in South Carolina in the past 20 years.

- Regional or county library service. South Carolina has adopted the county as the basic library unit, with the immediate goal of providing countywide service and the long-range goal of building, on this county-system base, multi-county regional library systems.

- Across-the-board strengthening. Since South Carolina was weak in almost all aspects of library service, when Federal funding became available a program was adopted that would enhance as many facets of library service as possible within the managerial constraints imposed by the small size of the State Library Board staff.

- Use of incentives. Both State grants-in-aid and Federal funding are allocated on a basis that makes the receipt of funds contingent upon adherence to specified standards and (in some instances) upon increases in local funding.

Because the State Library Board assessed its primary task as that of strengthening a whole range of library capabilities within the State, it chose to allocate support through specific program elements, or projects, primarily implemented directly by itself, rather than through local allocation. The State Library Board's development program has involved (1) improving basic library collections, including reference materials, adult fiction and nonfiction, children's and young-adult literature, and periodical holdings, (2) personnel recruitment, training, and placement, (3) salary supplements, (4) statewide reference and interlibrary loan arrangements, (5) statewide interpretation of library services to the public, and (6) assistance in forming countywide and multicounty systems.

RELATIONSHIP OF STATE AGENCY TO OTHER ORGANIZATIONS

South Carolina does not have a particularly strong State Library Association. The South Carolina State Library Association meets biennially, and its influence on library development in the State has been small. The State Library Board has, on occasion, used the Association membership as a sounding board before initiating a new library program, and it also has sought assistance from the Association when it needed program support, particularly when new library legislation was involved.

LIBRARY FUNDING

The Fiscal Year 1957 budget of the State Library Board (that is, the budget during the first year LSA support was available) was approximately $140,000. Since then the budget has increased fourfold, with the Fiscal Year 1968 annual budget amounting to $546,155. Of this amount, $435,944 was State grant-in-aid. Per capita library expenditures in South Carolina's 46 counties in 1957 ranged from a low of $.02 to a high of $.69, averaging $.52. Ten years later, in 1967, per capita support ranged from $.09 to $2.21, averaging $.95.

South Carolina has followed the practice of using local library funding coupled with State funding to meet the Federal matching requirement. When local funding is so used, it consists of funds from localities receiving LSCA support that particular year. The following chart shows LSA and LSCA Title I support for South Carolina, and State matching, for five fiscal years of the program.[1]

	FY 1957	FY 1964	FY 1965	FY 1967	FY 1968
Federal	$ 40,000	$173,223	$314,461	$432,051	$ 546,155
State	101,622	100,457	119,444	145,257	435,944
Local	0	207,306	414,311	326,159	265,769
	$141,622	$409,986	$848,236	$903,467	$1,247,868

[1] FY 1957 was the first year of LSA support; FY 1964 was the final year of LSA support. FY 1965 was the first year of LSCA support.

III.   LSCA PROGRAM

OVERVIEW OF ACTIVITIES

Local financial support and State grant-in-aid funds provide the basic support for South Carolina public libraries. LSCA Title I funds augment this basic support by funding the eight projects described below. Most of these projects were initiated during LSA. The first four represent grants that are made available, on a formula basis, by the State Library Board to all South Carolina libraries that have met the Board's requirements for participation in State and Federal programs; these grants have been made available annually. The second group of four are projects in which funds are granted for specified periods of time to county or regional libraries who apply, and are eligible, for them.

• Book Collection Improvement Project

   The State Library Board provides annual grant programs designed to improve local book collections. The allocation, initially $.04 per capita, is now $.10 per capita. It is provided only to county and regional libraries that meet certain minimum requirements. In general, these requirements are based on hours of opening, certain staffing requirements, and specified local support. All books must be selected through approved selection procedures.

   Initially, to help the libraries achieve a balanced collection, a different category in the book collection was emphasized each year. Emphasis was given in one year to reference material, in another year to adult fiction, and in another year to children's literature. When, in the opinion of the State Library Board, the libraries had achieved the objective of a balanced collection, the grants were continued but were to be spent at the discretion of the local library for books and materials needed to maintain and expand the collection. A particularly popular project, called "Books for the College Bound," was undertaken in 1962. Participating libraries received a collection of 200 books that had been carefully selected with the help of college faculties throughout the State as providing background reading desirable for a successful college career. In addition to the books, lists were supplied to the libraries for distribution to students both through service points in the libraries and through the schools. News releases were prepared and distributed to participating libraries for use in local papers, and several statewide releases were made by the State Library Board.

- Periodicals Project

  The State Library Board provides an annual grant to supplement local funds for the purchase of periodicals. Periodicals included in the project must be indexed in one of the periodical indexes and must not duplicate periodicals already on subscription to the library. In general, the selection does not vary, since one of the objectives is to build up back files of periodicals in business, science, and technology for reference use.

- Library Interpretation Project

  This project was inaugurated in 1961. It is a statewide public-relations program in which the State Library Board, through a contract with a private firm (Leslie Public Relations, Inc., in Greenville), provides assistance in a variety of public-information activities. The general aims of this service are to more fully inform the general public about existing public-library services and to encourage greater use of these services. It is also an attempt to provide people who do not use libraries with information about the services that are available and useful to them. It also publicizes the new programs of the State Library Board. The Library Board holds bi-weekly conferences with the publicist assigned to its account, at which time the field, reference, and administrative staffs discuss with him the programs being conducted and the special areas in which publicity or interpretation is needed. In some cases, a special news item will be given to him for preparation as a release, but, in general, he plans and prepares all releases for all types of news media. None are released until they have been screened by the Director.

  The publicist is available for conferences with local library staffs, or with their library boards, to plan publicity and public relations programs. His responsibility to a local library ends at that point, and the local library is responsible for its own releases and publicity. (The one exception would be in a demonstration area, where the public relations firm does prepare and handle a planned program of public relations and publicity for the period of the demonstration.) In the preparation of brochures, posters, and so forth, the object to be achieved, the facts to be presented, and the distribution are given to the public relations firm, which provides format, polishing, and final publication.

- Personnel Projects

  The State Library Board conducts several personnel projects (also called "programs") designed to recruit and train qualified professional and pre-professional (i.e., nonprofessional library employees, or students, being trained for professional status) librarians for South Carolina libraries, including internship, scholarship, inservice training, and salary supplement. The Board also conducts some training activities.

The Intern Program is designed to attract qualified young people to librarianship. Summer internships are provided for college students to give them an opportunity, under professional supervision, to explore the field of librarianship through work experience. In general, the internships are granted to college juniors or seniors to work in medium-sized or large libraries in the State during the summer. Once selected for an internship, the applicant receives a stipend of $200 per month. (This figure was initially $150.) (Table SC-1 gives a breakdown of recent data concerning this program.)

Table SC-1. Intern Program*

```
Total number of internships given, 1959-1966 . . . . . 117
Total number of internships given, summer 1967 . . . .  20
Total number who have received scholarships . . . . .  15
Total number who have attended library school on
 their own . . . . . . . . . . . . . . . . . . . . . .   6
Total number now working in S. C. public libraries . .  13
Total number known to be working in other libraries .  18
Total number applying for scholarships, 1968-1969 . .   6
```

---

*
 Source: Twenty-Fourth Annual Report, South Carolina State Board, July 1, 1966 - June 30, 1967, p. 11.

The recruiting for the Intern Program is tied in with the activities of the Library Interpretation Project. Recruiting is handled through news media, college papers, direct-mail solicitation, and contacts from lists provided by academic deans and department heads. All of the materials that describe the program, including the direct-mail letters, are passed through the public-relations firm for review.

The Scholarship Program is designed to increase the supply of adequately trained professional librarians for South Carolina public libraries. Each year, five or more scholarships of $2,500 each are awarded to college graduates of outstanding ability for one year's attendance at a graduate library school accredited by the ALA. The State agency encourages attendance at schools outside the South. Applicants must have a B average in their undergraduate work, a minimum of three months' experience working in a library (this requirement may have been met through an internship), and be under 35. Because the State Library Board requires that scholarship recipients have guaranteed jobs, at specific locations and salaries, before they enter graduate school, applicants are sponsored by the trustees of county or regional libraries. At the time the scholarship is granted, the recipient signs a contract with the Board, agreeing to accept the position and salary designated and to remain within the State for two years. The Board provides a subsidy to the employing library for the first two years of a scholarship graduate's employment; the amount of the subsidy can be up to $2,000 for the first year and $1,500 for the second year. The Scholarship Program has been reasonably successful. Most of the scholarship recipients have remained in the State.

Through an In-Service Training Program, the State Library Board makes opportunities for additional training in librarianship available to both pre-professional and professional library personnel who are already employed. Small scholarship grants are provided for regular courses in librarianship or for attendance at special workshops, institutes, or professional meetings that will contribute to the individuals' professional competence. South Carolina colleges offer a number of summer courses, usually of two weeks' duration, for this purpose. If presently employed librarians in the State attend these courses, the scholarship support consists of tuition, room and board, and fees. Usually about 12 pre-professional staff members are awarded scholarships each year to attend workshops in library science, and six professional librarians are given grants to attend the annual conference and the pre-conference institutes of the American Library Association (ALA). Occasionally, a grant will be given to a specific person (such as a grant recently made for the chief cataloger of the State Library Board to attend a month-long institute on cataloging held at the University of Illinois).

The Salary-Supplement Program is intended to relieve the pressure on local funds and to help local libraries compete for professional personnel. Certain requirements must be met: the recipient librarian must be under 65 and certified, and the local library board must certify the annual budget report and the existence of fringe benefits. Related to this, but provided in a somewhat different form, are salary grants. To qualify for grants, a regional or county library serving 50,000 or more population must employ, with local funds, one certified librarian for the first 50,000 population and an additional certified librarian for each 25,000 of population. The State Library Board will provide the salary for one additional librarian for each 50,000 of population above the first 50,000.

The final element in the personnel program provides travel grants for local library trustees to attend national ALA meetings, or the Southeastern Regional Library Association meetings. Generally, these are allocated to three to six libraries each year. The intent is to stimulate trustee attendance at meetings rather than to provide a

continuing grant for a particular library. Experience in
South Carolina indicates that library trustees who have attended
these meetings once will recruit other trustees to attend and
will themselves attend the meetings whether subsidized for travel
or not.

- Small Libraries Project

The Small Libraries Project was initiated in 1962 to explore the
possibility of extending service, through a contract with a well-
established county library, to a community library in a neighboring
county that was without countywide service. The project was
designed to provide the well-established library with an opportunity to study the possibility of regional development, to
provide the State Library Board with some indication of the
feasibility of contract service, and to provide the library
receiving service with expert direction and assistance (while,
hopefully, overcoming its fear of domination by a larger library).
Funds may be granted for a 3-year period.

During 1962-1963 this project was tried out in three locations,
only one of which was considered successful by the Library Board.
The successful one added a fourth county to a three-county region.
in 1964-1965, funds were offered to three more small libraries,
but only one of them could meet the requirements for participation.

- County Library Project

This project was established to encourage independent public library
agencies within a single county to consolidate into a strong one-unit
system serving the entire population. The amount of the grant
varies with the size of the population served and the objective
to be achieved: 35,000 - 45,000 population, $5,000 per year for
three years to cover the salary of a professionally qualified
librarian who will bring the new system up to an achievement
level that will allow it to join in a regional system; 45,000 -
74,000 population, $10,000 per year for three years to develop
the system to a point that it may join in a regional library;
75,000 and up population, a grant based upon $.25 per capita the
first year, $.20 per capita the second year, and $.15 per capita
the third year. This category has been used extensively on a
priority basis with funding granted to several counties per year,
usually on a 3-year demonstration basis. Greenville, Beaufort,
and Florence Counties have been considered successful county
demonstrations by the Library Board.

- Regional Library Project

Where local circumstances permit, it is the State Library Board's
goal to link county units of library service into multicounty
library regions. This project was designed to encourage the establishment of regional library systems composed of two or more counties

with a combined population of 100,000 or more. In awarding grants, the Library Board gives priority to regions that include at least one county that has not previously had countywide library service and in which there is reasonable assurance the program will be continued at the same level after the withdrawal of LSCA funds. Planning is generally done at the local level, with the assistance of consultants from the State Library Board.

- "Catch Up" Project

  The "Catch Up" Project was inaugurated in 1966 to help libraries for the first time qualifying for participation in the grant program to bring their service program more rapidly up to a good level. Two-year grants of $2,500 per year are made. These funds are used to acquire the books, materials, and equipment needed to help raise the level of service to that provided by other libraries in the State. In Fiscal Year 1967, three such grants were made.

In addition to the ongoing projects described above, three other projects, all completed, deserve mention. Two--the Carolina Materials and the Genealogical Materials Projects--were funded under LSCA Title I; the third--the Telefacsimile Project--was funded under LSCA Title III.

- Carolina Materials Project

  In an attempt to make much of the South Carolina historical material that was either out of print or available only in Charleston or Columbia available to the general public, the State Library Board, with the assistance of authorities in the field of South Carolina history, compiled a list of the 100 essential books on the subject. The Board then brought these books back into print through the Xerox process and deposited them in one library in each of the six Congressional districts that would agree to open its entire history collection to residents of the district. A later supplement added 25 more volumes.

- Genealogical Materials Project

  In providing State-level reference service, the State Library Board had a responsibility for reference in the field of genealogy. In order to discharge this responsibility, a cooperative agreement was worked out with the Caroliniana Library, which has extensive holdings in South Carolina local history of especial importance in doing any work in South Carolina genealogy. Under this agreement, the Caroliniana Library selects, houses, and services the genealogical material that is purchased by the State Library Board. This material remains the property of the State Library Board and is properly identified as the Board's property. This material is not supplied on interlibrary loan but its use is open to the general public on a reference basis.

- Telefacsimile Project

  During Fiscal Year 1967, the State Library Board used LSCA Title III funds to conduct a 3-month trial of the use of a Xerox Magnavox Telecopier linking the State Library Board with the Charleston and Greenville County libraries.

  The volume of reference and interlibrary loan requests handled by the State Library Board has always been large and is increasing rapidly. The Telecopier experiment was undertaken to determine whether this equipment would provide a means to (1) handle more quickly books and information urgently or immediately needed and (2) overcome the possibility of error in verbal transmission in relaying by voice information of a detailed or highly technical nature. The two libraries participating in the experiment with the State Library Board were carefully instructed not to relay by means of the Telecopier any requests other than those which were immediately or urgently needed or that were of a highly technical nature. Ordinary requests continued to be handled by mail or by telephone. At the close of the experiment, the conclusion was that although the equipment and its operation presented no problem, the quantity of the highly technical information requests did not warrant the maintenance of the telefacsimile communication system at present.

MANAGEMENT OF LSCA PROJECTS

Strong incentives have been present in the State Library Board's management of the LSCA program since its beginning. The allocation of both State aid and LSCA funds has been, and continues to be, contingent upon recipients' meeting quite detailed minimum library standards and/or local financial support. An additional management control is used with considerable effectiveness in South Carolina. The State Library Board employs comprehensive legal contracts between itself and the boards of local libraries that receive funds, and in turn requires that similar contracts be drawn between local boards when projects involve cooperative arrangements. These contracts not only stipulate the requirements that local boards must meet, but also specify the disposition of holdings and equipment should the recipients be unable to fulfill their obligations.

Aside from the State Library Board's explicit management procedures, three aspects of South Carolina's geographical and political environment contribute to the effectiveness of LSCA program management in the State. One is the relatively small size of the State, and of its library community--because of this, the strengths and weaknesses of each county library, and its staff, holdings, and problems, are well known by the Board's Director, Miss Walker. The second is the existence of an excellent State and interstate highway network in the State, which permits frequent personal contact between State and local people on their respective home grounds. The third is that the members of each county's governing body also serve as the county's representatives in the State General Assembly. In dealing with the members of the General Assembly in Columbia, therefore, the State Library Board is, at the same time, dealing with those who are responsible for local government. This circumstance permits the Library Board to monitor many local activities through personal contact with the representatives of local governments.

IV.   DESCRIPTION OF REPRESENTATIVE USES OF LSCA FUNDS

During the course of the survey, SDC visited, in addition to the State Library Board, two regional library headquarters and six county libraries. This section briefly describes library development activities at these eight locations.

Greenville County Library

Thirty years ago, the Greenville Municipal Library was one of the finest in the State. Since that time, the library declined until the loss of a greatly needed textile industry, in part because of the lack of local reference resources, prompted local business and civic groups to undertake a vigorous campaign to improve library services. In 1961, the State Library Board offered the Greenville County Board a grant of $45,000 if the city and county systems could be consolidated into a single county system. The Board worked with the county delegation in drawing up legislation to establish the new system, and, when it was established, a 3-year LSA demonstration grant was provided to facilitate the consolidation of all library services in the county--$22,000 the first year, $13,000 the second year, and $10,000 the third year. State aid was also made available to provide certain assistance in purchasing books, equipment, and other supplies.

The library's chief problem during the first year of the demonstration was a shortage of trained library personnel. Although money was available for enhancing book stocks and providing additional services--such as the book-mobile operation--the library was unable to obtain additional professional personnel to staff these new services. In this sense, the demonstration failed to meet either the Library Board's or the local people's expectations.

The 7-man Greenville County Library Board, composed of three city and four county members appointed by the county delegation, meets monthly and operates independently of other city or county services. At the time we visited Greenville we met with the board at one of its regular meetings. The board has been fortunate in obtaining considerable amounts of local private funding. Chief among these was a donation of $500,000 from a private local foundation for a new $2 million county library building to be funded by local, LSCA, and Appalachia funds. Though their building problems seem to be satisfied for the time being, they are still faced with the inability to staff key professional positions in the library. This is in spite of recent substantial salary increases for the professional staff, and a 20 percent increase in salary for nonprofessional staff members, paid for out of a 1/5-mill increase approved by the county delegation.

Laurens County Library

The Laurens County Library is the central library in a rural county. It operates two branches--at Clinton and Duckett--and a bookmobile service to outlying county areas. The existing library building was recently extensively remodeled and enlarged. The county owns the building and provides maintenance.

This library, in common with many other libraries in South Carolina, has had staffing problems. It is difficult to obtain personnel to staff the bookmobile service. The library has had three interns under grant from the State Library Board and considers the intern program valuable. They want to sponsor a scholarship applicant, but have not been successful in recruiting one.

Abbeville-Greenwood Regional Library

In July 1966, a 5-year regional library demonstration project was initiated for Abbeville and Greenwood Counties. The LSCA Title I grant of $25,000 was to be apportioned as follows: 1966-1967, 30 percent; 1967-1968, 25 percent; 1968-1969, 20 percent; 1969-1970, 15 percent; and 1970-1971, 10 percent. An additional grant-in-aid was provided, equal to $.50 per capita, to match "new money" over and above the required basic support of $.60 per capita. South Carolina State aid and other Federal project funds allocated on a formula basis were also available.

The Greenwood County Library was designated as the headquarters library and its Director, Elizabeth Porcher, as Director for the Region. Administratively, the Region is treated as a single unit with a unified staff and centralized ordering and processing. During the first year of regional operation a considerable portion of staff time was spent in establishing standard systemwide procedures for registration, circulation, reporting, and other activities.

Since Greenwood County already had a good level of library service, the immediate task was to improve library service in Abbevile County. Holdings in Abbeville County had never been cataloged, weeding was needed, and the physical facilities were extremely inadequate. To help with these problems, the State Library Board made a "Catch Up" grant to the Abbeville Library. The first step was the coordination of bookmobile service for the two counties. All bookmobile operations were transferred to the headquarters library. With the aid of an experienced consultant, new routes and stops were established, although the development of a complete extension service to rural areas was initially handicapped by the lack of a full-time extension librarian.

Considerable progress has been made in strengthening the library in Abbeville and the branch in Donalds. Book collections in both communities have been examined, worn and dated materials removed, and new titles added. The limitations of the existing library building in Abbeville have temporarily precluded the expansion of services at that location, although planning for

a new facility is under way. In Donalds the increased hours of service have
made possible greater use of the library. The opening of the Calhoun Falls
Library extended service to the western portion of the county. Thus, Abbeville
County is now served by three service points and a bookmobile, and its residents have free access to the resources of the headquarters library. It is
anticipated that, later during the demonstration period, service will be
extended to adjacent McCormick County.

The following is a tabulation of income received by the Abbeville-Greenwood
Regional Library in Fiscal Year 1968 from Federal, State, and local sources:

Federal (LSCA Title I)

Grant-in-aid	$ 10,708.00	
Demonstration Grant	6,250.00	
Book Collection Improvement Grant	6,576.30	
Abbeville "Catch-Up" Grant	2,500.00	
Salary Supplement	5,030.42	
Periodical Grant - Greenwood	622.53	
Junior Intern Grant	350.00	
Travel Grants	213.50	
Total Federal		$ 32,250.75
State Aid		13,152.60
Local		78,207.83
Total		$123,611.18

Florence County Library

In 1964, a 3-year demonstration project was initiated in Florence County.
This demonstration was made possible by an act of the General Assembly that
established a unified county library system by consolidating the existing
Florence City Library, which served the urban area, with the Florence
Circulating Library, which had provided limited bookmobile service in rural
areas of the county. The enabling legislation provided for local support
of the library by means of a 3-mill tax levied on School District One, plus
an appropriation of $.50 per capita for the remainder of the county.

To aid in the establishment of the new system, the State Library Board provided an LSCA Title I demonstration grant of $45,000, to be paid in decreasing allotments over the 3-year period. The initial allotment of $20,000 supplemented local income of $106,738 derived from millage and appropriation. The system also became eligible for other grants from State and Federal sources (State aid, scholarships, salary supplements, and other project grants), which totaled $48,815.34 for the 3-year period. In addition, the Florence County Library received book deposits of more than 4,000 volumes from the State Library Board and benefited from grants made through other agencies (scholarships, in-service training, and special collections) that amounted to $8,615.61. In total, the library system received $102,430.95 during the 3-year demonstration period.

At the time the demonstration began, the Florence County Library faced numerous problems. A large portion of the county population was receiving only token library service. Book and nonbook resources were limited in extent and uneven in quality. The staff was small. Buildings and equipment were badly in need of renovation or replacement. The value of the library as a community resource was recognized by only a small segment of the public.

Significant improvements in library service have become evident as a result of the demonstration project. A countywide organization was implemented; the library system now operates under a single board of trustees representative of all sections of the county. Administration is centralized under the library Director, who supervised the consolidation of existing library units and the expansion of services.

Library services are now more accessible to every county resident. The headquarters library, with its improved resources and facilities, is available to all, and services are carried to the people of the county by means of three branches and two bookmobiles. Discussions with other communities have been held to determine whether additional service points are needed. The number of registered borrowers has increased more than 25 percent since 1964.

During the demonstration period a comprehensive evaluation of the book collection was undertaken. Old, worn, and substandard titles were eliminated, and the existing 38,000-volume collection was strengthened by the purchase of 11,393 new titles. In addition, 4,000 books were placed on deposit by the State Library Board. Recently, the library became a depository for Federal documents. Special materials, however--such as films, recordings, music, slides, prints, and paintings--are lacking and will probably not be available until library income increases.

Throughout the demonstration period, the library was handicapped by a shortage of personnel. During the greater part of the period the Director was the only professional member of the staff. In 1967, two graduates of the State Library Board's scholarship program were employed, and in 1968 a third graduate was added to the staff. These additional staff personnel enable the library to provide contract support (LSCA Title I funded) to adjacent Williamsburg County, which ultimately may affiliate with Florence County to form a library region.

Charleston County Library

Charleston is one of the two largest cities in South Carolina. Because of this, the funding situation of the Charleston County Library System has probably been less desperate than that of most other libraries in the State. Its annual operating budget is approximately $375,000, most of which comes from local funds. The system is currently participating in a major demonstration grant, having been designated one of the five Area Reference Resource Centers in the State. The system is the largest in the State, consisting of a large headquarters library in downtown Charleston, 10 branches located primarily in suburban centers, and two bookmobiles serving rural areas. The staff of 70 includes 10 professional librarians. A handsome new branch facility was recently completed to provide service in a racially mixed area. The staff is currently involved in metropolitan-area studies concerning future locations of branch libraries (in conjunction with other county services). The overall library service is of very high quality compared to that in other areas of the State. In terms of the impact of LSA and LSCA Title I support, the system had shown less dramatic improvement than have other library systems in the State, chiefly because it did not have as far to go.

Aiken-Bamberg-Barnwell-Edgefield Regional Library

This regional library system was established in 1958 under a 5-year LSA demonstration grant. The first multicounty library system established in the State under LSA, it originally included Aiken, Barnwell and Edgefield Counties; Bamberg County joined in 1964 under an additional 4-year demonstration. The regional headquarters is located in Aiken; the region's two bookmobiles operate out of this facility. In addition, there are 12 branches, 9 community stations; and 11 school stations. The current operating income is approximately $145,000, of which $6,000 is State aid, $26,286 consists of LSCA Title I project grants, and the balance consists of local appropriations from the four counties.

The system's circulation figures have increased from 184,473 in 1958-1959 to 343,763 in 1966-1967. The increase is significant, and the pattern of the increase is equally so. In the earlier years of the demonstration, the most notable increase was in the smaller libraries. More recently, the larger communities have shown increases, possibly reflecting the increasing array of special library programs initiated in the larger libraries.

V.   EVALUATION

PROGRAM STRENGTHS

- Strong leadership in the State agency.

- A relatively compact State with a small library community well known to the State agency staff.

- Availability of State aid.

- Skillful use of "incentive" program management.

PROBLEM AREAS

- Low economic level throughout most of the State--financial status of public libraries was very low at the time Federal funding began.

- Lack of trained personnel.

CONCLUSIONS

In general, the improvement in library services in South Carolina over the past decade has been impressive. New buildings have replaced obsolete facilities, library branches have been added to expand local services, book and nonbook stocks have been strengthened, and a wider variety of library services are now available to the public. Local library staffs are extremely grateful for LSA and LSCA support. The administration of Federal funds by the State Library Board, in the person of Miss Walker, is highly thought of. The only concern communicated to the SDC study team was the possible loss of leadership if Miss Walker were to leave her position.

The marked effect of Federal funds on the improvement of library services in South Carolina is due, primarily, to the stewardship of a State agency that knows intimately the economic and political realities of the State.

VI.   BIBLIOGRAPHY

South Carolina State LSA and LSCA Title I annual plans, reports, and programs submitted to USOE during the period 1958-1968 (miscellaneous titles).

Arthur D. Little, Inc. Library Development Study of the Charleston County Library System. Cambridge, Mass., June 1968, 22 pp. (C-70220).

Busha, Charles H. A Prospectus of a Proposed Information Research Center Specializing in Textiles and Textile Technology for the Greenville, South Carolina, Area. South Carolina State Library Board, Columbia, S.C., 30 March 1965, 40 pp.

Busha, Charles H. and Landrum, John H. Telefacsimile Communication With the Xerox Magnavox Telecopier in Reference and Interlibrary Loans. South Carolina State Library Board, Columbia, S.C., July 1967, 22 pp.

State Budget and Control Board. Thirteenth Annual Report: South Carolina State Library Board, July 1, 1955 - June 30, 1956. South Carolina, 1956, 45 pp.

State Budget and Control Board. Twenty-Fourth Annual Report: South Carolina State Library Board, July 1, 1966 - June 30, 1967. South Carolina, 1967, 32 pp.

REGION V:

Illinois
Indiana
Michigan
OHIO
WISCONSIN

James G. Igoe, Library
  Services Program Officer, AVLP
  New Post Office Building
  433 West Van Buren St.
  Chicago, Illinois 60607

CHAPTER IX
OHIO

I.   SOURCES OF INFORMATION

The following organizations and persons were visited to obtain information
for this study (see Figure O-1 for a map of the State):

Date	Place Visited	Persons Visited
8/13/68 - 8/14/68	Ohio Library Association/ Ohio Library Trustees Association Columbus	A. Chapman Parsons, Executive Director
8/13/68 - 8/14/68	Ohio State Library Columbus	Joseph F. Shubert, Ohio State Librarian Ruth Hess, Head, LSCA Programs C. Edwin Dowlin, Head, Library Development Division
8/15/68	Regional Library Service Center Caldwell	R. Jane Thomas, Head
8/15/68	Bellaire Public Library Bellaire	Lois B. Walker, Librarian
8/15/68	Barnesville Public Library Barnesville	
8/16/68	Dayton and Montgomery County Public Library Dayton	William Chait, Director
8/26/68	Cleveland Public Library Cleveland	Dr. Fern Long, Adult Education Edward D. D'Alessandro, Deputy Director Treasure House Branch Quincy Branch
8/27/68	Cuyahoga County Public Library Cleveland	Lewis C. Naylor, Director Alice P. Aiello, Deputy Director, Research and Development and Promotion

Date	Place Visited	Persons Visited
8/27/68	Community Development Commission Cleveland	Glenn E. Nitschke, Planner
8/28/68	Mansfield Public Library Mansfield	A. T. Dickinson, Jr., Director
8/29/68	Cincinnati/Hamilton County Public Library Cincinnati	Ernest I. Miller, Director Jacob Epstein, Assistant Librarian and Head of Main Library Jane McGregor, Supervisor, Work with Children Virginia Kerr, Staff, Books/Jobs Project Elizabeth Lewis, Head, Extension Department
8/30/68	State Finance Department Columbus	Ed Troyer, Analyst Tom Williams, Analyst

Note: Also met with representatives of Opportunity Industrial Center, a private, nonprofit agency involved in employment counseling, training, placement, etc. (Cleveland and Mansfield).

Much valuable information was also obtained from the publications listed in the Bibliography in Section VI of this chapter.

II. BACKGROUND FOR LSCA OPERATIONS

THE STATE AGENCY

Although formally separated from the State Department of Education, the State Library is controlled and managed by a State Library Board whose five members are selected by the State Board of Education. The State Library Board has been legally designated as the agency responsible for receiving, and approving the allocation of, LSCA Title I funds. The Board appoints a State Librarian, who acts as the executive officer of the State Library and secretary to the Board. (See Figure O-2.) The Board also provides broad administrative guidelines and regulations for the internal management of the State Library.

Figure O-1.   Map of the State of Ohio

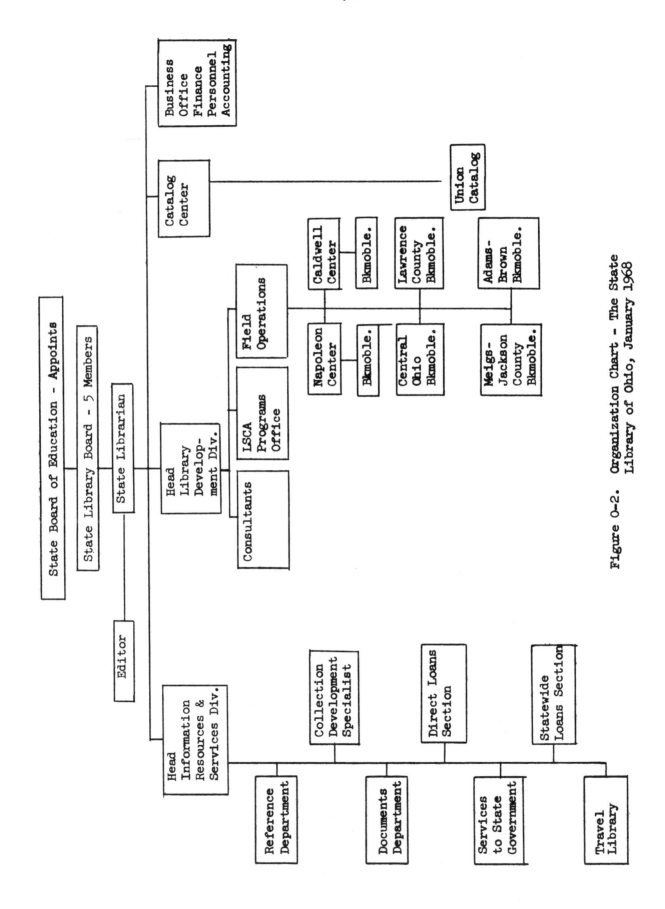

Figure 0-2. Organization Chart - The State Library of Ohio, January 1968

Legal Authority of the State Library

Many library activities are conducted without the benefit of permanent legislation. Some statutory laws, biennial appropriation acts of the legislature, and periodic statements of legal opinion by the State Attorney General provide the legal infrastructure supporting current operations of the State Library.

Even though the State Library's services are available to public, academic, school, and special libraries, the Ohio Legislature has not designated the State Library as the focal agency legally responsible for developing, coordinating, and administering library programs within Ohio. The State Library's influence on the development of library systems, the establishment of service standards, and the creation of new patterns of library services derives primarily from its control of State aid and LSCA funds. Because specific statutory authority has not been given to the State Library, it becomes incumbent upon the State Librarian to assume an active role in formulating and suggesting to the Board new program directions that he feels should be considered if library programs are to be responsive to the needs of Ohio's urban communities.

The State Library's Approach to Library Service

The State Library historically assumed leadership and consultive functions in county library service and extension work. It has served primarily as a service agency centering its attention on libraries in rural areas that have inadequate service and financial resources. Program planning and administration for some of these areas has been centralized at the State Library. To augment library services in these areas, the State Library has established two regional library service centers and has operated several bookmobile programs.

Regional centers, serving rural counties, provide such supplemental services as book loans, consultant services, loan of audiovisual materials, and so forth. Multicounty bookmobile service programs originally encountered resistance in some counties, as local librarians were apprehensive that accepting the service would lead to domination by the State Library. They also felt that the service might decrease their own circulation and thereby lead to cuts in their budgets by the County Budget Commissions. These fears have proved to be unfounded. Local autonomy has been preserved; and far from decreasing circulation, the bookmobile has proved to be a valuable public relations tool for providing vital library service to areas that would otherwise have none, for stimulating community interest, for alerting residents to the multitude of library services available to them, and for increasing the circulation of the local libraries.

According to the Directory of Ohio Libraries,[1] the State Library, in addition to the activities mentioned above, also provides the following services:

[1] State Library of Ohio. 1968 Directory of Ohio Libraries, with Statistics for 1967. Columbus, Ohio, pp. 8-9

- Inter-library loans

- Union catalog listings

- Periodicals and reproduction service

- Reference service

- Placement service

- Ohio documents bibliographical and depository program

- Consultant service

- Catalog and processing service centers (contract basis to public, school, academic and special libraries)

- Traveling library section

- Distribution of newsletters and publications by State Library to Ohio libraries

State Activities in Library-Development Planning

Until recently, library-development planning has been accomplished without a formal State master plan outlining long-range goals and programs. The statewide research studies, surveys, and so forth, which would have provided the foundation for formulating a viable master plan had not been undertaken since the statewide survey of 1935. Without a master plan, and without such surveys and studies, a weak framework has existed for effectively interacting with the LSCA program.

Under the administration of the acting State Librarian, Ruth Hess, LSCA Title I funds were used to initiate the first comprehensive survey of library services at State and local levels. The final report, by Ralph Blasingame, was entitled Survey of Ohio Libraries and State Library Services. This study has provided the basis for the current development of a formal master plan.

The current State Librarian, Joseph Shubert, provided opportunities for all interested library personnel, the academic community, and the joint executive office of the Ohio Library Association and the Ohio Library Trustees Association (OLA-OLTA) to participate in preparation of Ohio's library development plan. Recently, the proposed State master plan was formally presented to, and adopted by, the OLA-OLTA membership. Portions of the plan, together with projected costs, will be submitted to the Ohio Legislature in 1969.

LIBRARY FUNDING

Financial Support for the State Library

The Blasingame Survey found that, in Fiscal Year 1966, LSCA funds provided the major share (64.5 percent) of funding for the entire range of State Library operations, including both the State Library's operating budget and some of the costs of operating State-directed programs. The remainder of the funding (35.5 percent) was obtained from legislative appropriations and monies received for contract services rendered to the State's local libraries. That this is still the case indicates that the State Library continues to rely heavily upon LSCA, rather than legislative or local library support.

The legislature's previous attitude toward the State Library and its programs is evidenced by (1) the existence of numerous legal constraints, (2) limited statutory authority, and (3) the reliance upon appropriation acts (which automatically expire after two years) to support the operations of the State Library. However, this attitude is changing, as is shown by recent salary increases, the addition of some new staff positions, and an increased grant-in-aid subsidy for libraries serving the blind during the 1967-1969 biennial session. Table O-1 illustrates the pattern of biennial appropriations for the State Library from 1955 through 1969.

Table O-1. Legislative Appropriations for Library Services 1955-68

Biennial Year	State Library Operating Budget	Grant-In-Aid	Total
1955-1957	$241,612	$320,000	$534,612
1957-1959	254,338	352,000	606,338
1959-1961	326,868	543,600*	870,468
1961-1963	353,480	543,600*	897,080
1963-1965	337,000	554,600*	891,600
1965-1967	367,000	554,600*	922,050
1967-1969	491,130**	662,080***	1,153,210

*This figure includes $39,000 appropriation to Cleveland and Cincinnati Public Libraries for services rendered to the blind.
**Salary increases and new staff positions are included.
***A major portion of the increase in State aid can be attributed to an increase in the subsidy (from $13-$15 per reader), to both the Cleveland and Cincinnati/Hamilton County Public Libraries, which serve the blind.

LSCA funds have not stimulated additional library appropriations by the
State legislature. If grant-in-aid appropriations for local libraries
are used as one measure of LSCA's impact, the data in Table O-1 reveal a
tendency by the legislature to maintain spending close to previously
authorized levels and to view libraries as primarily a local financial
responsibility. The only large increases in grant-in-aid appropriations
have occurred in the 1959-1961 and the 1967-1969 bienniums. The major
percentage of the latter increase was a result of a raise in the subsidy for
services to the blind. In Fiscal Year 1966, however, LSCA funds were
required to maintain the $13 per reader subsidy originally intended by the
legislature because the number of persons using the service had increased
33 percent, while the legislative appropriation remained the same.

Another measure of LSCA's impact is the legislative appropriation for the operating budget of the State Library. Although the data in Table O-1 show that
allocations for its own operating budget increased slightly from 1959 to 1967,
the State Library has been unable to maintain sufficient staff positions
with only general revenue, and has been forced to subsidize its staff with
LSCA funds. The State Library has attempted to build and support a staff
with appropriations from the legislature; however, a majority of the staff
(approximately 142 of the 180 positions) are either wholly or partially
supported by LSCA Title I funds. Legal restrictions, such as Finance
Department approval of all new positions, have been barriers to staff
development. If LSCA funds were reduced, staff positions would have to
be reduced.

Discussions with various groups and persons suggested several possible
reasons why the State Library had remained on a budget plateau:

- The State Library previously lacked a master plan that would
  visibly demonstrate to the legislature that serious long-range
  planning and development were being undertaken.

- The fiscal conservatism of the legislature, in its behavior
  towards all State agencies, made budget increases difficult
  to obtain.

- The legislature did not consider the State Library as a
  useful adjunct of State government in terms of providing
  adequate library service to the legislature and other State
  agencies.

- The State Library was unable to clearly define its needs
  (probably aggravated by the lack of a master plan) and its
  role in urban areas for legislative members.

Three recent developments have tended to counter earlier criticisms of the State Library: (1) There is a general feeling that the current State Librarian has exhibited effective leadership qualities in dealing with the legislature, as evidenced by the increase in the 1967-1969 biennium appropriation; (2) a proposed State master plan has been developed that demonstrates that serious long-range planning has been undertaken, and this plan will be utilized to secure additional approappropriations; and (3) the present State Librarian has begun a program designed to encourage the legislature and State agencies to utilize the resources of the State Library.

Financial Support for Local Libraries

Local libraries are basically financed by a county-levied tax (uniform statewide). Also State grant-in-aid monies are an important supplement to this local tax support in a few rural counties. Although complicated legal procedures exist for levying a special library tax, local libraries within a county are, for all practical purposes, financed from a local situs intangibles tax (5 percent) levied upon such items as mortgages, bonds, and interest-bearing instruments. Under the legislation that instituted the tax in the 1930's, a local library board that agrees to make its resources available to all residents within the county can submit its budget directly to the County Budget Commission and receive first consideration for local intangibles taxes collected within the county.

Each County Budget Commission is composed of three members (County Auditor, County Treasurer, and County Prosecutor), who are authorized to distribute these taxes to various libraries within the county and make other decisions relative to the support of other local government activities. There are no statutory guidelines given to the Commissions for allocating intangibles taxes among the libraries. The Commission is not obligated to distribute the total amount of intangibles taxes for library purposes; a percentage may be returned to the cities on a situs basis. This arrangement results in pressures being exerted by cities upon the Commission to restrict the amount of intangibles tax given to libraries. An individual library's budget thus depends to a great extent upon the political ability of local librarians and library trustees to influence the Commission to allocate greater percentages of the tax for library purposes. (It is likely that, if libraries were forced to finance their operations with general revenue sources rather than with the intangibles tax, the local library community would have to engage even more actively in the political process if they were to receive an adequate share of the available revenue.)

The financing of local libraries by means of an intangibles tax has a direct bearing on the allocation of LSCA Title I funds. One reason is that intangibles taxes collected in a county can be spent only within that county; there is no statewide equalization formula for helping counties that have small intangibles tax revenues. (The present State grant-in-aid system attempts to alleviate this condition.) Table O-2 illustrates the financial inequities resulting from the lack of an equalization formula.

Table O-2. Intangibles Tax Collection and
Distribution: Selected Counties 1967*

County	Percentage of Intangibles Tax Distributed to Libraries	Per Capita Income of Libraries
Adams	100	$ .59
Brown	57	.69
Lawrence	100	.66
Meigs	71	.68
Jackson	47	.83
Cuyhoga	95	7.00
Wood	87	7.46

*Ohio Directory of Libraries, pp. 54-55.

The first five counties in Table O-2 are among the 28 counties in southeastern Ohio that have been designated by the Federal government as eligible
for Appalachia funds. Because of the extremely low per capita income of the
libraries in this area, LSA and LSCA funds have been used, in some instances
since 1957, to support bookmobile service to areas that the local libraries
cannot serve.

A second reason that local library financing difficulties are relevant to
LSCA Title I is that significant reductions in LSCA funds would further
sharply curtail library service in rural areas. Because of the declining
population and low income levels, sufficient intangibles tax revenue cannot
be generated to provide adequate support for library services. The situation
is not likely to improve and would be further aggravated if the intangibles
tax were removed, because the libraries would be forced to compete with other
municipal departments for limited general revenue. This situation would then
result in pressures by local libraries upon the State Library Board to
allocate even more LSCA funds to them.

Three forms of State grant-in-aid are allocated by the State Library Board.
The first form of grant-in-aid is given only to extension center libraries;
an extension center library is defined as:

> ...a county district library or a library which, with the
> approval of the State Library Board, has assumed responsi-
> bility for extending library service by means of branches,
> library stations, or traveling library service to all
> territory in the county not within the territorial bounda-
> ries of other established libraries with the county.[2]

[2]State Aid Rules for Ohio Libraries, June 11, 1968 (mimeo).

To be eligible for grants-in-aid, extension center libraries must demonstrate (1) that they are providing satisfactory service, and (2) that their activities are directed by either a head librarian certified by the State Board of Library Examiners or a graduate of a library school recognized by the State Library, or that arrangements for a person so qualified are being made by the extension center library. The grant-in-aid amounts are "based upon the per capita intangibles tax collection of the county in which the library is situated and upon the percentage of such collection allocated for library purposes of the county..."3 The grant-in-aid allowance formula is shown below.

Intangibles Tax Collection Per Capita	Grant-in-Aid Basic Allowance
$0 - 1.25	$6,000
1.26 - 7.70	5,000
1.71 - 2.61	4,000
2.62 - 3.45	2,500
3.46 - 4.00	1,500
4.01 and up	1,500

Two other forms of grant-in-aid payments are made. One is a flat payment of exactly $42 given to a library (other than an extension center library) that has received local intangibles tax support for the preceding three years and has attempted to get an increase in intangibles support from the County Budget Commission. The other is a payment given to libraries participating in the State Union Catalog that lend more books than they borrow in interlibrary loan; this payment is $2 for each book lent over the number borrowed.

III. LSCA PROGRAM

OVERVIEW OF ACTIVITIES

In Ohio's general approach to library development under LSA, there was little attempt to encourage cooperative arrangements, either within or between counties. Under LSCA, the State Library is encouraging cooperative arrangements among small and metropolitan libraries within a county. In Fiscal Year 1967, the library in the Dayton suburb of Miamisburg voted to

---

3Ibid.

affiliate with the Dayton Public Library. To help ensure that this affiliation would be successful, and to encourage other libraries to join similar
affiliations, the State Library granted LSCA funds to the Dayton Public
Library so that the Miamisburg Library could update its book collection and
upgrade its other services. So far, this cooperative venture has been quite
successful. The State Library is now also using LSCA funds to stimulate
multicounty contractual agreements such as: (1) Dayton/Montgomery County
Public Library and the Preble County District Library, (2) Akron Public
Library and Portage County Library joint operation of a branch library at
Magadore, and (3) the operation of the Loveland Branch (located in parts of
Hamilton, Claremont, and Warren Counties) by the Cincinnati/Hamilton County
Public Library. LSCA funds have provided, then, a preliminary framework in
which to encourage larger cooperative efforts, with numerous metropolitan
libraries perhaps serving as resource centers for additional services to
libraries in surrounding counties.

In addition to the Blasingame Survey, two studies, not funded under LSCA
but exemplifying recent local library planning, are:

> Regional Planning Commission Cleveland-Cuyhoga County, <u>Changing
> Patterns: A Branch Library Plan</u> for the Cleveland Metropolitan
> Area (1968). This is an excellent empirical study concerning all
> facets of library services within the Cleveland-Cuyhoga County
> area.

> <u>Service Program for Proposed Mayfield Regional Library of the
> Cuyhoga County Public Library (May 1968).</u> The study provides
> service guidelines for the Mayfield Regional Library, whose
> geographical location was selected as a direct result of the
> study mentioned above.

LSCA Project Proposal Procedure and Requirements

The allocation of LSCA funds is based upon project proposals submitted to the
State Library Board. The final approval of all LSCA projects rests with the
Board.

Currently, proposals are submitted throughout the fiscal year for LSCA funds
as the projects are developed locally. The State Library has not established
deadlines for proposals because local demand has not exceeded the supply of
LSCA funds available for special projects. However, local interest is being
stimulated and the increase in activity may result in the State Library's
having to impose certain deadlines for submission of LSCA project proposals.

Regarding the allocation of LSCA funds for special projects by local agencies, the State Library has published a statement outlining interim criteria and priorities for these projects.[4] Primary emphasis is placed upon tangible evidence of sound local planning, especially when several libraries or political jurisdictions are involved. The State Library follows a policy of gradually phasing out LSCA funds for locally directed projects that extend over several years. Therefore, local jurisdictions must demonstrate both a willingness and financial capability to assume long-range obligations connected with such projects. Generally speaking, the philosophy of the State Library has been that no LSCA grants should extend over five years. (Projects such as the LSA-funded bookmobile service to rural communities have been continued under LSCA because these areas are still financially unable to assume the full costs of the book-mobile operation.)

LSCA Matching Procedures

The State Library's budget was used to match Ohio's allotment under LSA. A combination of State and local funds is used for LSCA matching purposes. Since the budget of the State Library has remained relatively stable, more local funds (through contract services and intangibles taxes) are being used for matching the current LSCA allotment.

ALLOCATION OF LSCA TITLE I FUNDS

Two factors have influenced the early allocation of LSCA funds: (1) the history of Ohio's approach to library service and program development and the past emphasis upon extending library service to rural counties, and (2) political factors inhibiting the development of multicounty cooperative arrangements.

Historically, under both LSA and LSCA programs, the State Library has assumed the primary responsibility for planning and administering LSA and LSCA projects. Table O-3 illustrates the extent to which this philosophy affected the early allocation of LSCA funds; the table also illustrates a gradual change in this belief during the past two fiscal years, which have seen an increase in the proportions of locally administered projects.

---

[4]The State Library of Ohio, Interim Criteria and Priorities for Special Project Grants Under the Library Services and Construction Act, Title I (Services) Ohio Program, December 13, 1966, 4 pp.

Table O-3.   Administration of LSCA Projects 1965-1968

Fiscal Year	State-Administered*	Locally Administered**	Total
1965	6	2	8
1966	21	6	27
1967	16	13	29
1968	14	26	40
Total	57	47	104

*Includes statewide projects administered directly by the State Library and those administered on a multicounty basis through regional library service centers and bookmobile programs.

**Projects under the direct administration of a local or county library.

One possible reason why the State Library had to assume the early direction of the projects under LSCA was the general reluctance of libraries in urban areas to apply for LSCA funds. This reluctance could be attributed to several factors: (1) the previous lack of communication and interaction between the State Library and urban libraries under LSA, (2) a general feeling of independence on the part of urban libraries in their relations with the State Library, and (3) the acute shortage of local staff for administering special projects under LSCA. The lack of adequate staff, and the inability to recruit additional staff because library salaries could not compete with the high industrial wage scale in Ohio, were major factors in the failure, in Fiscal Year 1965, to initiate four proposed urban LSCA-funded projects. State Library consultants were utilized to stimulate local interest in applying for LSCA funds. Apparently, urban libraries have solved some of their personnel problems and their interest has been stimulated, as indicated by the recent increase in locally administered LSCA projects.

Traditionally, LSA and LSCA funds for State-directed activities have been allocated primarily to the projects listed below:

- In-service training by library school and State Library staffs

- Statewide union catalog

- Cataloging center for State Library and contracting public, school, and university branch libraries

- Bookmobile programs for rural areas

- Regional library service centers

To ensure that LSCA Title I funds will be used for programs that strengthen library service within the framework of the proposed State master plan, the State Library is also granting LSCA Title I funds to counties to conduct studies of their library services, to assess their current and past performance and to determine future areas of library service. LSCA funds for this purpose have been granted to Mercer, Lucas, and Franklin Counties, and other such grants are being planned.

A new approach to library service and planning indicated in the Blasingame Survey of 1968, mentioned earlier, may affect the future allocation of LSCA funds. The Survey recommended that certain State-directed programs--such as bookmobile centers, regional library service centers, and the Traveling Library Section--be phased out and transferred to local or regional centers, which would directly administer and finance these programs with State and local funds. This recommendation is incorporated in the proposed master plan; its effect would be to allow the State Library to concentrate on providing greater service to State government and to perform an even more effective consulting and leadership function. Moreover, LSCA funds could be released from supporting most of the State Library's service activities and be allocated for research studies and increased numbers of special projects. Whether these changes can be made depends on the legislature's willingness to appropriate sufficient funds to implement the State master plan.

REPORTING AND EVALUATION PROCEDURES OF STATE AGENCY

To monitor expenditures of LSCA projects administered locally, the State Library Board requires that a certified semiannual copy of expenditures be submitted to the State Library LSCA Office. Local library and State Library LSCA expenditures are audited by State examiners.

Aside from the routine auditing procedures, the State Library maintains contacts with local projects through periodic visits, conferences, telephone communications, and final reports.

Final reports serve as valuable feedback to the State Library and the Board concerning the successes, failures, and obstacles encountered in instituting innovative programs. For instance, the Cleveland Public Library submitted a report evaluating an LSCA-sponsored project that sought to combat the high illiteracy rates in several sections of Cleveland.

Information thus gained from LSCA projects has been made available to libraries throughout Ohio and other States. In order to disseminate this knowledge, the State Library provided LSCA funds that enabled the Cleveland Public Library to produce a film, entitled "Step a Little Higher," on experiences with their illiteracy program. The State Library also has recently funded, with LSCA Title I monies, a project by the Dayton/Montgomery County Library to produce a film on story-telling that also will be disseminated extensively.

IV.   DESCRIPTION OF REPRESENTATIVE USES OF LSCA FUNDS

The two projects described below provide good examples of the uses Ohio has made of LSCA funds in urban areas.

Books/Jobs Program

The Books/Jobs program is the first major attempt by the State Library to involve public libraries in new kinds of library service. The project has a budget of $371,000, with most of the money spent on materials ($234,000) and special experimental projects ($125,000) designed to find new methods for reaching the public. The project is the culmination of the efforts of the State Library, the Ohio Bureau of Employment, a steering committee, and vocational experts. As stated in the Books/Jobs brochure, the program has three objectives: (1) to enable libraries to obtain information and greater understanding of the needs of the unemployed, (2) to establish communication lines between libraries and agencies dealing with the unemployed, and (3) to provide pertinent materials to job seekers. This project provides an excellent case study illustrating the problems and obstacles in implementing an LSCA program in an urban setting in Ohio. As pointed out in the Blasingame Survey, some of Ohio's urban libraries have ignored the serious problems associated with a changing metropolitan center and have not developed the library service and materials to benefit the many disadvantaged groups (e.g., the unemployed and minority groups) who comprise a growing portion of the core city.

The Books/Jobs program has brought many urban libraries into contacts with other city agencies, minority groups, community agencies, and private organizations with whom they have had little or no previous contact. Listed below are some of the groups that have been contacted by librarians seeking to find unemployed to whom vital materials on vocational training could be given:

* Settlement houses

* NAACP

* Youth centers

* CORE

* PRIDE

* Opportunities Industrial Center (OIC)

* Churches

* Schools

* Civic and social clubs

The libraries' attempts to implement this program have met with several problems. Some librarians were reluctant to contact certain political or ethnic groups because they felt uneasy dealing with ghetto people. Other librarians felt they lacked a total understanding of the ghetto cultural patterns, which would require a nontraditional approach to instituting the Books/Jobs program. A high degree of militancy among ghetto residents posed obstacles to really finding the hard-core unemployed. Most of the target group (the unemployed) could be considered nonusers of library services; often, the only contacts a library has with ghetto residents are with those few who use library facilities. Many librarians, therefore, have developed few strategies or programs for reaching nonusers. Compounding this situation is the fact that libraries in ghetto areas have experienced decreases in circulation, and existing circulation is being maintained largely through children, for whom the Books/Jobs program has no relevance.

Rather than use the library as a primary distribution center for vocational materials, then, efforts have been made to find other distribution centers. Under the urgings of librarians Dr. Fern Long and A. T. Dickinson, the OIC centers in Cleveland and Mansfield, respectively, offered to provide time during their training sessions to library personnel. In Mansfield, Mr. Dickinson arranged for some Books/Jobs materials, covering all phases of vocational training and employment procedures (e.g., preparation of resumes); these materials will be placed within the OIC building so that there will be continuous access to these materials by both day and evening classes.

Although obstacles and opposition have arisen in some areas, and although libraries have varied their approaches in implementing this innovative program, Ohio libraries have taken a significant new step toward making the library more responsive to the demands posed by an urban community. The program has, however, only recently been initiated, and an intensive evaluation of its impact on the unemployed and underemployed cannot yet be made.

Library Service to Exceptional Children

The Cincinnati/Hamilton County project of demonstrating library service to exceptional (e.g., blind, retarded) children was an outgrowth of local interests and, since 1959, has been funded almost entirely by monies of the Cincinnati/Hamilton County Public Library. In Fiscal Year 1967, LSCA Title I funds enabled this library to increase its staff and develop even more creative programs for exceptional children.

The project is an excellent example of how an LSCA Title I project can support empirical research valuable to a multitude of social science disciplines. During the course of this program, the Cincinnati/Hamilton County Public Library, in conjunction with university research staffs, has recently completed a significant research study evaluating the successes and failures of various groups of children in the project. The results are to be published in various professional journals and in a report submitted to the State Library, and should be of immense value to librarians, scholars, and researchers throughout the country.

A great deal of local planning preceded the submission of the project proposal to the State Library Board. Many libraries apply for LSCA funds and are then unable to find staff to administer the program. The Cincinnati/ Hamilton County Library acquired the additional staff before it submitted the proposal for funding (but even then encountered difficulties in fully staffing the project). Even more significant is the fact that the program was, in a sense, a pilot project. The problems and obstacles to be confronted were identified, and imperfections in the program were refined, so that when the LSCA funds were granted, the preliminary planning had been done, staff time was not inefficiently spent in "gearing up" for the effort, and the project could begin immediately.

V.   EVALUATION

PROGRAM STRENGTHS

- Encouragement of cooperative library systems through the use of LSCA funds.

- Dissemination of information gained from LSCA projects to the academic and library community.

- Development of new library program strategies to meet the needs of Ohio's rapidly expanding urban communities.

- Encouragement by the State Library for local libraries to initiate systematic long-range planning and development.

- Development of strong consultive and leadership role by the State Library.

- Development of increased communication between the State Library and local urban libraries.

- Creation of an urban specialist position in the State Library.

PROBLEM AREAS

- Previous lack of systematic planning and research for effectively interacting with LSCA program.

- Continuing heavy dependence upon LSCA funds to support State Library staff.

- Lack of adequate interaction by local libraries with other municipal, State, or Federal governmental agencies in the development of library programs for their communities.

· Shortage of professional librarians in urban areas to staff special LSCA projects.

CONCLUSIONS

In the past a heavy percentage of Ohio's LSA and LSCA funds has been concentrated in State Library-administered programs; however, two new directions of administration, being emphasized by the State Librarian, may presage a different emphasis in future expenditures. One is the assumption by the State Library of a stronger leadership and consulting role; the other is the recent increase in locally administered projects.

The formulation of a State master plan has increased the likelihood that the State legislature will properly fund the State Library. If this support is obtained, LSCA funds could be released to be spent on more innovative special projects. Furthermore, as a result of the new policies being emphasized by the present State Librarian and his staff, it is probable that an even higher percentage of any future LSCA funds will be allocated to projects that deal with the growing urban problems in Ohio's metropolitan areas.

VI. BIBLIOGRAPHY

Ohio State LSA and LSCA Title I annual plans, reports, and programs submitted to USOE during the period 1958-1968 (miscellaneous titles).

Blasingame, Ralph. Appendix: Survey of Ohio Libraries and State Library Services. State Library of Ohio, Columbus, Ohio, 1968, 102 pp.

Blasingame, Ralph. Survey of Ohio Libraries and State Library Services. State Library of Ohio, Columbus, Ohio, 1968, 187 pp.

Cuyahoga County Public Library. Service Program for Proposed Mayfield Regional Library. Cuyahoga County, Ohio, May 1968, 17 pp.

Public Library of Cincinnati and Hamilton County. Demonstration of Library Services to Exceptional Children. Hamilton County, Ohio, 1967, 6 pp.

Regional Planning Commission. Changing Patterns, A Branch Library Plan for the Cleveland Metropolitan Area. Cleveland, Ohio, 1966, 160 pp.

State Library of Ohio. 1968 Directory of Ohio Libraries, with Statistics for 1967. Columbus, Ohio, 1968, 66 pp.

State Library of Ohio. Interim Criteria and Priorities for Special Project Grants Under the Library Services and Construction Act, Title I (Services) Ohio Program. Columbus, Ohio, 1966, 2 pp.

State Library of Ohio. Statements on Objectives and Methods and Related Policies. Columbus, Ohio, June 1968, 16 pp.

State Library of Ohio. Vital Information Arm of Government: Better Library Services for You. Columbus, Ohio, 1967, 20 pp.

CHAPTER X
WISCONSIN

I.   SOURCES OF INFORMATION

The following organizations and persons were visited to obtain information
for this study (see Figure Wis-1 for a map of the State):

Date	Place Visited	Persons Visited
8/12/68	USOE Regional Office Chicago, Illinois Region V	James G. Igoe, Library Services Program Officer

8/13/68
8/14/68
	Division for Library
	  Services
	Department of Public
	  Instruction
	Madison
		W. Lyle Eberhart, Director
		Richard J. Lederer, Adminis-
		  trative Assistant
		
		Jane Younger) Consultants
		Lucile Dudgeon (_ for Division
		Ione Nelson (for Library
		Jerry Young) Services
		John Kopischke, Director,
		  Reference and Loan Library

8/14/68	City of Madison Library Madison	Bernard Schwab, Director
8/14/68	Dane County Library	Donald Lamb, Coordinator
8/15/68	Southwest Processing Center Fennimore	Mrs. Barbara Bobzien, Director Gilbert Wood, County Board Member, Grant County

8/15/68	La Crosse Public Library and
	  La Crosse Library Develop-
	  ment System
	La Crosse
		Gertrude R. Thurow, City Librarian,
		  La Crosse Public Library and
		  Director, La Crosse Library
		  Development System

8/16/68	Baraboo Public Library Baraboo	Josephine Zipzie, Librarian Consultant
8/16/68	Sauk County Library Baraboo	Al Zipzie, Librarian

Date	Place Visited	Persons Visited
8/19/68	Wisconsin Valley Reference Service Wausau	Wayne R. Bassett, Director Carole Wessler, Reference Librarian
8/20/68	Multi-County Library System Ashland	William Sloggy, Director, Multi-County Library System Mrs. Florence Lyons, Librarian, Eagle River John Digert, Trustee, Multi-County Library System Member, Executive Board, Wisconsin Valley Reference System Chairman, Washington Township Board Member, Vilas County Board
9/4/68	Milwaukee Public Library Milwaukee	Richard E. Krug, City Librarian Vivian Maddox, Assistant City Librarian Nolan Neds, Supervisor, Neighborhood Libraries and Extension Services
9/5/68	Southeast Wisconsin Regional Planning Commission Waukesha	Eugene Molitor, Chief Land Use Planner
9/5/68	Shawano City-County Library Shawano	Mrs. Charlotte Sawyer, Acting Director
9/6/68	Menominee County Library Menominee County (formerly Menominee Indian Reservation)	Mrs. Lynne Skenadore, Librarian
9/6/68	Brown County Library Green Bay	Gerald A. Somers, Director

Much valuable information was also obtained from the publications listed in the Bibliography in Section VI of this chapter.

Figure Wis-1. Map of the State of Wisconsin

II.   BACKGROUND FOR LSCA OPERATIONS

THE STATE AGENCY

The agency designated to receive and disburse LSCA Title I funds in Wisconsin
is the Division for Library Services of the Wisconsin State Department of
Public Instruction. Formerly a separate entity known as the Wisconsin Free
Library Commission, it was incorporated into the Department in 1965. The
Division is now headed by W. Lyle Eberhart, Assistant State Superintendent
of Public Instruction and Director of the Division for Library Services.
Mr. Eberhart reports to the State Superintendent of Public Instruction,
William C. Kahl.

One of the seven divisions within the Department, the Division for Library
Services in turn encompasses a staff services unit and four functional units
and is linked to various advisory councils. (See Figure Wis-2, Partial Representation of Organization: Wisconsin State Department of Public Instruction.)
W. Lyle Eberhart, Division Director, coordinates LSCA program activities,
acting through the Public Library Services Staff and the Reference and Loan
Library Staff. Mr. Richard J. Lederer is Administrative Assistant to the
Division Director. Under State law the Division's charge is to "promote
the development of public library services and of school library services,
and to encourage the coordination of these library services with each other
and with other library programs of educational agencies"[1] reflects the
expanded responsibilities resulting from the 1965 reorganization.

LIBRARY DEVELOPMENT IN WISCONSIN

Wisconsin was among the first eight States to establish a State library
agency. The Wisconsin Free Library Commission, established in 1895 to aid
in the formation of new libraries and in the growth of those already
established, was an independent entity reporting directly to the Governor.
Overall policy direction rested with the Commissioners, while program
administration resided in an executive secretary or director, who was also
State Librarian. (This responsibility, formerly vested in S. Janice Kee,
Secretary of the Library Commission, is now assumed by the Director of the
Division for Library Services.)

Over the years, the Commission's duties and responsibilities have steadily
expanded, generally in the direction of increased extension service. In
1901, it was authorized to establish traveling libraries--literally "books
in a trunk." In 1905, it was given the task of holding librarians'
institutes and of encouraging the growth of adult study clubs throughout
the State. In 1921, and again in 1945, it was charged with setting
standards for librarians and issuing certificates to those who met stated
requirements of education, professional training, and experience. In 1945,

---

[1]State Plan for Library Services, Wisconsin State Department of Public
Instruction, Division for Library Services, 1967.

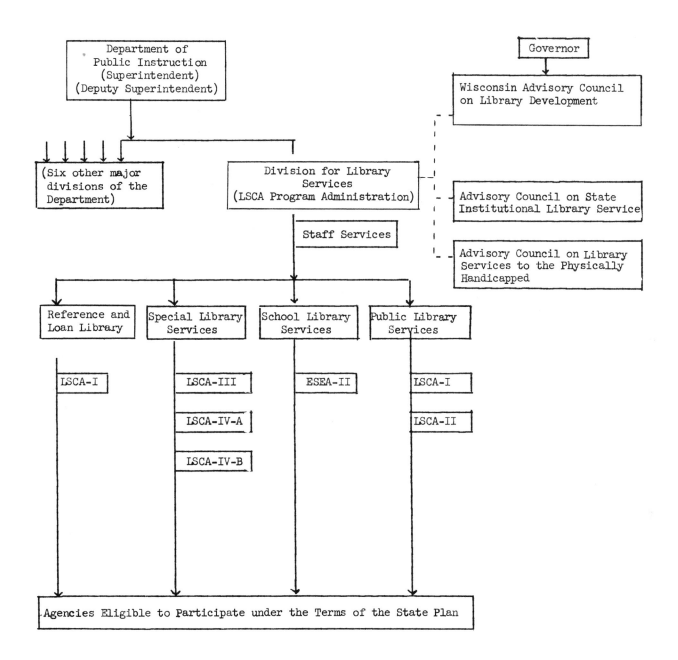

Figure Wis-2.   Partial Representation of Organization: Wisconsin
State Department of Public Instruction*

---

*Source: State Plan for Library Services, Wisconsin State Department of
Public Instruction, Division for Library Services, 1967.

the Commission was authorized to accept Federal grants. Other legislative
actions and appropriations enabled the Commission to assist both State
officials and public library personnel in completing files of State
documents, to maintain a legislative reference library, to draft bills for
legislators, and to select certain public libraries as depositories for
public documents.[2]

Wisconsin, in common with many other States, has adopted the concept of the
public library system as the most practical organization to meet the great
need for improved library services, particularly for the State's considerable
rural population. The development of library systems in the State can be
traced through the Wisconsin library literature published during the last
20 years. (See Section VI, BIBLIOGRAPHY, p.193.)

The public library-system concept is historically associated with the
multicounty Door-Kewaunee regional library demonstration of 1950-1952. This
prototype project aroused intense interest among the Wisconsin library
community, involved a special act of the legislature (passed over the Governor's veto), and set the stage for later LSA and LSCA projects. The project
grew out of discussions during 1947 and 1948 among a group of state librarians
and Library Commission personnel concerned with the State's rural reading
problem. The discussions resulted in two things: a plan, and a demonstration
project to test the plan. The plan[3] was Wisconsin's first attempt to set
forth the concept of a regional library system to meet the State's need for
more adequate library service, particularly in rural areas. The project was
an attempt to demonstrate what this approach might provide in enhanced
library service. Many of the ingredients found in the State's current
demonstration projects were present: a multicounty testbed, concentrated
planning efforts, designation of a central library, inauguration of bookmobile service, central processing, workshops for member librarians,
funding on a matching basis from a source outside the country (in this
instance, the State), and finally, after the demonstration period was over,
the problem of obtaining local funding to continue the service. This was
truly a landmark project in the eyes of the Wisconsin library community and
dominated the thinking behind library development in Wisconsin before the
more extensive LSA projects that began five years later.

In the development of library systems in Wisconsin, three major elements
of expanded library service have been emphasized:

- Library materials: Providing collections of real depth
  (particularly in central or system headquarters libraries)
  and making available a broad range of books and nonbook
  materials.

[2]Facing the 60s - The Public Library in Wisconsin; Part One, Findings and
Conclusions, Bureau of Government, University Extension Division, University
of Wisconsin, 1961.

[3]The Wisconsin-Wide Library Idea for Voluntary Education through Reading.
Wisconsin Free Library Commission, 1948.

- Professional services: Providing specialized staff positions (both in the major subject areas and in the major types of service) available to serve all users in the system area.

- Library networks: Providing the communications capability and other systems services necessary to link each local library user to the larger array of statewide resources.

For the better part of the past decade, the Library Commission, later the Division for Library Services, has explored various plans that divide the State into a number of library-system areas, each area containing at least one major resource library (see Figure Wis-3, A Tentative Wisconsin Library System Map). Though no firm geographic system configuration has been adopted as yet, the tentative configurations shown in Figure Wis-3 have served as a guideline for both continuing planning efforts and the implementation of specific projects. (In most of the configurations being considered, seven to nine areas are designated.)

Both the Commission and the Division have approached the decision to adopt a library-system area master plan with caution, in part out of keen appreciation for some of the technical problems involved, and also out of due respect for local "home rule." As in many other States, any issues arising between the State agency and the local jurisdictions are heightened by the fact that almost all funding for public libraries comes from local governing bodies; Wisconsin has no State grant-in-aid program. The State agency therefore chooses to achieve its planning goals indirectly, by influence through its strong extension program, rather than by direct interaction on the local level.

Technical considerations also play a role. The distribution of existing or potential central libraries in Wisconsin by no means always coincides with area configurations based upon other criteria such as distance, political boundaries, or local predilections. For those portions of the State where a "natural" library-system area does not exist, either actually or potentially, the State agency has tended to bypass the area (and the issue) temporarily, and to concentrate its efforts on more amenable areas. Thus, library-system development is incomplete, with several functioning multicounty systems, several multicounty systems based upon limited library service arrangements, and a number of single-county systems. Eighteen out of 72 counties do not have system-integrated library service.

The major portion of the Wisconsin public library law is contained in Chapter 43 of Wisconsin Statutes. In terms of intergovernmental arrangements for the creation of consolidated public library service, this body of legislation is generally permissive, although not necessarily facilitating: There is a lack of specific provisions empowering regional library systems to levy taxes. In Wisconsin, special-purpose taxing districts are not looked upon with favor except for schools and vocational education (the latter now under question). Established political units are used for general government operation.

Figure Wis-3. A Tentative Wisconsin Library System Map

In 1963, The Commission and the Wisconsin Library Association's Legislative Committee began a study on library law in Wisconsin and other States. The Committee advised a legislative program to update the Wisconsin library law, stressed the need for more uniformity in organizing library service, and recommended a State-aid program. One issue is particularly crucial. A key theme running through Wisconsin Library statutes is the provision that control be vested in independent local library boards. These, like independent school boards, have traditionally been considered advantageous because they are "outside of politics." More recently, however, librarians and others in Wisconsin have raised the question whether this independence might have been achieved at too high a price, causing decision makers to operate outside the effective communication channels. This insulation from the regular communication structures may pose a problem, particularly in view of the proliferation of high-level intergovernmental agencies.

RELATIONSHIP OF STATE AGENCY TO OTHER ORGANIZATIONS

Other Federal Programs

The School Library Services staff of the Division for Library Services, operating in part with ESEA Title II funds, coordinates with the overall public library program within the Department. The LSCA program staff has also provided consulting services for other Federal government programs, for example, the OEO-funded library project for migrant workers in Door County (see Section IV, p.184).

Other Libraries

There are three major State-operated libraries not under the administration of the Division.

- The State Historical Society Library

- The Legislative Reference Bureau Library

- The State Law Library

Library Associations

Wisconsin has a strong State association--the Wisconsin Library Association (WLA). This organization meets annually. Seven district library associations are affiliated with WLA and also meet annually, generally emphasizing matters of local library concern. There are close ties between these organizations and the Division for Library Services, and on issues crucial to both the Division and the profession--such as library standards--they become virtually a single task force operating within a framework of working and advisory committees.

Two other organizations exist: The Wisconsin Library Trustees Association (WLTA) is particularly active in matters concerning library legislation and financing; and the Friends of Wisconsin Libraries (FOWL) provides an organizational channel through which lay individuals and civic groups can assist in library development. The Division has designated one of its staff as a coordinator for interactions with these and other library organizations, including those extending beyond the State boundaries such as the regional and national associations, the Midwest State Library agencies, and the Assembly of State Librarians.

LIBRARY FUNDING

According to data for Fiscal Year 1967 (which is the last year for which figures are available), total public library income in Wisconsin was $11,564,987. Most of this income ($10,526,737) came from municipal appropriations. In comparison, in 1963 (the earliest year for which total income data were available to SDC), total public library income was $8,416,269.

Local library financing is provided on an appropriation basis. By translating the appropriations in mill rates, the following observation was made:

> The mill rate levied by local governments for library
> purposes has increased at about the same rate as levies
> for all local government purposes. Between 1958 and 1963
> local government levies for library purposes in cities
> with large- and medium-sized libraries rose from 49 cents
> to 57 cents per $1,000 of equalized property value. Over
> this same period expenditures for library purposes amounted
> to 1.9 per cent of total local government expenditures.
> This crude measure of the relative importance attached to
> library services by local units of government indicates
> that, while library expenditures are rising, they are not
> rising fast enough to reflect real improvement in their
> relative priority in the community budget. Moreover, these
> figures do not indicate that a rapid rise in municipal
> expenditures for libraries is in the offing. [4]

Table Wis-1 shows the percentage of revenues obtained from various sources in two recent years; Table Wis-2 compares various local levels for libraries to total local government expenditures for those same years.

---

[4] Department of Resource Development, State of Wisconsin, Public Library Services, 1965.

Table Wis-1. Percent of Revenue by Source, Large-
and Medium-Sized Public Libraries,
1958 and 1963*

Source	1958	1963
Local Appropriations	92.3%	86.7%
County, School District, and Town Payments	3.9	3.0
Payments from Contracts for Services	0.2	4.8
Gifts	0.3	1.3
Other**	3.3	4.2
Total	100.0%	100.0%

*Source: Department of Resource Development, State of Wisconsin, Public Library Facilities, 1965.

**For 1963, revenue derived from Federal and State governments represented an insignificant portion (less than 1-1/2 percent); more recently, this share has increased significantly.

Table Wis-2.   Municipal Mill Levy Rates for Large-
and Medium-Sized Libraries. Wisconsin
Public Libraries, 1958-1963*

Region	Mill Levy for Library Purposes 1958	1963	Change 1958-63	Library Expenditures as a % of Total Local Government Expenditures 1958	1963
Superior	.70	.73	+.03	2.2	2.3
Eau Claire	.44	.52	+.08	1.7	1.9
LaCrosse	.51	.58	+.07	2.1	2.3
Wausau	.50	.57	+.07	2.1	2.1
Green Bay	.48	.47	-.01	2.1	1.9
Oshkosh	.53	.60	+.07	2.8	2.8
Sheboygan	.68	.70	+.02	2.9	2.6
Madison	.39	.44	+.05	1.6	1.7
Milwaukee	.50	.59	+.09	1.8	1.8
Library Size					
Large	.50	.59	.09	1.9	1.9
Medium	.47	.52	.05	1.9	2.0
State Total	.49	.57	.08	1.9	1.9

*Source: Department of Resource Development, State of Wisconsin, Public Library Facilities, 1965.

The amount of LSCA Title I funding available to Wisconsin for library service since 1957 is indicated in Table Wis-3, along with State appropriations and local expenditures. Wisconsin has not reported local expenditures for all the fiscal years and, when it has reported, has used only those local expenditures relevant to the library service area to which the grant pertained.

Currently the LSCA program's operating budget comprises some State funds combined with an 8-1/2 percent retention of the overall LSCA Title I allocation to provide for administration of program activities.

Table Wis-3. Federal, State and Local Library
Expenditures in Wisconsin by Fiscal
Year: 1957-1968*

Fiscal Year	Federal	State	Local	Total
1957	$ 32,801	$ 53,830	$ -	$ 86,631
1958	111,390	116,041	-	227,431
1959	109,001	117,981	18,437	245,418
1960	164,495	131,252	155,664	451,411
1961	162,101	135,927	157,698	455,726
1962	180,303	214,665	180,303	492,766
1963	174,850	216,556	-	391,406
1964	179,990	233,075	-	413,065
1965	534,779	281,470	243,250	1,059,499
1966	495,012	251,971	938,405	1,685,388
1967	595,052	280,112	1,190,291	2,065,455
1968	745,365	338,153	(unknown)	1,957,744

*These figures were supplied by the Division for Library Services.

Comparison of per capita expenditures for library services over a period of years provides some measure of the increase in public library service in Wisconsin: In 1950, the per capita figure was $1.66, in 1963 it was $2.53, and by 1967 it was approaching $3. Although in terms of the decreased value of today's dollar as compared to the value of the dollar in the early 1950's, the increase loses much of its significance.

The following project from the Department of Resource Development estimates the costs of further improving public library service on a regional-system basis, as compared with a nonsystem basis:

> An attempt to bring all of the 84 proposed Type I and
> Type II[5] libraries in the State to the standards of
> Type I libraries would require an initial expenditure

---

[5]In Wisconsin, a Type I library is generally defined as the central library of the system; a Type II library is defined as a community library.

of more than $19,000,000 for additional bookstocks and an annual expenditure of more than $2,600,000 for book replacement. The proposed regional systems, on the other hand, would require an initial expenditure of less than $6,000,000 for additional books and an annual expenditure of less than $2,000,000 for book replacement.[6]

III. LSCA PROGRAM

OVERVIEW OF ACTIVITIES

The LSCA program in Wisconsin has two major emphases:

- Extension services, provided by the Division staff and funded in part by LSCA monies and in part by State appropriations for Division operating expenses.

- Specific library-development projects conducted at the local level (though coordinated by the Division staff) and supported by LSCA and local funds.

Extension Activities

The Division's extension work is performed by a field services staff of professional librarians (currently six in number), representing primarily the Public Library Services and the Reference and Loan Library units of the Division. Field services personnel are engaged in a variety of activities to promote and develop library service. Staff members work with and advise local library boards, county library committees, librarians, city, county and State officials, and lay people on library matters. During the period July 1, 1960 to June 30, 1965, approximately 3,000 consultations were provided by the staff. Most of these consultations occurred in local communities.

A significant goal of the extension program is to provide planning guidance for library development throughout the State. In addition, field services personnel also assist in training librarians in the State through on-the-job advice, workshops, institutes, exhibits, and publications. A small extension library for professionals is maintained at Division headquarters and is made available on loan to librarians, trustees, and the lay public. The collection contains the significant literature of local, State, and national library concern; it also includes film and 35mm slide materials on library buildings and services for use by librarians in working with architects, citizen groups, and public officials.

---

[6]Department of Resource Development, op. cit., p. 76.

A more specialized collection is the Children's Cooperative Book Center (CCBC), established in June 1963 (partly with LSA funding) by the Library Commission in cooperation with the State Department of Public Instruction, the University of Wisconsin Library School, and the University of Wisconsin School of Education. A field services staff member is supervisor of the Center. The CCBC is a noncirculating examination and research laboratory for all residents of the State interested in children's books and reading. The collection consists of current trade and reference titles, historical 19th and early 20th century titles, bibliographic aids, and exhibits of award-winning books.

The State agency is administrator of the Wisconsin Library Film Circuit, Inc., a nonstock, nonprofit organization that makes 16mm educational films available to public libraries in the State at a price far below the cost to any individual member library. The Film Circuit was partially supported out of LSCA Title I funds. The 30 libraries currently participating in the program pay a membership fee.

Periodic institutes on public library management provide an opportunity for city officials, library trustees, and librarians to come together to discuss library problems of mutual concern. To date, 13 such institutes have been held. Typical topics are: The Public Library and the Public School, Library Service for Adults, A Statewide Reference Service, and the Impact of Federally-Supported Programs on Wisconsin Library Service. This activity is partially funded under Title I.

Three study courses are coordinated under the Division's extension program:

- A scholarship program to encourage individuals to pursue a formal course of study toward a master's degree in library science exists and has been supported through use of LSA and LSCA Title I funds since 1959. In return for scholarship grants, students agree to work for two years in a Wisconsin library that is involved in area development.

- The University of Wisconsin Extension Division, Department of Library Science, conducts a directed study course to instruct individuals already working in libraries in the basic skills, operations, and philosophy of public library service. LSCA Title I grants have been provided annually for a limited number of attendees.

- Since 1965, Title I grants have also been provided for post-graduate study, primarily in library systems at the State University School of Library Science.

The following enrollment figures are typical of the three study programs:

	Graduate Study Grants	Directed Study Grants	Postgraduate Study Grants
1961	4	7	0
1962	2	7	0
1963	7	11	0
1964	4	15	0
1965	4	25	7
	21	65	7

The Division for Library Services is also responsible for establishing standards for public library service in Wisconsin. Current standards are set forth in a 1963 publication, A Design for Public Library Development in Wisconsin: Standards for Measuring Progress. This document resulted from a massive 2-year cooperative effort--partly LSA-funded--involving over 100 persons representing the Wisconsin Library Commission, the Wisconsin Library Association, and the Wisconsin Library Trustees Association. Standards were delineated for measuring the structure and government of library service, the service itself, book and nonbook materials, personnel, and organization of materials and physical facilities for large, medium-sized, and small public libraries.

In addition to library development program activities, the Division maintains the General Reference and Loan Library (formerly, "The Traveling Library"). In the Wisconsin library community, this library is known as the "State Library." Primarily an extension arm of the Division, it serves to supplement inadequate collections in the State by making the less-commonly-called-for materials available on a loan basis when they are needed. It has been partially supported by LSA funds and continues to receive LSCA Title I support. During 1966 and 1967, with LSCA Title I support, statewide library request actions were structured into Wisconsin's framework of public library systems. Formerly, reference and loan requests moved directly from the library of origin to the Division's Reference and Loan Library; however, in 1967 the Reference and Loan TWP net was expanded to include TWX to facilitate reference and interaction with systems, and local library requests are now handled through their system.

Selection of Local Library Projects for LSCA Funding

The second major emphasis of the LSCA program in Wisconsin is concerned with the specific library-development projects supported by LSCA.

The Division for Library Services has a significant role in the planning of new library projects throughout the State. Not only are requests for State and Federal funding forwarded to the Division for review and approval, but, in a more pervasive sense, there is little in the way of library planning activity that it does not become involved in, either directly on its own initiative or indirectly, through influence.

The criteria used by the Division to evaluate plans submitted by localities requesting LSCA grants are:[7]

1. Legal Basis

    a. The existence of a clear, legal basis for the establishment of governmental organization, control, and financial support of the proposed library operation.

    b. The number of unserved and/or number of inadequately served residents who will benefit by the public library operation.

    c. The agreement by the locality that its proposed public library service shall be free of charge to all members of the participating area.

2. Financial Support

    a. The relative financial ability of the locality to contribute toward the project or to provide necessary matching funds.

    b. The establishment of fiscal procedures involving reports regarding the disposition of all monies received in accordance with requirements prescribed by the United States Government.

    c. The agreement by the locality that the funds paid under this Act shall be expended solely for the purpose which paid.

    d. The relative financial ability of the locality to provide full, local support to carry on the project after the Federal grants are withdrawn.

    e. The intention of the locality to use diminishing amounts of Federal monies during the course of the program and the intention of the locality to take over wholly or in part the financial support of the ongoing library operation.

---

[7]The State Plan for the Further Extension of Public Library Service to Rural Areas, Wisconsin Free Library Commission, 1957.

3. Standards of Service

The extent to which the proposed library services will be moved toward adequacy according to the ALA[8] standards for public library service, or the extent to which existing services will be brought up to minimum standards and/or the extent to which quality services of existing public libraries will be extended to rural areas.

4. Citizen Participation

The degree to which the locality can provide evidence of citizen and/or official interest and participation in the proposed library operation. To assist localities in preparing their plan, the Free Library Commission[9] will (1) provide a detailed guide for submitting the required information, and (2) make available the help of a Public Library Consultant in drawing up the plan.

REPORTING AND EVALUATION PROCEDURES OF STATE AGENCY

Fiscal reporting, as mentioned above, is a requirement for every LSCA-funded project. Another useful tool for monitoring local library activities is provided by the mandatory requirement, established by legislation, for municipal and county library boards and committees to file annual reports with the Division. The Division's direction over standards for librarians is similarly mandatory. Financial and technical information on State libraries is assembled and published annually by the Division in the Wisconsin Public Libraries Service Record. For LSCA-funded projects, narrative reports are also required. It is common practice for a great deal of supplemental material to be submitted.

The State agency has also used, and continues to use, studies performed by organizations outside its own staff. The significant published studies have been mentioned previously. Generally, resource organizations within the State are used, although there have been exceptions.

IV.   DESCRIPTION OF REPRESENTATIVE USES OF LSCA FUNDS

Described below are several typical LSCA-funded library projects. Other projects could be included, but the following are probably sufficient to show how the Division for Library Services explores various means of fostering library development, and to show some of the problems and issues involved.

---

[8]Now the State standards described in "A Design for Public Library Development in Wisconsin: Standards for Measuring Progress," Wisconsin Free Library Commission, 1963.

[9]Now the Division for Library Services.

- ## Public Library Service Center of Southwest Wisconsin

This is a multicounty demonstration project organized around a limited number of library services. It is a typical example of the way in which the Division capitalizes on the emergence of local interest and assists in the development of an areawide library service.

In 1956, a group of librarians and library board members in southwest Wisconsin, who had been meeting informally for several years, adopted a set of bylaws and defined themselves as the Southwest Association of Public Libraries. Their original purpose in meeting was to discuss professional library matters of concern to the group. In 1958 the Association undertook to order books jointly on a trial basis, with the Library Commission providing consultant assistance in initiating joint-ordering procedures. The success of the trial run led to a plan for a permanent ordering and processing facility to serve a five-county area. This was proposed to the State agency in the fall of 1958, and with the availability of LSA funds, it became a 3-year demonstration project.

The center is located in Fennimore, a community in the heart of the primarily agricultural five-county area. The largest community has a population of 6,987. At the time the project was initiated, there were 25 public libraries, all small, some open only a few hours a week. Before the demonstration, the total annual expenditure for books and materials for the area was $14,742.

Since there was no strong central library around which to build a full range of services, funding support was granted on the premise that a single needed service--central ordering and processing-- would provide the organizational basis upon which other services and activities could be developed over time. This assumption has been confirmed, although further development has been modest. Bookmobile service was initiated at a later date and currently continues, and training workshops are regularly conducted for 9 months each year. A telelecture series, an experimental recorded lecture project jointly sponsored by the University Extension Service and the Wisconsin Library Association Adult Services Section (with the encouragement of the State agency), was one of the training elements utilized. Library service has been enhanced in the project, though the lack of a strong central library remains a basic impediment. Further improvements will probably depend upon linkages to external resource libraries, such as the Madison Public Library.

Local funding has supported the system's operation since the end of the demonstration period. Discussions with a county board member revealed no apparent problem in local government's assuming funding support. Grant County, the central and most wealthy county, assumed the administrative responsibility; the four other counties contract with it for service. [10]

• Wisconsin Valley Library Reference Service

Another multicounty project, initially organized around a single service, developed in an 11-county area in north-central Wisconsin.[11] This large, sparsely populated and economically poor area contains 39 small libraries, only one of which--the Wausau Public Library in Marathon County--has sufficient resources to warrant designation as a central library.

In 1963, an LSA grant was initiated to strengthen the reference and information resources of this library, to extend these resources to the entire 11-county region, and to conduct training workshops for library personnel. Initially, the project was funded under a 2-year LSA grant, the money being used primarily to strengthen the reference resources at the Wausau Public Library and provide additional reference-staff assistance. The grant was extended an additional year under LSCA Title I and has since been continued annually, but funding is now limited to only a few of the elements specified in the original grant.

The regional service is operated by a Board of Trustees appointed from the participating counties. Contracts between each participating county and the Board provide for local financial support. Counties are assessed on a formula based on (1) county population, (2) county assessed valuation, and (3) county income. The Wausau Public Library contracts to furnish housing (an LSCA Title II grant helped defray the cost of a structural addition to the headquarters building). Through Fiscal Year 1965, LSCA Title I funding totaled $126,750. The combined local expenditures for the regional area were $574,860 in 1966, and the continuing Federal grant was $16,000 in 1967.

The system utilizes WATS and TWX links to the State Library for reference requests that cannot be met from system resources. Training within the regional area is coordinated by the headquarters staff. Member librarians select topics and choose workshop locations;

[10]At the time the funding issue was presented to the various county boards, civic agitation for another service was presented--a multicounty guidance center. The campaign for this latter service was unsuccessful, but it serves to illustrate the growing variety of services competing with library services for funding.

[11]Later reduced to 10 counties.

the headquarters then sends out staff members to conduct workshop sessions (with an occasional assist from Division consultants when available). The system unites in one organization a large number of isolated small libraries. A board with regionwide representation provides support and an articulate voice in dealing with local taxing bodies. The resources of the central library have been strengthened considerably and are available upon request.

However, the 10 counties represent a large number of diverse interests, and distances are considerable, precluding the short-travel, face-to-face interaction that would be possible if the regional area were smaller. Although local funding support has been provided up to the present, some local governments apparently have difficulty in meeting even modest funding obligations. In this sense the project presents the usual difficulties of providing library service in sparsely populated rural areas.

- Fox Valley Library Program

This program represents a loose federation of six libraries--Oshkosh, Appleton, Brown County, Manitowoc, Sheboygan, and Fond du Lac--which cooperatively give interlibrary loan and reference referral service to approximately 55 libraries in 15 counties. In 1964, each of the 55 libraries entered into an agreement with the Division for Library Services and received an LSCA Title I grant, which, during this first year, was used primarily to strengthen individual library holdings in reference and subject fields. During this initial period, the Fox Valley Steering Committee played an important advisory and communicating role. The grants during the following two years were made between the Division and each of the six larger libraries, which, in turn, contracted with the surrounding community libraries. The stress was upon reference referral and interlibrary loan, with the six libraries acting as resource centers for nearby community libraries. A TWP circuit connects the six libraries and the Division's Reference and Loan Library. Workshops have been important educationally but even more because they developed a feeling of unity. This is particularly noted among reference librarians who have come to rely upon each other's strengths. The area coheres geographically, economically, and is relatively affluent. In most of the area, library service is adequate even though not superior and political considerations are such that unification along system lines is proceeding slowly.

- Sauk County Library Service

This project is typical of many single-county library-development projects in the State. Where inauguration of a multicounty regional library service is not immediately feasible, the short-range goal is to strengthen a single-county system that could then become a part of a larger unit of service in the future.

Modest Title I grants are usually provided to such systems. In this instance, the two most recent annual grants ($5,811 and $6,886 for Fiscal Years 1967 and 1968 respectively) have been used to supplement local support for specified categories such as salaries, books, and equipment. Local funding provides $35,000-$40,000 annually. The Sauk County Library Board contracts for services with the public library in the city of Baraboo, which has been designated the central library for the system. New acquisitions and other books are rotated among 10 member libraries and, in addition, there is a bookmobile service for rural areas in the county.

• Southeast Wisconsin Regional Library Survey

In July 1968, a 2-year regional library survey was undertaken in seven counties of southeastern Wisconsin, the State's most rapidly growing urban area. There are 153 local units of government within the region, including Milwaukee and its suburbs, Racine, and Kenosha. Approximately 45 percent of all tangible wealth in the State is contained in this area. The first year of the study is being funded by an LSCA Title I grant in the amount of $96,908.

In addition to public libraries, the survey will include many other library facilities that affect public library service: one State University, seven private colleges and universities, four university centers, one county teachers college, one technical and professional college, 11 vocational and adult education schools, public school libraries and special libraries.

The survey is being made by the Southeast Regional Planning Commission, an organization created in 1960 to assist local governments in planning and developing their regional areas. The Planning Commission is an agency whose perspective ranges across a wide spectrum of factors, including physical, economic, demographic, social, and educational. The Commission has recently been instrumental in influencing decisions concerning the location of several planned libraries on the basis of demographic and transportation factors. In this survey it intends to consider not only existing library facilities, but projected information resources such as computer data banks of the various governmental agencies. The Commission works closely with Division staff personnel.

• Disadvantaged Projects

The Division has funded projects directed toward three differing groups not adequately supplied with library service: Indians, the urban disadvantaged, and migrant workers. One such group is represented by the Menominee County Library Service. This county, recently created by the State, was formerly the Menominee Indian Reservation. The Menominee Tribe, electing to become independent of the Bureau of Indian Affairs, now maintains its own governmental services. The State agency provides a modest annual Title I grant of approximately $8,000, in part to develop the county library collection. Another portion of the grant is paid directly to nearby Shawano City-County Library for reference referral, walk-in service, and consultant services. The county librarian, granddaughter of a former tribal chief, is building her collection primarily for the Indian children and young adults, since the number of adult readers in the county is negligible. (Similar support is provided for a more scattered Indian population in the Multi-County Regional Library System in northwest Wisconsin.)

A program directed toward an urban disadvantaged group is found in two inner-city neighborhoods, Lapham and Forest Home, in Milwaukee. The Milwaukee Public Library has received Title I grants of $11,396, $8,946, and $39,230, in Fiscal Years 1966, 1967, and 1968 respectively, to provide a special library service, initially in the Lapham area as a pilot program, and currently in both areas. A community librarian is employed to work with community organizations and agencies in the area. Specialized collections including paperbacks are being acquired, a gift program is being developed, and training opportunities created. In many instances particular elements of library service (such as children's story hours and young-adult discussions) are brought into private homes and community gathering places, since techniques of bringing materials and programs into the immediate area are basic to this "outreach" program and racial turmoil has often made street travel hazardous.

Although not funded under LSCA, a library service to a third type of disadvantaged group is worth mention. In 1965, the Door County Library, located in a prominent cherry-growing area, applied for an OEO grant to provide library service to Spanish-speaking migrant workers, primarily from Texas and Mexico. Funds were used for the salary of a specially trained person and for special materials and equipment to provide library service, primarily for the migrant workers' children during the summer harvest season. The Division provided consultant assistance. A similar program was conducted in Dodge County under a 1965 Title I grant of $992.

· Statewide Projects

A number of separate Title I projects can be described under the general category of strengthening statewide library capabilities. Although not all categories have been funded each year, the list is generally representative. (These activities are conducted within the Division for Library Services.)

Project or Activity	Fiscal Year 1968 Grants
State Reference and Loan Collection (includes strengthening holdings and maintaining TWX nets linking it with regional systems and major resource centers)	$150,796 (partial)
Cooperative Children's Book Center	$ 10,550 (partial)
Special resources for public libraries (includes microfilming of basic periodical holdings)	$ 57,000
Interlibrary services (a contractual arrangement whereby Milwaukee Public Library provides resource services on referral from the Reference and Loan Library to regional centers for materials not practicable to be held locally)	$ 55,978
Scholarship programs	$ 12,000
Statewide surveys	(occasional and varying)

V.   EVALUATION

PROGRAM STRENGTHS

- Organization of the State Agency. The recent reorganization placing the agency within the Department of Public Instruction has undoubtedly strengthened its capabilities. It is no longer an independent single-function agency reporting directly to the Governor. The channel upward is less direct, but the considerable resources of the Department of Public Instruction are available, and, more important, public library linkages with educational systems are now more feasible.

- Extension Service. Wisconsin has a long heritage of State-supported extension services. Public library extension services represent a part of this heritage and provide both direction and assistance in public library development throughout the State. The program offers a wide range of features, including planning consultation assistance, surveys, book and nonbook collection strengthening, reference and interloan capability, personnel scholarships and training.

- Regional Systems. Wisconsin has established the basis for a true public library regional system configuration. Many of these regional systems are in being and others are in process of development. Network linkages between system central libraries and the State agency have increased the operational effectiveness of the entire statewide system.

- Supporting Organizations. The Division is supported in its library development activities by strong professional and lay library organizations.

PROBLEM AREAS

- Legislation. Wisconsin lacks legislation that would facilitate the establishment of regional public library systems as tax-levying entities.

- State Aid. No State grant-in-aid program currently exists. The Division for Library Services lacks both the funding resources and the potential planning and coordination leverage those resources might provide in furthering public library development in Wisconsin. (As of this writing, a State grant-in-aid program is being presented for legislative approval.)

- Personnel. Wisconsin has a shortage of trained librarians. A survey conducted in 1965, by the Library School of the University of Wisconsin (see Section VI, BIBLIOGRAPHY), found that the public libraries in the State were deficient in both the number and educational level of their personnel. The authors of the 1965 survey report estimated that it would cost $2,987,000 annually in additional salaries to employ an adequate number of trained library personnel. This is 53 percent more than the amount paid in public library salaries in 1963.

  Looking to the single within-State source of trained personnel, the University of Wisconsin Library School, the prospects of alleviating this shortage are not promising. Currently the University is conferring approximately 100 graduate library degrees per year with an increase to 150 projected by 1970-1971. However, only 60 percent of those receiving degrees accept employment in Wisconsin, and of those only 14 to 15 percent have been employed in public libraries. Based on the projected total number of graduates above and the percentage expected to accept public library employment, it is difficult to see how the shortage will be alleviated.

Currently, the Division is attempting to augment the number of trained librarians in the State. Portions of Federal grants are frequently used for salaries for additional staff personnel, and the Division's scholarship program previously described is an attempt to bring in trained people. The Friends of Wisconsin Libraries has, as part of its library-support function, a recruitment program. However, more will need to be done. State aid in the form of salary supplements would be helpful.

CONCLUSIONS

Wisconsin provides a good example of a well-managed State library program. As noted above, there is evidence of many areas of strength, and the problem areas tend to be those facing most of the other States--inadequate funding and a shortage of trained personnel. The unique problems of partially inadequate State library legislation and a needed State grant-in-aid program have long been recognized and corrective action is being initiated.

VI. BIBLIOGRAPHY

Wisconsin State LSA and LSCA Title I annual plans, reports, and programs submitted to USOE during the period 1957-1968 (miscellaneous titles).

Baumann, Ruth. Facing the '60's: The Public Library in Wisconsin. Bureau of Government, February 1961, 126 pp. (Report NS 9)

Division for Library Services. An Annual Report 1 July 1959 - 30 June 1960. Madison, Wisc., 1960, 21 pp.

Division for Library Services. Proceedings of the Eleventh Institute on Public Library Service. Madison, Wisc., 1966, 110 pp.

Division for Library Services. Wisconsin Public Libraries Service Record: Statistical reports for period of 1962-1968 (miscellaneous titles), Madison, Wisc.

Library Development & Legislation Committee. Public Library System: Development for Wisconsin. Madison, Wisc., 1968, 16 pp.

The Library School of the University of Wisconsin, Financing Public Library Systems in Wisconsin: A Fact Resource Paper with Analysis of Basic Data in Terms of a Public Library Area System Network for Wisconsin, Madison, 1965.

Southeastern Wisconsin Regional Planning Commission. Comprehensive Library Planning Program Prospectus. Waukesha, Wisc., April 1968, 35 pp.

Wisconsin Department of Resource Development. Public Library Facilities: Wisconsin Development Series. Madison, Wisc., 1965, 92 pp.

Wisconsin Free Library Commission. A Design for Public Library Development in Wisconsin: Standards for Measuring Progress. Madison, Wisc., 1963, 53 pp.

Wisconsin Free Library Commission. The Idea in Action: A Report on the Door-Kewaunee Regional Library Demonstration, 1950-1952. Madison, Wisc., 1953, 87 pp.

Wisconsin Free Library Commission. Wisconsin Library Bulletin. Madison, Wisc. Special issues containing LSCA-State Plans:

    Vol. 60:6A (Supplement Nov.-Dec., 1964), pp. 401-463.
    Vol. 61:6A (Supplement Nov.-Dec., 1965), pp. 51-540.
    Vol. 63:5 Supp. (Supplement Sept.-Oct., 1967), pp. 341-384.
    Vol. 64:2 Supp. (Supplement March-April 1968), pp. 137-176.

Wisconsin Free Library Commission. Wisconsin Library Commission: A Five Year Report July 1, 1960 to June 30, 1965. Madison, Wisconsin, 1965, 39 pp.

REGION VI:

Iowa
KANSAS
Minnesota
Missouri
Nebraska
North Dakota
South Dakota

William D. Cunningham, Library
    Services Program Officer, AVLP
    601 East 12th St.
    Kansas City, Missouri 64106

CHAPTER XI
KANSAS

I.   SOURCES OF INFORMATION

The following organizations and persons were visited to obtain information
for this study (see Figure K-1 for a map of the State):

Date	Place Visited	Persons Visited
10/28/68	USOE Regional Office Kansas City, Mo. Region VI	William D. Cunningham, Library Services Program Officer Thain McCormick, Director, AVLP
10/29/68	Kansas State Library Fifth Floor, State House Topeka, Kansas	Denny R. Stephens, Kansas State Librarian
10/30/68	Kansas Information Circuit Topeka	Mary A. Hall, Administrative- Coordinator
10/31/68	State Budget Division Topeka	James W. Bibb, Director Alden Shields, Budget Analyst, (Recreation, Historical, and General Government Agencies)
	Kansas State Library Topeka	State Library Staff: Mrs. Jeanice Thomas, Administrative Assistant to the State Librarian Mrs. Claire Vincent, Director, LSCA Title II Mrs. Virginia Manley, Editor, Kansas Library Journal Rita Gatz, Secretary
11/1/68	State Library Advisory Commission Topeka	Mrs. D. C. Meuli, (Rep. selected by Kansas Federation of Women's Club) Mrs. Josephine Churchill, (also 1st Vice President of Northeast Kansas Library System) Dr. Richard A. Farley, (also Director of Libraries, Kansas State University, Manhattan, Kansas)

Date	Place Visited	Persons Visited
11/1/68	Research Office of the Kansas Legislative Council Topeka	Richard Rein, Researcher
	Office of the Attorney General Topeka	J. Richard Foth, Chief of Municipal Law
11/2/68	Northeast Kansas Libraries System Oskaloosa	Mrs. Louise S. Barker President (and Trustee) Oskaloosa Public Library Earl Means, Vice President, NEK (and Trustee of Everest Public Library, former President Trustee Section, KLA) Leo Hack, Administrative Consultant, NEK LeRoy G. Fox, Johnson County Librarian (former Kansas State Librarian) Rep. John D. Bower, Past Chairman, Committee on Education, Kansas Legislative Council and Chairman, House Education Committee
11/4/68	Southeast Kansas Library System, Iola Free Public Library Iola	Lucile Wagner, Administrative Librarian, Southeast Kansas Library System and Librarian, Iola Free Public Library Raymond L. Willson, SEK Consultant and Head of Technical Services, Iola Free Public Library
11/4/68	Parsons Public Library Parsons	Richard Combs, President of SEK and former Mayor of Parsons Jane Mast, Librarian
11/4/68	Chanute Public Library Parsons	Mrs. Gene Gray, Librarian
11/4/68	St. Paul Kansas Public Library St. Paul	Mrs. Irma Habely, Librarian William O'Bryan, Library Trustee

Date	Place Visited	Persons Visited
11/5/68	Wichita Public Library Wichita	Ford Rockwell, Librarian and Member of K.I.C. Robert Gadberry, Trustee and V.P. of 4th National Bank of Wichita
	Legislative Committee of KLA Wichita	Mrs. Barbara MacGregor, Chairman
11/5/68	Moundridge	Sen. Joseph C. Harder, Chairman of Education Committee, Kansas Legislative Council and Chairman of Senate Education Committee

Much valuable information was also obtained from the publications listed in the Bibliography in Section VI of this chapter.

II.   BACKGROUND FOR LSCA OPERATIONS

THE STATE AGENCY

The agency presently having legal authority to receive and disburse LSCA funds in Kansas is the State Library, an independent entity reporting directly to the Governor. Actual LSCA program administration is supervised by the State Librarian. The State Library Advisory Commission acts as a body of consultants to the State Librarian and to the Governor and also reviews the annual plans of all library regional systems.

History of the Kansas State Library

Created by the Kansas Legislature in 1868, the State Library was placed under the supervision of the State Supreme Court in 1873. Its primary function was to develop and maintain a journal library for the use of the legislature, the Supreme Court, and State agencies; its emphasis was thus on legal publications and State and Federal documents. General books, as well as periodicals, on social, economic, and political problems were soon acquired, making the State Library a significant research and resource center for the general public and students.

In 1899, at the instigation of the Kansas Federation of Women's Clubs, the State legislature also created the Traveling Libraries Commission, a separate agency. The purpose of this Commission was to provide local library service to communities without public libraries, to provide long-term loans of books

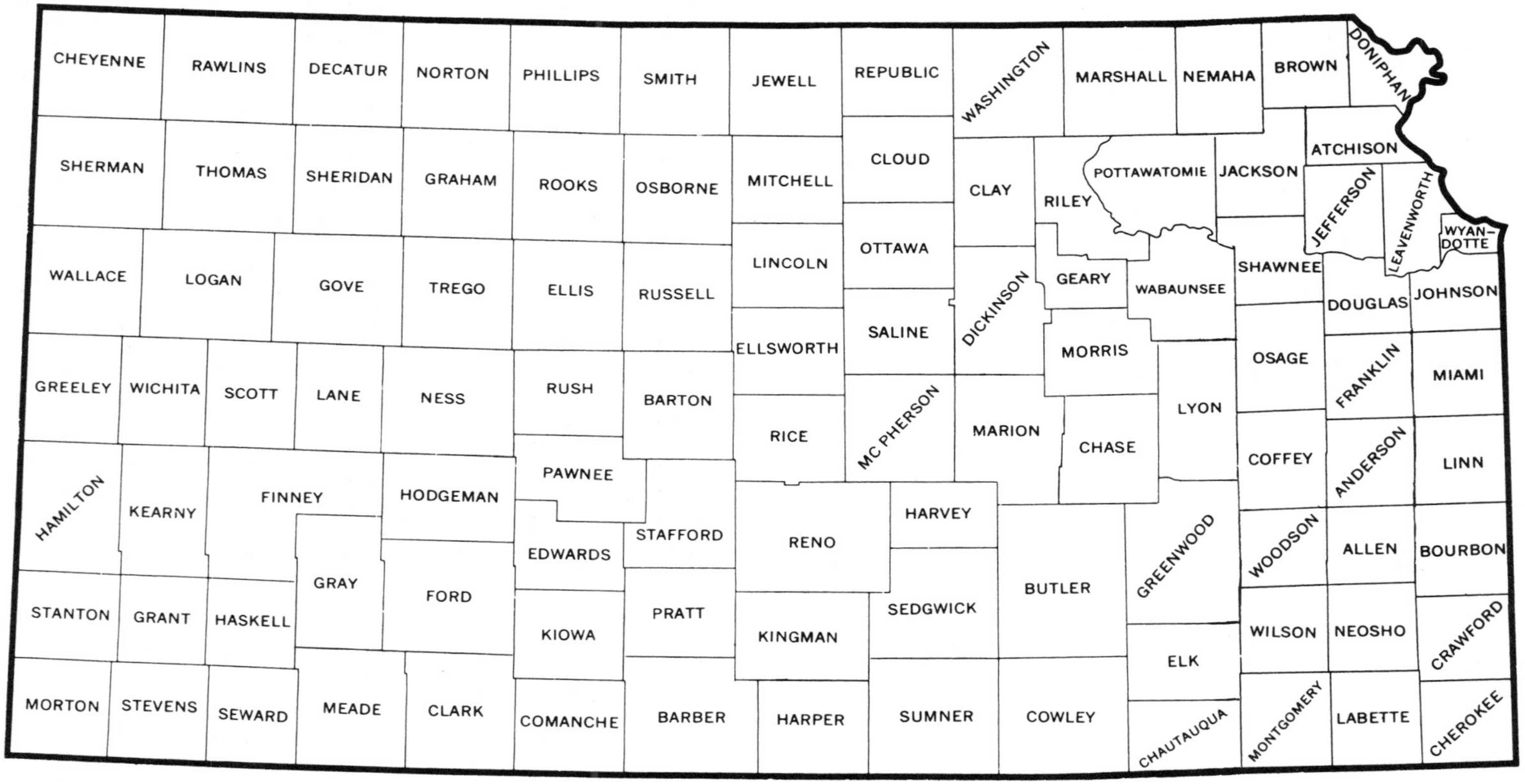

Figure K-1. Map of the State of Kansas

to local groups, and to supplement the collections of limited local libraries. The Commission's initial collection included adult and children's literature, mostly fiction.

The Commission was designated in 1949 as the Kansas agency authorized to enter into agreements with the Federal government for library services and funds. In 1957 its powers were enlarged to enable it to establish rural branches or service centers, provide consultative services, establish standards, and provide demonstration libraries. This organization, under the leadership of Miss Zelia French, proposed the original State plan in July 1957 and assumed responsibility for receiving and dispensing LSA funds. Initially, the Commission concentrated on providing bookmobile demonstrations, with mixed success. In November 1962, it was able to successfully conclude the first regional district library demonstration in Pottawatomie and Wabaunsee Counties. Another successful demonstration was concluded in Wyandotte County. It soon became apparent, however, that it would be a long, drawn-out process to provide sufficient library service to the 105 counties in Kansas under the present system.

In 1963, at the request of the Governor, LeRoy G. Fox accepted the office of State Librarian, subject to two conditions: A new law must be enacted combining all of the State's libraries into one organization, and he must have authority to implement a statewide plan of action. The same year, the legislature passed such a law, containing several important provisions: (1) all library functions in the State government were transferred into the State Library; (2) the Traveling Libraries Commission was abolished and its functions merged into the Public Library Extension Department of the State Library; (3) the responsibilities of the State Library were defined to include general public library leadership in the State; and (4) qualifications for the office of State Librarian were specified (a degree from an accredited library school and at least five years' experience in library administration). The most important feature of the 1963 act was the removal of the State Librarian from direct supervision by the Supreme Court. He was made an appointee of the Governor, and both appointment and removal from office were made subject to the approval of the State Chief Justice. A State Library Advisory Commission was also created to serve both the Governor and the State Librarian as consultants and advisors on general library policies.

In 1965, the legislature enacted the Kansas Systems Law,* upon which is based the future of library development in the State. This act created the present arrangement of seven regional library systems and also provided the impetus for organization of the Kansas Information Circuit. The development of the regional systems and that of the Information Circuit are due almost entirely to the availability of LSCA funds; both are described in detail in this chapter.

_____

*The official title of this law is the Regional System of Cooperating Libraries Law but in this report it will be referred to as the Systems Law.

In 1965, Mr. Fox resigned his position as State Librarian and an acting State Librarian was appointed. The present State Librarian, Denny Stephens, was appointed in February 1967.

Organization of the State Library

The State Library contains the following departments: Reference, Law, Extension, Legislative, Cataloging, and Administration. The Extension Department provides material for loan, in person or by mail, to libraries or individuals. In 1964, the bulk of the Department's collection was distributed to various small and medium-sized libraries throughout the State, on a long-term loan basis, to supplement their inadequate collections. The current collection of adult nonfiction serves mainly to support reference service and interlibrary loan service to all types of public libraries and individuals in Kansas.

The State Library employs 38 people. Fifteen can be considered professionals; they occupy positions ranging from Librarian I through Librarian III levels. There are no full-time extension consultants to public libraries at the present time. Staff people are available on an informal basis to librarians who are willing to go to the State Library for consultation. (Since one of the functions of the regional library systems is to provide consultant service, it was felt that full-time State consultants would not be necessary.)

State Library Advisory Commission

The 1963 Library law creating the State Library Advisory Commission describes the Commission's responsibilities as follows:

> The state commission shall consult and advise with
> the state librarian from time to time and suggest
> or recommend to the governor and the state librarian
> such policies, management and services as will best
> promote and advance the use and usefulness of the
> state library and its extension services for the
> residents of the state.[1]

Six of the seven members of the Commission are appointed by the Governor for 4-year overlapping terms. (No member may serve for more than two consecutive terms.) The seventh member and chairman is the Chief Justice of the Supreme Court. One member must be a librarian from the University of Kansas or Kansas State University, and at least one member must be a representative of the Kansas Federation of Women's Clubs. The Commission is also charged with the responsibility of justifying new programs at the Governor's Budget Hearing and the Ways and Means Committee meetings.

---

[1]Source: Kansas State Statute 75-2546.

With the passage of the Systems Law in 1965, the Commission acquired its only real authority. During the planning stages of systems, the Commission now reviews and approves all grants. It is also responsible for adopting rules and regulations establishing standards.

RELATIONSHIP OF STATE AGENCY TO OTHER ORGANIZATIONS

Kansas Library Association

The Kansas Library Association has been deeply involved with the State Library development and regional system development. Members have participated in all phases of library and related work, from developing library publicity to lobbying for library legislation. As of April 2, 1968, the Kansas Library Association had a total membership of 642, of whom 191 were public librarians and 165 trustees and citizens.[2]

When the Systems Law was originally proposed by the State Librarian, a series of seven regional meetings was held throughout the State to familiarize librarians and trustees with the need for new library approaches. The Association cosponsored all seven of these meetings and actively engaged in creating support among local librarians, trustees, and Friends of Libraries groups. In addition to the regional meetings, the Association held local meetings to inform a broader public of the need for further library development. These meetings created a ground swell of library support from which the System Law eventually emerged.

The Kansas Library Association engaged, directly and indirectly, in lobbying activity throughout the State through its Legislative Committee. Committee Chairman Mrs. Barbara MacGregor assisted greatly in getting the bill passed before opposition could be effectively organized by farming groups, county commissioners, and property owners (who were concerned about an increase in the ad valorem taxes for municipal services, including but not limited to libraries).

HISTORY OF STATE AID TO KANSAS LIBRARIES

The State of Kansas has not provided direct aid to public libraries. The State legislature has, however, provided support for libraries by passing legislation highly favorable to the extension of library service and the development of library systems (see History of Kansas State Library, above). In addition, the Kansas Legislative Council has recommended the passage of a direct State-aid-to-libraries law and has supported the request of the State Librarian for a $1,500,000 appropriation as a direct State grant.

---

[2]Kansas has 352 people working full time in public libraries and 459 working part time. Of the 642 members of the Kansas Library Association, 101 are members of ALA and 31 are members of the Mountain Plains Library Association. Twenty-seven belong to other library associations.

LSCA-State Matching Procedure

With the acceleration of Federal assistance to public libraries under the 1964 Library Services and Construction Act, a reorganization was effected in the State Library to make maximum use of the available Federal funds. In essence, a shift was made from an emphasis on direct State use of the Federal funds to the utilization of regional library systems. During the first seven years of Kansas's participation in the LSA program, the Traveling Library Commission had followed a policy of using only its own State appropriation for matching Federal grants; as a result, Kansas was able to claim only a little more than 60 percent of the funds actually allocated to it.

The original Kansas plan submitted in 1964, adding the State Library budget for matching purposes, would have made Kansas return to the Federal government more than $45,000 in Title I money alone. To prevent this, the State Librarian, in the same year, submitted a revised plan whereby, under a 1-year contract, the budget of the Wichita Public Library was also counted as part of the State's matching money. This contract has been renewed each year. As a result of the inclusion of this money, Kansas was able to receive the full amount of Federal funds. Table K-1 contains the amount of LSA/LSCA Title I funds allotted to Kansas from 1957 to 1968 and the amount returned because of insufficient State matching funds. Beginning with Fiscal Year 1970, the budget of the combined regional library systems will be used as the State's matching requirement.

Recent Developments in State Aid Plan

The Education Committee of the Kansas Legislative Council recently surveyed Kansas public libraries and formulated recommendations to the State legislature. Their recommendations are based on the concept that library service is no longer a matter of local option (such as a zoo or swimming pool) but is a legitimate State function for which the State has an obligation to provide funds just as it does for roads and vocational education. The Committee made the following recommendations: (1) that the governing body of the regional system include only members elected from the participating district boards; (2) that libraries other than those open to the general public be eligible to become members of the regional system, so that all of the major general libraries (except law libraries) may be linked together and that there may be an interchange of services between public and private agencies on a contractual basis; and (3) that all system boards submit annual budgets to the State Advisory Commission and to the State Librarian for review and approval, so that the submission of request for funds may be in accordance with general State budgetary procedures.

Table K-1. Kansas LSA/LSCA Title I Allotment*

Fiscal Year	Allotment	Payment	Allotment Lost
1957	$ 40,000	$ -	$ 40,000
1958	88,002	71,649	16,353
1959	104,329	64,543	39,786
1960	128,820	76,570	52,250
1961	128,820	75,902	52,918
1962	123,408	75,758	47,650
1963	123,408	76,537	46,871
1964	123,222	78,216**	45,006**
1965***	338,647	338,647	-
1966	338,647	338,426	221
1967	455,789	455,789	-
1968	455,789	455,789	-

*Source: Research Department, Kansas Legislative Council, Survey of Library Services in Kansas, p. 52; conversation with William D. Cunningham, Library Services Program Officer, Region VI.

**Later changed to $123,222 and 0, respectively, with revised budget.

***Note the large increase in funds in 1965 due to passage of LSCA. (Approximately 41 percent of the population of Kansas lives in areas containing more than 10,000; these areas had been ineligible for funds under LSA.)

In view of the Education Committee's report, and the State Librarian's request for $1,500,000 from the State in the next fiscal year, it seems there may well be a change in the legislature's historical attitude toward library aid. If the $1,500,000 line item for Fiscal Year 1970 is passed by the legislature, it will be used as a State grant to the regional library systems. Of this money, $50,000 plus $0.50 per capita will be distributed to each system. Generally, the State Librarian is hopeful about the possibility of passage during the current legislative session. Furthermore, if this request is granted, the State Library will then be able to shift most of the LSCA Title I funds towards the development of a statewide cataloging and processing center. This proposed switch in funds is explained in greater detail in the section, ALLOCATION OF LSCA TITLE I FUNDS.

LOCAL LIBRARY FUNDING

Kansas contains a large number of economic planning districts that have the legal authority to establish and collect taxes. According to the League of Kansas Municipalities, there are approximately 1,255 special districts (fire, cemetery, and hospital districts, and so forth). In addition to the special districts, there are 105 counties, 600 incorporated cities, 1,500 townships, and 300 school districts. Kansas's population of over 2,265,000 is widely distributed; only four counties have a population base large enough to support standard library services on a single-county basis.

One result of the existence of these many taxing authorities is that property owners are distinctly inhospitable to proposals that would increase their taxes. Almost three-fourths of the public libraries rely on property taxes for the major part of their income. It is the opinion of many State administrators and legislators that property taxes will not be increased for any purpose other than, possibly, education. Property taxes, therefore, cannot be used as a basis for increasing support to libraries on a local or regional level; libraries may, in fact, face a cut in funds in the future. State aid from general funds seems to be the major potential source of increased funds for libraries, hence the State Librarian's request for $1,500,000 in the next fiscal budget. It is hoped that this initial State grant-in-aid request (which is supported by the Kansas Library Association) will lead to an annual appropriation to the regional library systems.

In general, libraries go to their city, district, township, or county with a prepared budget. The concerned body prepares a total and assigns an amount to the libraries. The total amount requested for a library must be within the tax limits set by the State legislature. The attached chart (Table K-2) gives the current mill levies for all classes of cities, counties, townships, and districts. The maximum levy is called the Aggregate Mill Levy. Most library levies are within the Aggregate, but the legislature has authorized some additional levies outside the Aggregate, which also are indicated in Table K-2. The usual result is that libraries can receive their outside-the-aggregate funds, but must fight harder for their fair share of the aggregate levy due to the normal competition with other departments.

Table K-2. Maximum Library Tax Levies*

First class cities over 150,000 (Witchita)	4.4 mills (shared with several other services)
120,000 - 200,000 (Kansas City)	2.5 mills
35,000 - 150,000 (Hutchinson, Salina, Topeka)	2.5 mills (library levies directly - outside aggregate)
Less than 50,000 (10 cities)	2 mills (1 mill outside aggregate)
Second class cities (91 cities)	3 mills (2 mills outside aggregate)
Third class cities (516 cities)	2 mills (inside aggregate)
Counties (105 counties)	1.5 mills (outside aggregate)
Urban area counties (Johnson County)	2 mills (1/2 mill inside aggregate)
Townships (1,500 townships)	1 mill (outside aggregate)
District (Pottawatomie-Wabaunsee)	1.5 mills (outside aggregate) levy limits applying to counties
District (Louisburg)	1.5 mills
Regional library systems (7 authorized library systems)	.5 mill on property outside current library taxing areas levying more than .25 mills

*Based on: Jeanice Wellons. Kansas Library Trustee Handbook, Kansas State Library, 1968.

The State legislature has also passed a Home Rule Amendment that allows cities, upon vote of the City Council, to assume the tax levy of the next higher class of city. Although this amendment enables cities to obtain a higher millage tax for the library than was formerly possible, the Home Rule Amendment has rarely been used for public library purposes.

III.   LSCA PROGRAM

OVERVIEW OF ACTIVITIES

Development of Systems

In 1964, the State Library received a grant of $15,000 to perform a library survey of the State and determine the most efficient method of allocating LSCA funds. In Fiscal Year 1965, Kansas received $605,495 through LSCA, of which $338,647 was Title I money. The State Librarian requested the Research Department of the Kansas Legislative Council to perform the survey and perhaps provide the basis for the introduction of a proposed systems legislation. This highly respected group began the survey in March 1964 and published a report entitled "A Survey of Library Services in Kansas" in October 1965, while the legislature was still in session. This report provided basic information on the status of public libraries and pointed out the urgent need for joint planning. The Regional Systems of Cooperating Libraries Law (otherwise referred to as the Systems Law) passed the legislature on April 27, 1965.[3] The Systems Law created seven grant areas (multicounty regions) as a starting point for eventual regional system development. Each grant area received an LSCA Title I appropriation to use for operating expenses until it could receive tax funds. Figure K-2 shows the boundaries of each grant area and their initial appropriations. The State plan has successfully developed seven regional systems based on these grant areas.

Regional library system boards have been created with the authority to levy an ad valorem tax of 1/2 mill except in those areas now being taxed on a regular basis of 1/4 mill or more for library services.[4] Those areas that at present do not have a history of regularly taxing 1/4 mill or more for library services must then pay an appropriate systems tax. The system money is to be used within a system in a manner that will allow all libraries to share in its benefits.

[3]Senate Bill 498, incorporating some necessary amendments, was passed by the legislature in March 1968, after considerable effort by the State Library, the Kansas Library Association, and other interested groups.

[4]Even after a system is officially designated as eligible to begin collecting taxes, it must wait until January of the next fiscal year to start collecting them. This delay has resulted in a need for further grants enabling systems to operate until tax monies are actually available.

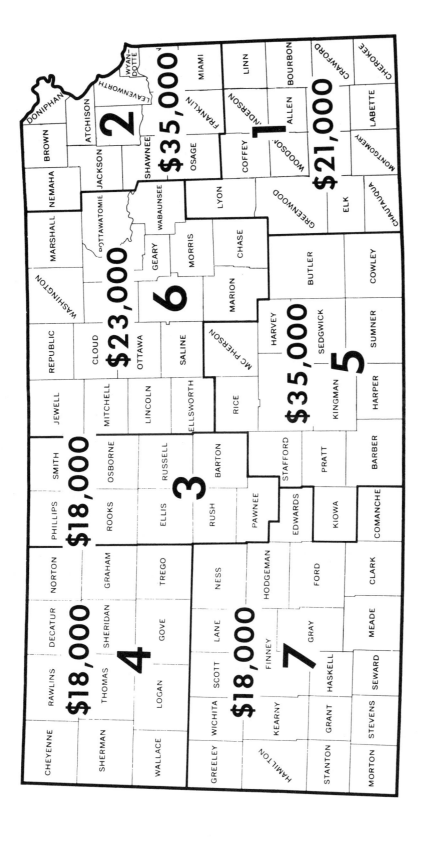

Figure K-2. Original Systems Grant Areas

Most of the State's public libraries are members of the regional systems covering their respective areas. A variety of reasons have been given in the few cases where libraries have not joined, most of these reasons are based on uncertainty about the responsibilities and privileges of membership and the fear of losing autonomy or exchanging a possible relatively favorable local taxing structure for the system tax. These few libraries, however, are finding the advantages of system affiliation and the additional available service too great to resist, and most of them are investigating their objections to determine if they are valid.

The present boundaries of the seven regional systems, their official names and counties that belong to a system are shown in Figure K-3.

System Operation

The following paragraphs describe the operation of the seven regional systems established and initially supported by LSCA funds.

The Systems Law provides that a local library will not sacrifice control over its own operations by choosing to join a system. Each local library board continues to operate its own library and manage its own budget; however, a library participating in a regional system is not permitted to charge for any service to a citizen who lives within the territory covered by the system.

The local library board of each member library has the responsibility for electing one member to serve as its representative on the regional library system board. The Governor of Kansas also has the power to appoint, to any system board, representatives from territories that are not within the district of any participating library in the system. The membership of a library system board is thus constituted to represent all of the areas within the region.

The system board, in turn, has the authority to create an executive board which may conduct the regular ongoing business of the system in all areas except preparation of the annual budget. Only the system board itself can prepare the annual budget and present it to the State Library Commission for approval.

The Systems Law also specifies the territory and name for each of the seven legally designated systems. Rules for membership in a system by a participating library, and for withdrawal from the system, have been clearly detailed by a recent set of regulations passed by the State Library Advisory Commission as authorized under the Systems Law. The rules for admission into a system are as follows:

REGIONAL SYSTEMS OF COOPERATING LIBRARIES

NWK – NORTHWEST KANSAS LIBRARY SYSTEM
CKL – CENTRAL KANSAS LIBRARIES
NCK – NORTH CENTRAL KANSAS LIBRARIES
NEK – NORTHEAST KANSAS LIBRARIES
SEK – SOUTHEAST KANSAS LIBRARY SYSTEM
SCK – SOUTH CENTRAL KANSAS LIBRARIES
SWK – SOUTHWEST KANSAS LIBRARY SYSTEM

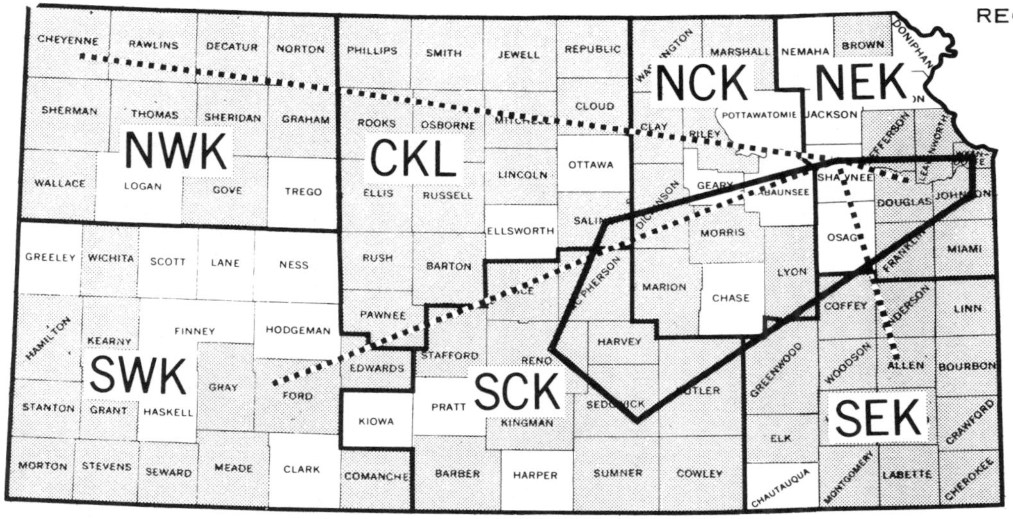

REGIONAL INTERLIBRARY LOAN CENTERS

DODGE CITY
HUTCHINSON
IOLA
LAWRENCE
MANHATTAN
SALINA
ST. FRANCIS

KANSAS INFORMATION CIRCUIT

TOPEKA
KANSAS CITY
JOHNSON COUNTY
WICHITA
HUTCHINSON
SALINA
STATE LIBRARY

AREA DECLINED PARTICIPATION IN REGIONAL
SYSTEM OF COOPERATING LIBRARIES

REGIONAL SYSTEM OF COOPERATING LIBRARIES

KANSAS INFORMATION CIRCUIT LIBRARIES

REGIONAL INTERLIBRARY LOAN CENTERS

Figure K-3. Regional Systems of Cooperating Libraries
and Kansas Information Circuit Libraries

54-1-3. **Admission to Regional System of Cooperating Libraries.** Any library desiring to participate in a regional system of cooperating libraries which has theretofore been established by the state library advisory commission shall file a petition to participate in said regional system of cooperating libraries with the regional system of cooperating libraries' board of trustees, and said board shall, if it approves the petition to participate, petition the state library advisory commission to include said library as a participating library in such regional system of cooperating libraries. If such petition is approved by the state library advisory commission, the petitioning library shall become an official participant in the regional system of cooperating libraries and shall have regional system of cooperating libraries board of trustees representation. Such library shall be entitled to services of the regional system of cooperating libraries one year from the 1st day of January following the approval of said petition by the state library advisory commission, unless financial contribution or other agreement by such library is agreed upon between the board of trustees of the regional system of cooperating libraries and the petitioning library and approved by the state library advisory commission to authorize services at an earlier date.

The rules for and consequences of withdrawal from a regional system are as follows:

54-1-12. **Withdrawal from Regional System of Cooperating Libraries.** A library participating in a regional system of cooperating libraries may petition the state library advisory commission for withdrawal from said regional system of cooperating libraries if such petition for withdrawal is presented to the state library advisory commission no less than one year prior to the time that the regional system of cooperating libraries is required to publish its annual budget....

54-1-13. **Same: Opinion of Regional System Board of Trustees.** Prior to approval of a petition for withdrawal from a regional system of cooperating libraries the state library advisory commission shall seek the advice and opinion thereon of the regional system of cooperating libraries board of trustees from which the library is petitioning to withdraw....

54-1-14. <u>Same: Hearing.</u> The state library advisory
commission shall within thirty (30) days after the
receipt of a petition for withdrawal from a regional
system of cooperating libraries by a participating
library set a date for a hearing to consider said
petition....

54-1-15. <u>Same: Transfer of Property.</u> Books,
furniture, equipment or other property purchased for
a library participating in a regional system of cooperating libraries and paid for from regional system of
cooperating libraries or state funds shall be the
property of the regional system of cooperating
libraries. In the event a participating library should
petition the state library advisory commission for withdrawal from the regional system of cooperating libraries
and such withdrawal is permitted by the state library
advisory commission all books, furniture, equipment, or
other property which has been purchased with regional
system of cooperating libraries or state funds shall be
returned to the regional system of cooperating libraries
upon demand of the regional system of cooperating
libraries' board of trustees....

The State Library Advisory Commission, as prescribed by law, has the
following authority over systems operations:

• The annual plan for a system must be approved by the
  Advisory Commission and each system must have its
  accounts audited on an annual basis.

• A system is permitted to employ a person as the systems
  librarian providing that person meets the qualifications
  for certification set by the Advisory Commission.

Except for these limitations, each system is permitted to operate internally
according to its own concept of the needs of the region. The system may
provide for any administrative service necessary for system operation.
Systems also have the right to determine how funds and materials are to be
allocated. One system, for example, has chosen to divide the money equally
among the participating libraries. Others have decided to invest the
majority of funds into developing a strong core library upon which the
other libraries may draw for supplementary material. Some are investigating
the possibility of regional ordering and processing of books instead of
relying on the proposed State processing system. Interest in building
strong audiovisual and record collections, whether in each library or on a
rotating basis, has also been generated. In general, then, each system has
chosen to interpret the needs of its region rather than follow a single
statewide plan.

Kansas Information Circuit

The Kansas Information Circuit, a TWX network connecting the leading libraries in the State, is a direct result of the passage of the 1965 Systems Law. Its organization and development are described in detail in Section IV.

ALLOCATION OF LSCA TITLE I FUNDS

The State plan has successfully created seven regional systems; all but two are receiving their tax funds and the last two will start receiving theirs in January 1969. Also if the budget submitted for Fiscal Year 1970 is approved, a State grant-in-aid program for the regional systems will be available, and LSCA Title I monies now allotted for regional systems aid and support will be shifted into developing a State central cataloging and processing center for public libraries.

The creation of an agency to provide this centralized service will mean a change in emphasis in the State plan. Originally, the State Library used LSA funds for direct aid, usually in the form of book-mobile demonstrations. With the passage of LSCA, a change in emphasis developed with the creation of regional library systems. Presently, another change is occurring, as the State Library moves to provide statewide library service, and as systems become more self-supporting. This development--from direct aid to local libraries. to the development of regional libraries, to strengthening the State Library--is a natural evolution. As local libraries become less dependent on LSCA funds, the State Library can then develop statewide service to supplement and enhance local service.

In Fiscal Year 1967, roughly 5 percent of the LSCA Title I funds received by Kansas were retained by the State Library for adminis-tration and special projects. Fiscal Year 1968 saw a little over 10 percent of the funds so used. The Fiscal Year 1969 allotment, including the proposed allotment for central processing, will result in the following allocations (this breakdown reflects the proposed usage of all Title I funds after allowing for the grant to the Kansas Information Circuit, discussed below):

Activity or Service Proposed for Fiscal Year 1969	Percent of LSCA Title I Funds Available after Grant to KIC
Retained at State Library:	
Administrative and General Services	2.0
*State Reference Service to Public Libraries	7.5
*Interlibrary Loan Program (includes 21 percent granted to systems and returned to State Library for Loan Program)	30.5
Central Cataloging and Processing for Public Libraries	36.0
Consultant Services	1.0
**System Library Grants (over and above the 21 percent used for Interlibrary loans)	23.0
Total	100.0

*Includes budget for books and periodicals which is 8 percent of the total LSCA-I allocation of $455,689.

**In addition to System Library Grants, Interlibrary Loan Program includes grants to six public libraries for purchase of materials and performance of interlibrary loan service in cooperation with the State Library.

If the State grant request is approved by the Kansas Legislature for Fiscal Year 1970, and if the central processing service is approved, about 70 percent of the Title I funds will stay with the State Library. If it is not, the plan will call for continued support of the regional systems so that the State will retain only 13 percent.

There is evidence that planning by the State Library has reached a point where the creation of a central processing facility is almost a certainty. Therefore, it can be assumed that if not this year, surely the next will see such a function added to the State Library.

Kansas Information Circuit (KIC) Allocation

The Kansas Information Circuit (KIC) has received an annual appropriation of $96,000, totally derived from LSCA Title I funds, from its first full year of operation to the present. The five participating public libraries receive

$12,000 each and the Topeka Public Library receives $36,000.[5] The State
Library and Kansas State University Library do not receive Title I funds but
are participating because of their belief in supplying the needs for State
residents while receiving State funds. The fact that KIC has never received
an increase in its appropriation is one of the major reasons why the participating libraries favor the inclusion of KIC into the State Library.

REPORTING AND EVALUATION PROCEDURES OF STATE AGENCY

The State Library sets reporting requirements for the systems that are roughly
equivalent to those the State Library must meet in reporting to the Federal
Regional Program Officer. All LSCA funds granted to the systems must be
audited and accounted for in detail. Each system board must submit an annual
plan and report to the State Advisory Commission similar in detail and
content to the annual report submitted by the Kansas State Library to USOE.

Evaluation of the regional library systems is performed by means of the
Library Advisory Commission's annual review of each system. The Commission
has the authority to withhold Title I funds if annual plans do not meet
minimal requirements. It is this fiscal control, rather than direct legal
authority, which enables the State Library to develop evaluative procedures.

IV.   DESCRIPTION OF REPRESENTATIVE USES OF LSCA FUNDS

NORTHEAST KANSAS LIBRARIES SYSTEM

This report will concentrate on the Northeast Kansas Libraries System as a
representative sample of the seven systems. Although each system is unique,
the general approach to system development can be more clearly grasped by
an in-depth study of one system.

The Northeast Kansas Libraries System (NEKL) was originally called Grant Area
II (see Fig. K-2, map of original grants). It was designated a system in
November 1967, with 19 libraries signing resolutions to participate. In
Fiscal Year 1968, the Northeast Kansas Library received $35,835 from the
State Library under LSCA Title I as a system planning grant. Although the
system was formally accepted as a legal regional system in 1967, by State
law it cannot become a taxing body until January 1969. If the 1/2 mill levy
were immediately available, the system would raise approximately $167,075.
However, the Fiscal Year 1969 budget is estimated at $85,000, as a result of
the difficulties of getting all the counties to participate immediately.

---

[5]The Topeka Public Library receives $12,000 as a KIC member. Because of
its proximity to the State Library, it was designated as KIC headquarters.
Since this library was fulfilling as many requests as all five other
participating libraries combined, in addition to serving as headquarters,
it receives an extra grant of $12,000. It receives another $12,000 for
the director's salary and related expenses.

There are 14 counties within the system; two (Johnson and Wyandotte Counties) will be exempt from the systems tax, as they already have a history of providing a regular tax of over 1/4 mill for library services.

As an indication of how the system organization has stimulated local interest, Table K-3 contains a comparison between the local mill levy for libraries within the region for 1965 and 1968.

As one of the newest regions, the NEKL System has not advanced much beyond the planning stage, although member libraries and trustees have a long and active history of library involvement. Their biggest problem is in integrating the large and small libraries. The role of the larger libraries has not been defined well enough yet to allow the development of a working relationship between them and the small libraries. As a result, continuous planning and coordination meetings will be necessary before the member libraries can learn to resolve individual differences and work together.

Because of the need for a comprehensive plan that would alleviate any fears of the various libraries and enhance their cooperative efforts, five objectives were developed by the NEKL trustees. This plan is a good example of the work now being undertaken by all of the seven systems. Although the details of the planning are not the same (just as the problems are not the same) in all of the systems, the thorough approach of the NEKL System is common to all.

Objective 1

The NEKL, through implementing policies adopted by the system board, through the services of an advisory committee (including professional librarians), and through the assistance of other friends of libraries, will offer programs to local libraries that are not available either in the local community or in any member library of the system. These programs will bring the full range of library services to the citizens of Northeast Kansas.

A number of strategies have been developed to accomplish this objective. Some of these strategies are: developing a system adminstration through a system librarian, providing nonbook and supplementary collections, supporting the development of library associations and other systems, informing local people about system services, providing consultative services and workshops to help improve local libraries.

The accomplishment of this objective is expected to be completed over a 2-year period. Each strategy involves several distinct short-term tasks, each of which has a clearly defined goal. The administrative strategy will involve such tasks as writing fiscal, policy, and personnel manuals; continuously reviewing progress in all areas of development; and reporting annually on these efforts. The strategy of special collection building will include the development of access to all types of audiovisual material by permanent,

Table K-3. Mill Levies for Representative Local Libraries in Northeast Kansas in 1965 and 1968*

Library	1965	1968
Hiawatha	.91	1.92
Horton	2.40	2.70
Everest	1.71	1.46
Meriden	-	1.00
Oskaloosa City	.47	.68
Oskaloosa Township	-	.50
Valley Falls	.50	.50
Norton Township	-	.25
Ottawa	2.27	2.68
Richmond	1.02	.86
Wellsville	.82	1.52
Louisburg	.43	-
Miami County Library District #1	-	1.50

*Source: Meeting with trustees and librarians of Northeast Kansas Libraries System, Oskaloosa, November 2, 1968.

long-term, or rotating loan, or by special loan from a core collection.
The consultative strategy will involve hiring specialized consultants who
will visit libraries, provide written reports of recommendations, and hold
workshops and seminars.

Objective 2

The NEKL, through centralized purchasing, cataloging, and processing of
books, will provide every citizen of Northeast Kansas with convenient and
planned access to the collections of Northeast Kansas libraries. This
objective is based upon the final adoption of central processing by the
State Library. If a statewide centralized agency is developed, additional
NEKL activities might include a special contract with the Kansas City
Library, contract with an outside agency, or development of a regional
cataloging and processing center for the member libraries.

Objective 3

By building adequate local collections, the NEKL will provide every citizen
with a source of current and standard material in his community. The only
strategy for this objective is to evaluate the present 20 libraries in terms
of facilities, hours of service, collection, and need. Once an evaluation
is made, the system librarian and the system board can formulate recommendations as to types of materials needed, quantities, and direct book grants.
By Fiscal Year 1970 this objective should be an important part of the
system interim policy.

Objective 4

Through a system of adequate materials collection and personnel, the NEKL
provides every citizen of Northeast Kansas with information services. It
will utilize the system's headquarters, the Lawrence Public Library, to
fill periodical requests, participate in KIC as a means to acquire material
outside the district and to provide an increased reference collection so
that it can function as the system's resource center starting in 1969.

Objective 5

The NEKL, through a system of core libraries, will offer interlibrary loans
to citizens of Northeast Kansas. The strategies involved in this objective
include continued affiliation with the Kansas Information Circuit, and the
development of a communication network linking Lawrence, Ottawa, Leavenworth,
and Johnson County public libraries to provide an intra-system resource for
retrieval of materials and information.

KANSAS INFORMATION CIRCUIT (KIC)

From its inception, all funds for the KIC network have been provided by LSCA Title I. It originated in 1965, when the State Librarian contacted the head librarians of the largest Kansas public libraries and proposed that they make their holdings available on an interlibrary loan basis to public libraries throughout the State and to individuals who do not have direct access to a local library. Six libraries were approached: Johnson County, Wichita, Hutchinson, Salina, Kansas City, and Topeka public libraries. The six librarians, with their respective boards, agreed to the proposal, and the Kansas Information Circuit began operation on September 27, 1965. Each library hired additional personnel and purchased teletype equipment, duplication equipment, and office supplies. The formation of this system immediately made more than a million volumes in collective holdings available to Kansas citizens. The inclusion, in 1967, of the State Library and the Kansas State University Library made a total of 3,000,000 volumes available. The area of coverage for the KIC network is shown in Figure K-3. Mary Hall, former Head of Adult Services at Topeka Public Library, became the first Director of the Kansas Information Circuit as the need for coordinated leadership became apparent. Under her leadership, the Circuit was able to adopt a manual of operation and the present set of procedures.[6]

Requests enter KIC in one of two ways. Some are mailed to the State Library from individual citizens who do not have a local library, or whose library is not part of a regional system. Other requests are teletyped to Topeka Public Library from KIC libraries. Books that are in the Topeka collection are either mailed directly to the requesting libraries or sent to the State Library by messenger. Requests for books not found at Topeka are put onto the TWX circuit, on a rotating basis, to the other five participating libraries.

By the end of the day--or, at the latest, the next afternoon--the Topeka Public Library will notify the State Library and each of the participating libraries of the results of the search. (This 1-day to 1-1/2 day turn-around time is a significant accomplishment.) If a book belongs to a Circuit library but is currently in circulation, the Circuit's response will so indicate, so that the requestor can contact the owning library directly rather than tying up the KIC with repeated requests. KIC will accept only verified author and titles of books and publications to be reproduced. No school assignments nor subject searches are accepted by KIC.

---

[6]The Director must deal with the public library staff involved in the KIC network at other library locations without having any administrative authority over these people. In June 1969, when KIC is scheduled to become part of the State Library, it is hoped that the Director will receive the necessary authority to carry out her responsibilities.

The percentage of requests filled by the Circuit stays consistently between 65 percent and 70 percent while, at the same time, the quantity of incoming requests has constantly increased. Figure K-4 shows the numbers of requests received and filled by KIC from its inception through July 1968.

The network has constantly tried to increase its usefulness by devising alternative methods of operation. Efforts have been made to determine ways in which the percentage of unfilled requests might be reduced. One such experiment occurred in March 1968, when KIC headquarters conducted a 2-week experiment with the Denver Bibliographic Center. The 237 verified requests that the eight KIC libraries were unable to fill were teletyped to the Bibliographic Center, which was able to furnish locations for 194 members, or a little over 80 percent.

The future of KIC will be dependent on the State Library, and the Kansas Library Association. Members of both these organizations are devoting much study to the optimum use of the network by the regional library systems.

V.   EVALUATION

PROGRAM STRENGTHS

LSA and LSCA have been very successful in Kansas in creating seven regional library systems and the Kansas Information Circuit. Local support has been increased and has led to the strengthening of local library service. As an example of library growth, the following table contains a summary of visitors, circulation, and costs for a typical small library:

Table K-4. Visitors, Circulation and Costs:
Everest, Kansas, Public Library

		Books Checked Out of Library		
Year	Visitors Per Month	Total Per Month	Total For Year	Total Costs Per Book
1962	49	44	528	.847
1963	63	79	948	.444
1964	110	172	2,064	.184
1965	151	256	3,072	.164
1966	217	361	4,327	.129
1967	243	420	5,044	.122

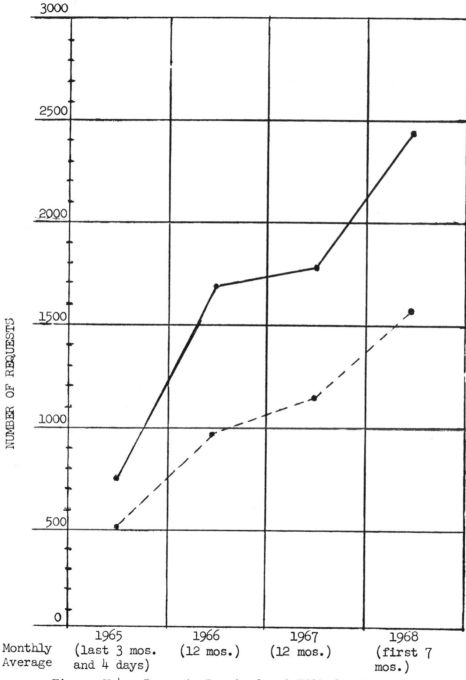

NUMBER OF REQUESTS

| Monthly Average | 1965 (last 3 mos. and 4 days) | 1966 (12 mos.) | 1967 (12 mos.) | 1968 (first 7 mos.) |

Note: Prior to April 1967, the Searching Circuit Libraries were the six Public Libraries of Topeka, Johnson County, Wichita, Hutchinson, Salina, and Kansas City. In April 1967, the State Library became the seventh Searching Library and in June 1967, the Kansas State University Library became the eighth Searching Library on the Circuit.

Figure K-4. Requests Received and Filled - Kansas Information Circuit

Legend: The solid line represents the monthly average of all requests incoming to KIC Headquarters. The broken line represents the monthly average number of requests filled by all Circuit Libraries, combined.

It is interesting to note the circulation increase of over 100 percent due to a donation of 1,000 books from the State Library Extension collection. Circulation has continued to increase because of participation in the NEKL Regional System.

The tremendous increase in regional activity and the growth of the Kansas Information Circuit (as reported in Section IV) are good indicators of the vitality of the overall library program in Kansas.

PROBLEM AREAS

Recently, there has been serious discussion among the library community as to the proper role of the Commission in relation to the State Librarian. On the one hand, the Commission is simply an advisory body; on the other, it is, in effect, the trustee for all of the library systems. The Kansas Library Association has recently adopted a resolution requesting that the State Library Advisory Commission drop the term "advisory" and become, in effect, the State Library Board. The Kansas Library Association also believes that the State Librarian should be appointed by and answerable to the Commission rather than the Governor. The present Librarian concurs with this resolution and is exploring legislative action to implement it. (A member of the Kansas Library Association has recently been asked to approach the Chief Justice and ask that he delegate his appointive and removal authority to the Commission. This would be the first step in eventually placing full responsibility over the State Librarian with the Commission.) The Commission, however, appears reluctant to take on these added responsibilities. The members of the Commission receive no compensation for their time and services, except for actual expenses and travel to attend meetings. Most of the members feel unable to assume the additional obligations that would fall upon them if the proposed changes were enacted into law. Unless some way is developed to compensate the members for their time, they will most likely continue to be reluctant to aid in supporting legislative action on the proposed changes.

Another possible problem arises with respect to the future role of the Kansas Information Circuit. Its imminent incorporation as a division of the State Library may cause a disruption in activity, as the large-library members will continue to want a strong voice in its operation. On the other hand, the reverse might be true: The prestige of the State Library may give KIC a greater dimension and an even more dynamic role in providing quick and efficient service to all of the system-affiliated libraries.

Two more problem areas are worthy of mention, though neither poses a serious obstacle to the further development of the State's library system:

- The present Systems Law contains no equalization factors that would enable the poorer areas to receive additional support beyond that available from the systems tax.

- The regional systems have not yet developed enough capable administrators to become autonomous and continued guidance is necessary. In addition, there is occasionally friction between the newly established system libraries and the large urban libraries. The solution to these two related problems seems to lie in the continuing strong leadership provided by the State Library.

CONCLUSIONS

The library program in Kansas has seen a marked expansion of services on all levels. This very growth, which is primarily due to the availability of LSCA funds, has created a need for a strong central agency, a need admirably filled by the State Library. The present management of this agency has been notable for its effective leadership and its wise use of LSCA funds. The legislature's creation of the library systems as taxing bodies is also to be commended, as this act will enable the systems to grow quickly into effective organizations.

The State still needs to continue planning in depth and to preserve flexibility to meet changing needs. Further, the State Library must maintain its position of leadership for some time, in order to overcome any factionalism among the disparate elements of the newly formed systems and to form an effective lobbying force for the passage of State grant-in-aid legislation.

LSCA will continue to play an important role in Kansas, even with the passage of a grant-in-aid law. LSCA funds will still be needed to supplement the income of the systems, particularly those in the poorer regions. There will also be the need for special projects (such as demonstrations and central processing services) that can only be supported by LSCA.

In summary, LSCA will play an important though not indispensable role in Kansas for some time to come; and with continued good management of LSCA funds, the State may well develop one of the nation's most successful library systems in the not too distant future.

VI. BIBLIOGRAPHY

Kansas State LSA and LSCA Title I annual plans, reports, and programs submitted to USOE during the period 1957-1968 (miscellaneous titles).

Bugwin, Martin & Associates. St. Paul Kansas Comprehensive Plan 1968. Kansas, 1968, 50 pp.

Foster, Robert D. Library Resource and Service Center of Kansas, Wichita, Kansas, September 1968, 54 pp.

Fox, LeRoy G. Annual Report to the State Library Advisory Commission. Topeka, Kansas, 16 October 1964, 12 pp.

Hall, Mary A. Kansas Information Circuit Annual Reports and Supplementary Statistics (Manual of Procedure) covering the period of 1966-August 1968 (miscellaneous titles).

Kansas Legislative Council, Research Department. Kansas Tax Facts: A Handbook on State and Local Taxes. Topeka, Kansas, October 1965, Publication No. 252, 51 pp.

Kansas Legislative Council, Research Department. Kansas Tax Facts: 1968 Supplement. Topeka, Kansas, 16 October 1968, 24 pp.

Kansas Legislative Council, Research Department. A Survey of Library Services in Kansas. Topeka, Kansas, 1965, 62 pp.

Kansas State Library. Kansas Public Library Statistics, 1965. Topeka, Kansas, 1965, 42 pp.

Kansas State Library. Kansas Public Library Statistics, 1966. Topeka, Kansas, 1966, 85 pp.

Kee, S. Janice. Public Library Development in Kansas Since 1966: A Review Including Recommendations. Kansas State Library Advisory Commission, Topeka, Kansas, 1966, 53 pp.

Knecht, Fred W., ed. Kansas Public Library Laws. Kansas State Library, 1968, 70 pp.

League of Kansas Municipalities. Kansas Tax Rate Book. Topeka, Kansas, 24 pp.

Manley, Virginia, ed. Kansas Library Bulletin. Kansas State Library,
Topeka, Kansas, 32 pp. Spring, Summer-Fall 1965; Winter, Spring, Summer-
Fall 1966; Spring, Summer, Fall 1967; Winter, Spring Summer 1968.

Marcoux, Dale C. and Leach, Hugh V. Library Resources Survey Kansas Institutions. Kansas, December 1967, 76 pp.

Moore, Mary A., Hall, Mary A. and Fox, LeRoy G. A report on seven regional
meetings of the Kansas Library Association held to review Preliminary Fund-
ings of a Survey of Kansas Public Libraries conducted by the Education
Committee of the Legislative Council and to discuss these findings in light
of 'Interim Standards for Small Public Libraries'. Kansas Library Association,
Merriam, Kansas, 9 November 1964, 26 pp.

Northeast Kansas Library System. Barker, Louise S., Chairman. History of
the Use of L.S.C.A. Funds in Encouraging Inter-Library Operation, Education,
Concerning Library Standards, and Finally Leading to Legally Constituted
Systems, Kansas, 1965, 20 pp.

Wellons, Jeanice. Library Trustee Handbook. Kansas, 1968, 76 pp.

REGION VII:

ARKANSAS
Louisiana
New Mexico
Oklahoma
Texas

S. Janice Kee, Library Services
   Program Officer, AVLP
   1114 Commerce St.
   Dallas, Texas 75222

CHAPTER XII
ARKANSAS

I.   SOURCES OF INFORMATION

The following organizations and persons were visited to obtain information
for this study (see Figure A-1 for a map of the State):

Date	Place Visited	Persons Visited

9/16/68	USOE Regional Office
	Dallas, Texas
	Region VII
		S. Janice Kee, Library Services
		  Program Officer
		George Hann, Regional Assistant
		  Commissioner
		William G. Cummens, Acting
		  Director, AVLP
		Dr. Harold Haswell, Director of
		  Educational Research

9/17/68	Arkansas Library Commission
	  Headquarters
	Little Rock
		Mrs. Frances Neal, Librarian and
		  Executive Secretary
		Freddy Schader, Administrative
		  Assistant and Consultant

9/18/68	Arkansas River Valley
	  Regional Library
	Dardanelle
		Mrs. Katharine Keathley, Regional
		  Librarian
		Nola Ellis, Library Consultant
		Mrs. Helen Birkhead, Administrative
		  Assistant
		Mrs. Helen Bunting, Interlibrary
		  Clerk
		Mrs. Katie Murdoch, Reference
		  Librarian and Consultant
		Bobby Piercy, Bookmobile Assistant
		Harold Ford, Chairman, Arkansas
		  River Valley Regional Library
		  Board and former Franklin County
		  Judge
		John Chambers, Member at Large of
		  Arkansas Library Association Board
		  and 1967 National Library Week
		  Chairman for Arkansas
		Lyn Stringer, President, Dardanelle
		  Chamber of Commerce
		Bill Woodson, President, Rotary
		  Club and Member of Dardanelle
		  City Council

-230-

Date	Place Visited	Persons Visited
		Bill Newsom, Regional Library Trustee of Pope County
		Charles A. L. Fore, Regional Library Trustee of Pope County
		E. B. Wilson, Yell County Library Trustee
9/18/68	Arkansas Library Commission Jacksonville	Kenneth Wilson, Member
9/19/68	Ozarks Regional Library Fayetteville	Mrs. Carol Wright, Regional Librarian
		Howard Clark, Springdale Library Trustee, and Chairman of Arkansas Library Association Trustee Division, Member of Arkansas Library Commission
		David Gates, Rogers Library Trustee and Member of Benton County Library Board
		J. R. Kennan, Ozarks Regional Library Board, Chairman
9/20/68	North Arkansas Regional Library Harrison	Mrs. Evelyn Griffiths, Regional Librarian
		George Severson, Chairman, Marion County Library Board and Member, Regional Library Board
		Mrs. Bob Newton, Board Member
		R. A. Cox, Active Member, Arkansas and American Library Association (former Mayor of Harrison)
9/30/68	Little Rock Public Library Little Rock	Library Staff
	Pulaski-Perry County Regional Library System Little Rock	Mary Sue Shepherd, Librarian
	State Capitol Building	Ralph Liverman, Budget Analyst, Educational Affairs
	Arkansas Library Commission Little Rock	Mrs. Bessie Moore, Coordinator of Economic Education, Arkansas State Department of Education and Chairman of Arkansas State Library Commission
		Mrs. Cynthia Pitts, Head, Order Department

Date	Place Visited	Persons Visited
10/1/68	Stuttgart Public Library Stuttgart	Mrs. Sylvia Mills, Librarian
10/1/68	Jefferson County Public Library Pine Bluff	Mrs. George Dorsett, Librarian State Senator Morrell Gathright
10/2/68	Cloc Regional Library Magnolia	Mrs. Florence J. Bradley, Regional Librarian
10/2/68	Union (Barton) County Public Library El Dorado	Lucille Slater, Librarian
10/3/68	Northeast Regional Library Paragould	Mrs. Kathleen Sharp, Regional Librarian
10/3/68	Paragould Daily Press Paragould	Barlow Herget, Managing Editor
10/3/68	Wonder State Manufacturing Company Paragould	W. L. Gatz, President and Local Civic Leader
10/3/68	Jonesboro Public Library Jonesboro	Elizabeth Malone, Regional Librarian, Crowley Ridge
10/4/68	White River Regional Library Batesville	Mrs. Terry Griffith, Librarian G. H. Moore, Chairman, White River Regional Library Board and County School Supervisor Mrs. P. F. Lindsey, Board Member Mrs. Jim Barnett, Board Member Mrs. Harney Chaney, Board Member William E. Coats, Superintendent of Schools Mrs. O. E. Jones, Sr., Owner, Batesville Guard P. F. Lindsey, Manager, Batesville Chamber of Commerce Peyton Golden, Citizens Committee for Libraries

Date	Place Visited	Persons Visited
		Mayor Richard Sturch
		John W. Edwards, Chairman of Board, First National Bank
		Mrs. John W. Edwards, Friend of Library
		H. D. Bailey, Jr., President, Chamber of Commerce

Much valuable information was also obtained from the publications listed in the Bibliography in Section VI of this chapter.

II.   BACKGROUND FOR LSCA OPERATIONS

THE STATE AGENCY

The Arkansas Library Commission has been legally designated as the agency responsible for receiving and allocating LSCA Title I funds and State grant-in-aid appropriations.

The Commission was created in 1935 and received its initial appropriation in 1937. It is composed of seven members--one member from each of the four Federal Congressional districts and three members selected at large. Each member serves a 5-year term. In accordance with Arkansas public library law, members are appointed by the Governor from lists submitted by four groups: (1) the State Department of Education, (2) the Arkansas Federation of Women's Clubs, (3) the Arkansas Congress of Parents and Teachers, and (4) the American Legion Auxiliary, Department of Arkansas.

During the 1967-1969 biennial session of the legislature, the Commission (originally located within the State Department of Education) was established as a separate agency reporting to the Governor.

The Commission appoints a State Librarian currently Mrs. Frances Neal, who has the administrative responsibility and legal authority for implementing Commission policies, procedures, and directives. In addition to acting as an administrator, the State Librarian also serves as the Executive Secretary of the Commission.

LEGAL AUTHORITY AND RESPONSIBILITIES OF STATE AGENCY

In 1937, the Arkansas Library Commission was given legal authority to serve as the coordinating agency for library service in the State. The Commission has accordingly formulated policies and directives to guide

PUBLIC LIBRARIES IN ARKANSAS

BY ARKANSAS LIBRARY COMMISSION 1968

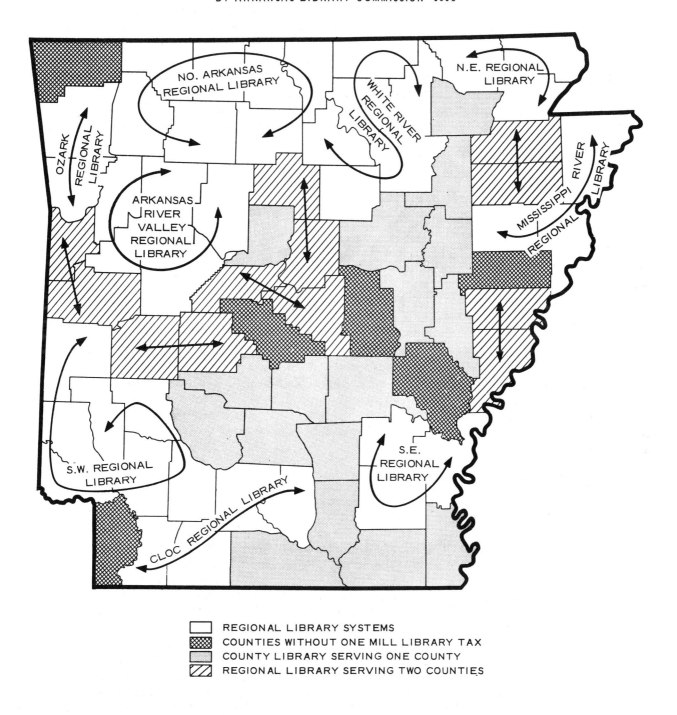

REGIONAL LIBRARY SYSTEMS
COUNTIES WITHOUT ONE MILL LIBRARY TAX
COUNTY LIBRARY SERVING ONE COUNTY
REGIONAL LIBRARY SERVING TWO COUNTIES

Figure A-1.   Public Libraries in Arkansas by
              Arkansas Library Commission 1968

public library development; local library policies and programs must be in accord with these in order for the libraries to receive State grant-in-aid or LSCA funds. In addition, counties are required to have passed a countywide library tax in order to qualify for State aid or Federal funds.

The Arkansas Library Commission headquarters serves primarily as a service agency for county and regional (multicounty) libraries. To implement the Commission's service commitments, legal authority was given by the legislature to provide a multitude of library services through the following departments located at the Commission's headquarters in Little Rock:

- Administration

- Reference and Order

- Technical Processing

- Circulation

- Catalog

- Consultant Service

Through these departments, county and regional libraries can receive such services as: (1) centralized purchasing and processing of books selected locally, (2) a centralized book selection center, (3) interlibrary loan privileges, (4) access to the Commission's central cataloging facilities, and (5) workshops and other in-service training programs for local librarians and trustee groups conducted at the Commission, or regional library, headquarters.

GENERAL APPROACH TO LIBRARY DEVELOPMENT

Even before the enactment of LSA and LSCA legislation, the Commission had encouraged the development of county and regional (multicounty) library systems. For example, the first Regional Library System was established at Clarksville, Arkansas, in Johnson County, now a part of the Arkansas River Valley Regional Library at Dardanelle. This first regional library, composed of Johnson and Franklin Counties, joined Arkansas River Valley Regional Library in 1958. (See Figure A-1.) Primary attention of the Commission is currently focused upon encouraging individual county libraries to join together in new regional library systems or to affiliate with existing contiguous systems. As shown in Figure A-1, there are currently 16 single-county library units and 53 counties that have formed some regional arrangement for library service. Regional libraries serve areas ranging from two to seven counties. In addition, the Commission has funded bookmobile programs to stimulate community support in four of the six remaining counties that have failed to pass a countywide library tax.

HISTORY OF STATE AID TO ARKANSAS LIBRARIES

Since its formation, the Commission has worked to increase State grants-in-aid to county and regional libraries. Legislature appropriations had for some time remained on a plateau, with only minimal increases from year to year. A significant departure from this budget plateau has occurred as a result of the past two biennial legislature sessions: During the 1965-67 session, the Commission was successful in doubling the State grant-in-aid appropriation (from $160,000 to $320,000 per year); the appropriation was further increased (to $400,000 per year) in the following 1967-69 session. The State-aid appropriations are important because they are used as matching funds to qualify for LSCA allotments.

The State grant-in-aid program for county and regional libraries is administered by the Arkansas Library Commission. The six grant-in-aid categories, and requirements for such grants, are listed below:

STATE AID GRANTS[1]

*ESTABLISHMENT GRANT:

$1.00 per capita (1960 census) for the purchase of an initial book collection for counties meeting the following requirements:

1. A library organized under the County Library Law of 1927.

2. One mill library tax.

3. THE HEAD LIBRARIAN APPROVED BY THE ARKANSAS LIBRARY COMMISSION

4. Suitable quarters for the library.

5. Budget approved by the Arkansas Library Commission.

6. AT LEAST TWENTY PERCENT OF INCOME SPENT FOR BOOKS.

7. Quarterly reports sent to Arkansas Library Commission.

8. Librarian attends annual meeting of Arkansas Library Association, and workshops and institutes of Arkansas Library Commission.

---

[1]Arkansas Library Commission, Public Libraries in Arkansas: Fifteenth Biennial Report (Little Rock: Arkansas Library Commission, 1967), p. 20. Revised July 1, 1967.

*CONTINUATION GRANT - County annual grant - effective July 1, 1967.

>10 cents per capita (1960 census) plus $1000 for one mill tax.
>Requirements: same as for establishment grant.

*MULTI-COUNTY - annual grant - effective July 1, 1967.

>10 cents per capita (1960 census)

>$1000 per county for one mill tax.

>$2000 per county in region for extension of service from one headquarters to 2 or 3 counties.

>$3000 per county in region for extension of service from one headquarters to at least 4 counties.

>Requirements: Same as establishment except two or more counties must cooperate.

DEMONSTRATION GRANTS, 1942 -

>Multicounty units may qualify for demonstration grants for two year period for purchase of books and equipment and for payment of salaries. Amount varies according to need, area, population served.

>Requirements: Same as establishment and multicounty grant.

EQUALIZATION GRANTS, 1961 -

>Multicounty units may qualify for equalization grants to enable counties to have equal financial support for public library service. Amount varies according to need, area, population served.

>Requirements: Same as establishment and multicounty grant.

PERSONNEL GRANTS

Scholarship Aid

>$100 per semester hour for a maximum of 18 hours in Library Science at a Library School accredited by the American Library Association to staff members of libraries receiving state aid provided recipients present transcript of acceptable credit and remain in the position for one year following grant of aid.

<u>Institutes and Workshops</u>

> Actual expenses of librarians and trustees of public libraries
> to attend workshops and institutes sponsored by the Arkansas
> Library Commission in the state for in-service training are
> granted.

*Revised July 1967.

LIBRARY FUNDING

Economic conditions and legal restrictions influence now, as they have in
the past, the level of funding for the state and local library programs.
Arkansas is a poor state, ranking 49th in per capita income ($2,090 in
1967) and having limited industrial resources.

Arkansas is, however, a study in contrasts. A wide range of economic and
social strata exists within the State. Some areas are experiencing rapid
increases in population growth and industrial resources; many other regions,
relying solely upon an agrarian or lumber economy, are depressed. Because
of these economic conditions, there has been severe population declines in
the depressed areas, resulting from the migration of residents to urban
communities (such as Little Rock and Fayetteville) where better employment
opportunities exist.

State constitutional restrictions have a profound effect upon local
government. For instance, the Constitution has restricted the property
tax levy to 5 mills for support of traditional municipal services, such as
police and fire protection. If library services are desired, an additional
(above the 5 mills) levy is required; however, this levy is restricted by
law to 1 mill.

According to a recent survey of Arkansas libraries by Gretchen Schenk (see
Section VI, BIBLIOGRAPHY), this millage restriction guarantees that local
libraries will be placed in an inferior position from the standpoint of
expanding their services.

<u>Financial Support for the Arkansas Library Commission</u>

The Commission's current activities are supported from three sources:
(1) State appropriations for operating expenses, (2) LSCA Title I funds,
and (3) local funds (both State grant-in-aid and the 1-mill tax) for
contract services, such as centralized book processing.

While the Commission was under the State Department of Education, financial
support was derived from the Public School Fund. The 1967 legislation,
making the Commission a separate agency, placed it in the position of
competing with the other State agencies for the limited amount of available

revenue. During the past two biennial legislative sessions, despite the significant increase in State grant-in-aid monies, the Commission has obtained only a slight increase in appropriations for the operating expenses of its own headquarters.

Financial Support for Local Libraries

In 1940, the State Constitution was amended to allow cities having more than 5,000 people to levy a maximum of 1-mill for library services. An additional amendment (in 1947) included a provision allowing the 1-mill tax to be levied on a countywide basis. (The 1-mill tax is particularly important because without it the county cannot receive either Federal or State funds.) Only six counties (out of 75) have not voted the 1-mill library tax on a countywide basis. However, some of the larger communities within these counties (e.g., Stuttgart, in Arkansas County, with a population of about 10,000) have voted a 1-mill city library tax. Counties that lack the library tax may place a referendum on the ballot during a general election to determine whether the tax will be assessed on a countywide basis, cities in these counties already having the library tax, however, are ineligible to vote on this referendum.

Under the present legal restrictions, counties or communities that have an increasing population and a rapidly expanding industrial complex are denied the opportunity to vote additional millage for library services to meet the expanding needs of their population and local industries. In order to bypass the 1-mill restriction, some communities, such as Springdale and Rodgers, have instituted an additional, voluntary 1-mill assessment for library services. So far, there has been great success in collecting this voluntary assessment; however, questions have been raised about whether it conflicts with the State constitution.

The Arkansas Library Commission has waged a long, hard battle to convince the populace to institute the library tax on a countywide basis. Two primary factors have hindered its endeavors. First, there is general public resistance to imposing additional taxes within some communities or counties. Second, in some counties, there are large concentrations of land holdings, and many of the landholders have resisted both the additional library tax and the lifting of the legal ceiling on general municipal levies because the increase would fall primarily on them.

Some county and regional libraries have received additional funds through the efforts of county judges who have included a request for additional monies for libraries in their budgets to County Quorum Court. (The county judge, a key political figure in most southern communities, also has the legal authority to appoint a county library commission of six trustees once the 1-mill tax is passed.)

During the SDC survey, various individuals and groups expressed the belief that there will be additional pressure for lifting the 1-mill ceiling and increasing the legislature's appropriation to the Library Commission when all 75 counties have voted the library tax. Such statewide support would reinforce the Commission's demands that more funds be appropriated by the legislature, it could also prompt the State legislature to appropriate funds for a new State Library Commission building and remove the Commission from its extremely limited quarters.

During the past general election, the populace voted to establish a constitutional convention for the purpose of revising the outdated State constitution and presenting the revised constitution for ratification in the general election in 1970. During the formulation of a new constitution, library members and trustees hope to be able to remove the 1-mill ceiling and recodify existing public library laws.

However, the final source of funds for county and regional libraries, as mentioned previously, is the State grant-in-aid administered by the Arkansas Library Commission.

III.   LSCA PROGRAM

OVERVIEW OF ACTIVITIES

As under the LSA program, LSCA money continues to support and supplement what could be considered traditional library activities, such as the purchase of new books and materials. Because of limited Federal funds and because of other economic factors, the Arkansas Library Commission has continued the same program categories initiated under LSA. Since the main need has been to upgrade basic library services, the Commission has not allocated LSCA monies for the development of special or innovative projects for urban or rural areas.

ALLOCATION OF LSCA FUNDS

Two philosophical factors have influenced the present allocation of LSCA funds in Arkansas: (1) the emphasis upon extending library service to rural areas previously unserved or without adequate service, and (2) the emphasis by the Commission upon strengthening the State agency headquarters services and encouraging, supplementing, and strengthening regional (multicounty) systems.

Under both LSA and LSCA, the Arkansas Library Commission has assumed the primary responsibility for the allocation of LSA and LSCA funds. The Commission has stipulated that, in addition to having the necessary county tax support, local library policies must be in accord with the Commissions stated policies in order to receive LSCA monies. LSCA funds continue to be allocated to two general program categories: (1) State agency activities and (2) multicounty activities. Each of these program categories is described in more detail in the following section.

IV.   DESCRIPTION OF REPRESENTATIVE USES OF LSCA FUNDS

LIBRARY COMMISSION ACTIVITIES

The funds retained at the State level ($61,870/$148,229 in Fiscal Year 1967) are utilized to support and supplement the increased staff, books, equipment, and operating expenses required for the centralized processing that serves public libraries throughout the State. Funds are also spent on workshops and in-service training courses that are conducted for local librarians and trustees at regular intervals at the Commission's headquarters. Federal funds have been crucial in supplementing these two primary activities.

MULTICOUNTY ACTIVITIES

LSCA funds have been allocated to local multicounty libraries to supplement State and local resources and provide for additional staff, equipment, and supplies. Regional libraries use some LSCA monies for new books, which are then centrally purchased and processed at the Commission's headquarters in Little Rock. Other LSCA funds have been used to provide (1) in-service training programs for local librarians and (2) periodic workshops for both librarians and trustee groups. Such training programs are conducted at the local level.

Federal funds have supported and encouraged the development and expansion of regional library systems and have provided bookmobile service to areas which have been previously unserved or which have not voted the 1-mill county library tax.

In counties lacking the 1-mill tax, bookmobiles are used to stimulate and arouse local interest in and support for library services.

V.   EVALUATION

PROGRAM STRENGTHS

- General upgrading of basic library services throughout the State

- Success by the Commission in developing regional library systems for more effective library service

PROBLEM AREAS

- Lack of adequate library personnel for handling the increasing workload at the Commission's headquarters and at regional library systems

- Existence of a 1-mill tax ceiling at the local level for the support of library services

- Low per capita support of county and regional libraries

- Absence of special projects to cope with growing urbanization of the State

CONCLUSIONS

Both LSA and LSCA funds have had a direct, tangible impact upon public library development throughout Arkansas. Although the amount of Federal funding has been small in comparison to other States, the Arkansas Library Commission has judiciously allocated these funds to upgrade basic library services for the people of Arkansas.

The increased political involvement by a group of knowledgeable individuals, interested in library services and its importance to the improvement of the educational level of the citizens of Arkansas, has resulted in significant increases in State grant-in-aid during the past two legislative sessions. Their actions have also resulted in increased legislative interest in providing a State Library building needed to house the expanding operations of the Arkansas Library Commission.

The primary, overriding factors, which will continue to affect all aspects of the administration of the LSCA program, are the general economic conditions existing within the State. Not only are there limited financial and industrial resources in Arkansas, but constitutional restrictions further negate any efforts to sufficiently fund even basic library activities. The fact that county and regional libraries are currently receiving only $1.23 per capita (from State and local sources) indicates much work is still to be accomplished in financing library services and in educating the Arkansas public about the value of libraries to them.

Unless the 1-mill restriction is removed and the legislation continues to appropriate increased grant-in-aid (as they have done during the past two biennial sessions), it will be necessary to continue expending LSCA funds to supplement the same basic library services as under LSA, both at the State agency level and at the regional systems level.

VI.   BIBLIOGRAPHY

Arkansas State LSA Title I annual plans, reports, and programs submitted to USOE during the period 1957-1968 (miscellaneous titles).

Arkansas Economic Expansion Commission. <u>Accelerating Economic Growth in Arkansas: Survey/Recommendations</u>. Little Rock, Ark., 1 October 1964, 186 pp.

Arkansas Library Commission. <u>Public Libraries in Arkansas: Fifteenth Biennial Report</u>. Little Rock, Ark., 30 June 1967, 60 pp.

Neal, Frances P. "The State Library: An Essential Agency." <u>Wilson Library Bulletin</u>. 42:8 (April 1968) pp. 804-810.

Schenk, Gretchen K. <u>Survey of the Arkansas Library Commission and Public Libraries of Arkansas</u>. Arkansas Library Commission, Little Rock, Ark., January 1965, 57 pp.

REGION VIII:

Colorado
Idaho
Montana
UTAH
Wyoming

John Andrew Fisher, Library
    Services Program Officer, AVLP
    Federal Office Building
    19th & Stout Sts.
    Denver, Colorado 80202

CHAPTER XIII
UTAH

I.   SOURCES OF INFORMATION

The following organizations and persons were visited to obtain information
for this study (see Figure U-1 for a map of the State):

Date	Place Visited	Persons Visited
9/30/68	USOE Regional Office Denver, Colorado Region VIII	John Andrew Fisher, Library Services Program Officer Ray Minnis, Regional Adult Education Program Officer Charles O'Conner, Director AVLP
9/30/68	Center for Bibliographic Research Rocky Mountain Region, Inc. Denver	Phoebe Hays, Director
10/1/68	State Library Commission Salt Lake City, Utah	Russell L. Davis Director State Library Staff: Arlene Grover, Technical Processing Librarian Mrs. Martha R. Stewart, Circulation Librarian Amy Owen, Acquisitions Librarian Carol Oaks, Consultant for Children's Libraries Max L. Collotzi, Construction Auditor Paul A. Buttars, Bookmobile Librarian Gerald A. Buttars, Special Services Librarian Parris G. Cobb, Recording Librarian
10/3/68	American Fork City Library American Fork	Mrs. Frank Greenwood, Librarian
10/3/68	Springville Public Library Springville	Mrs. Paula O. Jones, Librarian

Date	Place Visited	Persons Visited
10/4/68	Davis County Library Farmington	Mrs. Helen Gibson, Librarian Stanley M. Smoot, Chairman, Davis County Commissioner Chairman, Trustee
10/4/68	University of Utah Salt Lake City	Richard W. Boss, Acting Director of Libraries and President of ULA
10/5/68	Salt Lake City Library Salt Lake City	Robert E. Thomas, Librarian
10/5/68	Brigham Young University Provo	Donald H. Trottier, Librarian
10/21/68	State House Salt Lake City	Melburn Coombs, Budget Director Carlyle Larsen, Assistant Budget Director
10/21/68	Salt Lake County Library Midvale, Utah	Mrs. Ruth V. Tyler, Librarian
10/21/68	Utah State Library Salt Lake City	Mrs. Vivian H. Howard, Retired, Acquisitions Consultant
10/22/68	Weber County Library Ogden	Guy Schuurman, Librarian
10/22/68	State Library Commission Salt Lake City	Dr. Everett L. Cooley, Former Director of Utah State Historical Society; now, University of Utah Archivist and Curator of Western Americana, Member of Utah Library Commission
10/23/68	Sevier and Wayne Counties Bookmobile Richfield	Merlin K. Partridge, Book- mobile Librarian
10/23/68	Richfield Public Library Richfield	Mrs. Rachel Peterson, Part- Time Librarian for Richfield Public Library and Part-Time Clerk for Bookmobile

Date	Place Visited	Persons Visited
10/23/68	Sanpete County Bookmobile Centerfield	Christopher G. Parry Bookmobile Librarian
10/23/68	San Juan County Bookmobile Gouldings Trading Post	James A. Greenhalgh, Bookmobile Librarian
10/24/68	Aneth Elementary Boarding School for Indians Aneth	Thomas Sloan, 4th Grade Teacher
10/24/68	Salina Elementary Public School Salina	Kendal Wilkes, 4th Grade Teacher

Much valuable information was also obtained from the publications listed in the Bibliography in Section VI of this chapter.

II.   BACKGROUND FOR LSCA OPERATIONS

THE STATE AGENCY

The State agency designated to receive and administer LSCA funds is the Utah State Library Commission, appointed by the Governor with the advice and consent of the State Senate. Nine members are chosen for six-year overlapping terms. The law of 1957, creating the Commission, specifies that one member shall be recommended from each of the following agencies: the State Department of Public Instruction, the Law Library Board, the Legislative Council, and the State Historical Society Board. Of the five remaining members, at least two must be from rural areas. The Secretary of State is a member ex-officio. Further, the law encourages membership of people who are actively concerned with, or knowledgeable about, libraries.

The Commission, an independent entity reporting directly to the Governor, appoints with his consent the Director of Libraries (official title: State Librarian), who is charged with the immediate responsibility for the State Library. The Library is thus the agency for carrying out State library policy and disbursing LSCA funds. Though the Commission has supervisory power over the State Librarian, it has limited itself to establishing policy and has permitted Mr. Russell Davis (State Librarian since 1957) to exercise full executive authority in administering LSCA and State funds.

The Utah State Library has four divisions: Administrative Services, Extension Services, Reference Services, and Special Services (see Figure U-2). At the time of its founding, the Library had only one professional librarian, the Director; it now has a staff of 50 including eight professionals.

Figure U-1. Map of the State of Utah

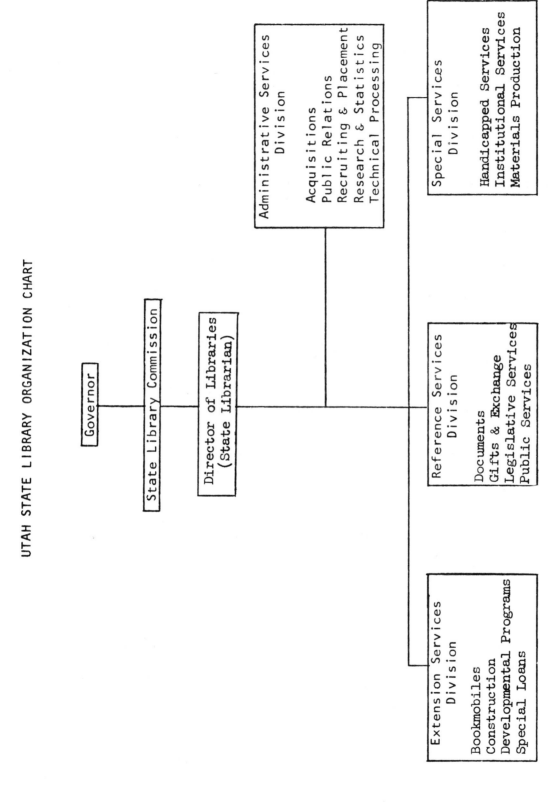

UTAH STATE LIBRARY ORGANIZATION CHART

Governor

State Library Commission

Director of Libraries
(State Librarian)

Administrative Services
Division

Acquisitions
Public Relations
Recruiting & Placement
Research & Statistics
Technical Processing

Special Services
Division

Handicapped Services
Institutional Services
Materials Production

Reference Services
Division

Documents
Gifts & Exchange
Legislative Services
Public Services

Extension Services
Division

Bookmobiles
Construction
Developmental Programs
Special Loans

Figure U-2. The Utah State Library Organization

HISTORY OF STATE AID TO UTAH LIBRARIES

Perhaps more than in many other States, the history of library service development in Utah has been affected by that of the State itself, as well as by geographic considerations. Settled largely by members of the Church of Jesus Christ of Latter Day Saints (referred to as the Mormon Church or LDS) who were seeking religious asylum, Utah is the 12th largest state in area, with 84,000 square miles. However, it ranks only 26th in population; the 1967 Department of Commerce population estimate was 1,007,000, up from the 1960 census of 890,827. Overall density is 12.4 persons per square mile, compared with the national average of 55.9. (The Department of Commerce estimate for New York State in 1967 was 383 persons per square mile.) The literacy rate, on the other hand, is unusually high as a result of the Mormon Church's emphasis on education.

The State is mostly composed of desert and mountain regions with some farming area. Original settlers clustered around the Great Salt Lake, only gradually spreading out into nearby regions. Even today the population is closely packed into the north-central or Wasatch Front region, comprising Weber, Davis, Salt Lake and Utah Counties. These counties contain approximately 90 percent of the population and all eight of the cities over 10,000--Salt Lake County alone has half the entire State population--in only 20 percent of the land area. The remainder, a population of about 100,000, is spread out over more than 68,000 square miles. The American Library Association has established a recommended minimum population base of 150,000 for the formation of any library system, and Utah would encounter difficulties in forming even one such system in the entire region south of the Wasatch Front.

The State's tax base is rather narrow because so much of the land is owned by the Federal government in the form of national monuments, national parks, armed forces bases, and Indian reservations. Few cities in Utah have tax bases sufficient to create effective local municipal government providing general municipal services. With the exception of a few large cities, the county has thus become the most effective form of government.

Before the Library Services Act was passed in 1956, Utah was the only State without a State Library, and only Arizona and Utah were without State extension services. Not until LSA money became available was Utah able to create a Library Commission and a State Library. In 1957 the State appropriated to the Library $100,000 from the general fund to be spent over a two-year period. In Fiscal Year 1958, the Library was ready to submit a proposal to the Federal government and to begin developing public library service throughout the State. The amount of State appropriation has increased each year at a rate of 5 to 10 percent. In 1967, the legislature appropriated $115,300 for the Library's budget, and in 1968 the total was $192,461. In Fiscal Year 1969, the budget was increased by 20 percent; the next largest increase for any State agency was 10 percent, with an average of 5 percent for all other agencies.

RELATIONSHIP OF STATE AGENCY TO OTHER ORGANIZATIONS

Other Federal Agencies

The services provided by the Special Services Division of the State Library
are more than 50 percent funded by the Library of Congress. The State of
Utah contributes $40,000 of the $90,000 budget for this division. This
division of the State agency serves the blind and handicapped, not only in
Utah but in several other western states.

Utah Library Association

The Utah Library Association has not played a strong role in library
development in Utah. It has had little if any effect in lobbying for
greater State aid to local libraries, and its 20-year efforts to create a
State Library (prior to LSA) were without avail. The annual meeting, the
Association's primary activity, serves merely as a forum for the exchange
of local library information.

LIBRARY FUNDING

Federal (LSCA) monies appropriated to Utah in Fiscal Year 1968 amounted to
$245,448; this amount was more than matched by State-aid funds, which amounted
to nearly $200,000, allocated to the State Library. State funding for fiscal
1969 is expected to be further augmented by $96,000 in county taxes raised
for payment of contractual bookmobile services.

The amount of potential financial support available for libraries from local
revenues varies widely from county to county. The legal limit (3 mills) has
rarely been reached, and local library income ranges from a high of $863,000
for Salt Lake County to a low of $4,000 for Sevier County. One reason for
this wide variation is that State law leaves to the cities or counties the
decision whether to fund local libraries. (The State Library has made an
unsuccessful attempt at passage of a law requiring local governments to
assign revenues to libraries.) Despite the low millage rate and the permissive language of the statutes, some counties--San Juan, Davis, and
Salt Lake are prime examples--have steadily increased their aid to libraries.
In the main, however, local efforts are largely dependent upon State and
Federal funding as disbursed by the State Library.

III.   LSCA PROGRAM

OVERVIEW OF ACTIVITIES

Since the entire Utah State Library exists mainly as the result of LSA and
LSCA funding, a brief summary of its overall program is appropriate.

The State Library Commission, hence the State Library, has broad powers delegated to it by the legislature. Of particular importance is its legal authority (as established under Section 37-4-4 of the Utah State Law) to:

- Provide bookmobile service;

- Develop regional and multi-county library systems;

- Act as the State agency for receiving State and Federal funds;

- Act as the State depository and distributor of State documents (including both official documents and all such State Library holdings as books, films, microfilms, records, etc.); and

- Provide standards for, and certification of, public libraries throughout the State.

Concerned initially with acquiring the staff, space, and basic collections to begin operations, the Library now has developed an active program, using LSCA funds entirely for bookmobiles and for the purchase of books for the central reference collection. Other monies are used for administrative and technical services, consulting, research activities, and special services. State Library policy has supplemented the efforts of the State's 52 public libraries, most of which had been small and isolated; emphasized the use of bookmobiles to reach areas heretofore without service; and stimulated greater public interest in, and support for, library services. The program is described more fully in Section IV.

ALLOCATION OF LSCA TITLE I FUNDS

Immediately after formation of the State Library, as soon as initial staffing and acquisitions were under way, an informal survey of the State was conducted to determine what services should be provided at once. Two priorities emerged from this survey: providing bookmobile demonstrations in counties where there was no countywide service, and developing regional library systems. It quickly became apparent that the State had neither the facilities nor the personnel--nor, indeed, enough widespread interest--to develop regional systems. The State Librarian therefore concentrated on bookmobiles and, through these, on stimulating public support for the eventual formation of systems. The Library has channeled 98 percent of its allocated LSCA funds into the bookmobile demonstrations; the remaining 2 percent is used to provide the central reference collection maintained at the State Library and also used by all of the bookmobiles and local libraries.

REPORTING AND EVALUATION PROCEDURE OF STATE AGENCY

Formal reporting and evaluation procedures have not yet been developed for
the bookmobile demonstration program.

IV.   DESCRIPTION OF REPRESENTATIVE USES OF LSCA FUNDS

Although Utah's LSCA funds are used almost exclusively for the bookmobile
demonstrations, this service is such an integral and important part of the
overall State Library program that it is desirable to devote this section
to the State agency as a whole, with particular attention to LSCA expenditures. (The Library program, in fact, exists only as a direct result of
the allotment of LSA/LSCA funds.)

ADMINISTRATIVE SERVICES

Nonlibrary functions such as public relations, research, technical
processing and administration are handled by the Administrative Services
Division and are funded out of State and local appropriations.

The largest single activity of this division is the acquisition and
processing of books, both for the central reference collection and for
local libraries. The Division contracts with local libraries (negotiating
through the county governments) to perform centralized processing services
--purchasing books at the request of the contracting libraries and providing
complete cataloging, processing and shipment. The State passes along its
volume discount to assist local libraries in increasing their own purchases.
Twenty-seven libraries now participate in this program. The following
chart* (Table U-1) contains a summary of the services that had been provided
to the 16 most active libraries as of January 1968.

---

*Source: An Annual Report 1967, Utah Public Library Service, prepared
by the Library Commission of Utah.

Table U-1. Purchasing and Processing Services
Provided to Representative Counties
as of January 1, 1968*

	Ordered		Processed
	Titles	Copies	Totals
Duchesne County Library	276	279	227
Emery County Library	71	256	202
Ephraim City Library	131	141	155
Fillmore City Library	204	204	228
Hurricane City Library	26	26	46
Manti City Library	13	13	11
Grand County Library	404	404	579
Morgan County Library	548	548	515
Mt. Pleasant City Library	138	146	612
Murray City Library	165	187	685
Price City Library	6	6	0
St. George City Library	202	203	199
Salina City Library	42	42	565
San Juan County Library	390	879	1,341
Spanish Fork City Library	66	67	63
Springville City Library	285	286	284
Other	362	400	2,377
Totals	3,329	4,087	8,089

*These figures do not contain the totals for the State Library Commission
itself. These totals are: 2,834 titles and 31,030 copies ordered and a
total of 29,012 processed.

The State Library is also beginning a study on ways to automate and improve
the processing system and to provide a book-form catalog of holdings
in the State, showing their locations. No attempt is made by the Division
to acquire or make known nonbook materials, which may eventually be of
tremendous value to small cooperating libraries and bookmobile collections.

This division also handles acquisitions for the Reference Services Division,
using that portion of the LSCA funds (2 percent) retained specifically for
increasing the central reference collection.

EXTENSION SERVICES

The State Library's developmental program, special loans, and most
consulting services are handled by the Extension Services Division out of
State and local monies. (Construction projects, also managed by this

division, are funded by LSCA Title II allocations.) Consulting services are limited by the lack of full-time personnel. The present staff attends to consulting requirements on special assignments apart from their regular duties. In 1967, 51 public libraries received 1,643 hours of consulting services from nine staff members who logged 103,576 travel miles. In addition, three workshops (one for public librarians and two for bookmobile personnel) were held. No effort was made to recruit full-time consultants, though these positions do exist on paper.

Bookmobiles

All bookmobile demonstration projects are conducted by the Extension Services Division. These services are funded entirely by the 98 percent of LSCA funds devoted to this project with the addition of State funds. Expenditures include books, materials, personnel, training, bookmobiles, and equipment maintenance. (Local appropriations for additional contractual bookmobile service, beyond the demonstration period, amount to approximately $96,000 in 1969 and are expected to increase.)

Because most of Utah's population unserved by libraries is thinly dispersed over a large area, it was clear that the only way to provide library services to that population would be through bookmobiles. Accordingly, a plan was developed whereby bookmobile demonstrations would be held in a county for a period of one to two years, the duration depending on the size of the county, and the relationship of the demonstration start date to the fiscal year start date. During the demonstration period the State would supply the vehicle, the personnel, and the books. At the end of the demonstration, the county could elect one of three alternatives:

- Contract the State for service. The county would have to pay predetermined costs ranging from $1,000 to $15,000 per year, depending on the economic conditions in the county, while the State would fully administer the service and be responsible for maintenance, upkeep, personnel, and books.

- Take over the service on its own and be responsible entirely for the maintenance of the bookmobile, the purchase of books, the driver-librarian, etc.

- Remove the service entirely from the county.

To date, bookmobile demonstrations have been held in 17 of the 27 counties in the State; all of the demonstrations have led to continuing library service. (Two county supervisory boards, with new incoming commissioners, voted to discontinue library service. However, a campaign on the part of the local population immediately caused the commissioners to reverse their decision.) Sixteen counties are operating under the first alternative (contracting for service); the 17th, San Juan County, elected to purchase the bookmobile and provide adequate headquarters and books, but requested that the State retain administrative control and be responsible for hiring and training the driver-librarian. The State now has 13 bookmobiles in operation besides the one now being operated by San Juan County. These bookmobiles travel 157,441 miles and serve a population of 181,287. A bookmobile makes a complete round, on the average, in two weeks. Utah's bookmobiles have a total collection (including the headquarters collections but not including the Reference Center collection) of 194,250 volumes. In 1967, circulation was 955,348, and per capita circulation was 5.27 books. Together the bookmobiles make 8,904 stops, and give 19,138 hours of service each month. Each bookmobile has an average circulation of 1,000 to 1,300 books per day, which is twice the 1956 ALA standard. Two supervisors, one for Northern Utah and the other for Southern Utah, are responsible for scheduling and operating the State's 13 bookmobiles.

The three bookmobiles observed by SDC contained ephemeral collections. Roughly half of the collection was adult and juvenile fiction; the other half was divided more or less equally among religion (of which most works were on Mormonism), the history of the American West, World War II, and general nonfiction. The composition of the collections, therefore, appears to be dictated by the desires of the community rather than to serve as reference collections. Most of the communities served by the bookmobiles are too small to support movie theaters or other public recreation facilities. Because the LDS religion prohibits drinking coffee, tea, or alcoholic beverages, people do not frequent coffee shops or taverns to meet informally when they have free time. Television and radio reception is poor, and some areas are too isolated to have telephone service. The bookmobile, therefore, is a major source of recreational activity, and bookmobile schedules are announced on the local radio stations, published in local newspapers, and displayed on community bulletin boards.

REFERENCE SERVICES

Acquisitions for the State Library's reference collection are made by the Administrative Services Division from LSCA funds. The collection itself is managed by the Reference Services Division, which also has developed (out of other monies) a reference system for local libraries. This system utilizes a WATS telephone network linking all public libraries with the central reference collection. (Large public libraries are also linked to the academic libraries by a separate teletype network supported by other than Title I funds.) The extent of the central reference collection is indicated in Table U-2.

Table U-2.   State Library Commission Book Reference Collection

	Net Holdings Jan. 1, 1967			Acquisitions			With-drawals	Net Holdings Jan. 1, 1968		
	Titles	Copies	Volumes	Titles	Copies	Processed		Titles	Copies	Volumes
AUDIT										
Fiction	1,786	150	1,936	363	99	462	4	2,145	249	2,394
Non-Fiction	9,568	2,178	11,746	660	137	797	14	10,267	2,315	12,529
Total	11,354	2,328	13,682	1,023	236	1,259	18	12,412	2,564	14,923
JUVENILE										
Fiction	369	0	369	53	0	53	0	422	0	422
Non-Fiction	0	0	0	0	0	0	0	0	0	0
Total	369	0	369	53	0	53	0	422	0	422
Grand Total	11,723	2,329	14,051	1,076	236	1,312	18	12,834	2,564	15,345

Based on data from: An Annual Report 1967 Utah Public Library Serviced, Prepared by the State Library Commission of Utah.

The State Library is also chartered to maintain and distribute State documents and publications, and to provide a legislative reference service, but lack of personnel and storage facilities has prevented any effort to fulfill these requirements.

SPECIAL SERVICES

Although the Special Services Division receives no LSCA Title I funds, it is a significant part of the State plan. The Division is concerned with providing large-print books, talking books, and tape recordings to the blind and handicapped in Utah and in several other states. The Division also provides part-time consulting services to State-operated institutions, hospitals, and special schools. In 1967, nine agencies received 21 hours of consulting services; during 1968, the figures increased sharply.

V.   EVALUATION

PROGRAM STRENGTHS

The composition of the State Library Commission as prescribed by law provides safeguards against appointments made for purely political purposes. It further ensures a membership composed of some who are knowledgeable about State government, as well as at least two who know the impact of the library program on the rural community.

The main asset of the Utah State Library system is the State Librarian. The incumbent is a strong and highly capable individual, and the Commission has wisely permitted him to take the lead in developing and administering the entire program, including LSCA. Under his direction, the State Library has played a vigorous role in library development in Utah; indeed, for most of the State, the State Library is the local public library.

The State Library's program has done much to end the isolation in which the 52 public libraries had operated. These libraries, mostly small, under-staffed, and understocked, have been in great need of support. Librarians were originally fearful that the State's program (for example, the book-mobile service) would compete with their local efforts; but they now see the State's program increasing public demand for services. Because of this increased demand, ultimately the local libraries may look forward to a higher level of funding. The central reference library's WATS linkage has also been helpful in knitting these solitary units into the beginnings of a system, as has the State's central purchasing and processing activity. In effect, because of its influence and relative strength, the State Library has established the pattern for general library policy and service throughout Utah.

The single most effective arm of the State program is the bookmobile service. As a result of the demonstrations, interest in libraries has been greatly increased and new libraries have been developed.

The success of the bookmobiles may be measured in two ways: (1) the adoption of bookmobile service on a permanent locally supported basis by every county in which a demonstration was conducted; and (2) the increase in tax support for existing local libraries and for the State Library as a direct result of the public interest aroused by bookmobiles. State legislators are well aware of their constituents' strong desire to have bookmobiles in their own counties; thus the State Library has a tremendous reservoir of goodwill with rural legislators. Increased support at the State level is graphically demonstrated by the following figures:

- Total tax receipts for libraries have increased roughly 300 percent since 1958, from $927,129 to $2,909,015, while population has increased roughly 12 percent. Per capita income in a comparable period (1955-1967) has increased approximately 60 percent.

- Book stock has increased by over 100 percent since 1958, from 1,327,273 to 2,388,760.

- Per capita spending for libraries has risen from $1.47 in 1961 to $3.14 in 1967.

At the local level, Davis County has recently begun an extensive building project to replace its existing headquarters and housing. The county also has developed a combination of school and public library service under the County Librarian that is rare in the United States. This development grew out of the State Librarian's intervention with County Commissioners on behalf of the County Librarian. He was able to convince the County Commissioners of the inadequacy of service and the need for new approaches and library development. The American Fork City Library, also, in addition to receiving the maximum tax allotment, receives all surplus funds from the general municipal revenue. Other communities have raised impressive sums for their libraries through such activities as dances, bake sales, and auctions. Only four counties in Utah are now without some sort of countywide library.

As an indication of increased support, some of the more populous counties (such as Weber, Salt Lake and Davis) are now beginning to discuss the possible formation of a multicounty system.

The bookmobile driver-librarian providing a generalized reading service at his stops is doing more for a community than providing library service. He is the community's contact with the cultural and knowledgeable outside world. He is the man providing a major source of their recreational needs. He is not only a librarian, but in his way a community asset enabling people to live where they are and yet feel part of the state, the country, and the world.

It is impossible for this report to relate the smiles observed on people's faces when the bookmobile arrives at a typical stop. The handshaking, the greetings, and the first name basis of everyone concerned could well be sufficient justification of importance of this service.

The initiative and awareness of the individual operating the bookmobile are most important. The State has been very lucky in attracting a number of people to work for it who are qualified in this manner. Most of the driver-librarians are local people who have a college education and wish to reside in their local area. They take the position, in some cases at a lower salary than elsewhere, because they enjoy the work. Their enthusiasm for their job is necessary to overcome the adverse conditions such as long isolated drives between stops, rotating the collection and cleaning their vehicles.

PROBLEM AREAS

Dependency of Local Libraries on State Agency

The very strength of the program has created a dependence upon the State Library that will probably never be overcome. The success of the book-mobiles, for example, may encourage the feeling that this working program should not be interfered with but rather continued under State direction. This dependency is to some extent increased by the State Library's own definition of itself as a service agency rather than an administrative arm of the State government. It has not yet sought to coordinate and develop local libraries; instead, it is an active participant at the local level. State and Federal monies are thus spent on projects initiated and carried out by the State rather than by local agencies. By this definition, the State cannot tailor its programs to meet the needs of individual communities, but must develop statewide programs that will be effective in all areas.

Limitations in Service

Despite increased support, the State Library's program is inevitably limited by the lack of funds, personnel and facilities. Specific areas needing attention are:

1. The LSCA-funded central reference service. This is too
   small to be of much resource value to libraries. As of
   January 1, 1968, there were only 10,267 adult nonfiction
   titles available; the bookmobile collection is much larger.
   Those who used the WATS telephone reference service stated
   that the reference librarians could not provide adequate
   service and that requested materials were usually not part
   of the collection. The collection needs to be developed
   extensively, and librarians need to be more thoroughly
   trained in reference service, before it will have an
   impact on the public libraries or the general public.

2. The authorized but nonexistent collection of State
   documents. The lack of this has created severe problems
   for the academic and research libraries, as well as for
   State legislators.

3. Personnel. Well-qualified library personnel are scarce
   in Utah. Public libraries do not attract professional
   librarians because of the unusual working conditions and
   low salaries. There are fewer than a dozen professional
   librarians now working in public libraries in Utah.

   Of the 13 bookmobiles, only two are manned by professional
   librarians and only one has a degree from an accredited
   library school. (However, the ability of these people to
   relate to the public, satisfy their needs for recreational
   reading, and be able to maintain the bookmobile in working
   condition tends to offset any lack of professional
   education.)

   The State and local libraries have no plans to provide
   special scholarships or cadet programs in order to attract
   people to the library profession. The lack of personnel
   staffs limits library development on the State and local
   levels. It is only because of the State's having such an
   unusually high literacy rate among its population that it
   is able to attract nonprofessional librarians who, by dint
   of education and experience, have become reasonably successful in handling many of the public's requests. Only
   when someone gets into very sophisticated areas of research
   does the lack of professional library personnel become
   noticeable. However, the three leading academic libraries
   are extremely cooperative and have offered their facilities
   to the public at large; in this way, they have attempted to
   bridge the gap in public library service. Workshops created
   by the State agency have been fairly successful in training
   librarians to be more effective.

4. Limitations in Scope of Program. The State has thus far
    limited itself to providing the classical type of book
    service. No attempt was made to create a large audiovisual
    and nonbook service outside of the special services directed
    towards the blind and handicapped. The State does not have
    any library service specifically designed for ethnic or
    minority groups. For example, the American Indian population
    in the State is quite large; yet they are almost totally
    ignored.

PROSPECTS FOR REGIONAL SYSTEM DEVELOPMENT

The sparseness of the population in most of Southern Utah makes regional
library development an impossibility in the near future. Most areas are
unable to maintain adequate headquarters for bookmobile service, let alone
support strong county or regional library service. Because of limitations
in county taxes for libraries, it appears that the State will be operating
the bookmobile supplemental service in Davis and Weber Counties. In other
words, the State will be operating some bookmobile service in every county
in Utah except Salt Lake County in the immediate future and as long as
LSCA Title I funds are available.

Salt Lake, Davis, and Weber Counties are, at present, the only area in Utah
where a multicounty system may eventually develop. These counties constitute
the only area where the development of services has already progressed to a
relatively advanced level, where there are metropolitan areas of sufficient
size, wealth, and population density to support such a system. Even so, this
area has a long way to go before it will be able to obtain the necessary
funds and legislative action to create an appropriate taxing system. Local
jealousies and political quarrels must first be resolved before any multicounty system can be established. The State Library will play a crucial
role in the laying of the groundwork for such a system. The political
astuteness and prestige of the State Library are necessary to bringing the
local units of government into a concerted effort to establish a multicounty
system.

CONCLUSIONS

It is apparent that the State Librarian clearly saw the needs of the State
and answered these needs as efficiently and effectively with the limited
funds at his disposal. With the limited funds available bookmobile service
provides the only answer for large areas containing few people. Furthermore,
the decision to have a generalized reading collection has made this service
of immediate value to people hungry for recreational reading. Had the State
attempted to provide traditional library service with emphasis upon reference,
the public would probably not have responded as quickly and enthusiastically
to the service available. Without LSA and LSCA, Utah would not have had a

State Library, and the local libraries would still be very anemic. Without the present dynamic leadership, the State Library would probably not have developed so quickly and effectively, and as a result the local libraries would not have begun their own development. It was evident that the library community in Utah was too minuscule for effective accomplishment and that without the Federal "seed money" from LSA and LSCA there would be an entirely different library situation today.

The loss of LSCA funds would mean the end of any further library development in the State: State funds would not be increased to match the loss of LSCA funds, and the present service would be sharply curtailed. Most counties would not develop their own library program. There is not enough of a local tax base for the majority of counties to pay the full cost of the equivalent level of service now rendered by the State Library's bookmobiles.

The State Library has made itself sufficiently important that it is doubtful that it would ever have its own budget cut, even if LSCA funds were no longer available. There would not, however, be an attempt by the State to make up for the loss of LSCA funds.

If Utah were to receive 10 times the present amount of money, the general consensus of those connected with the program is that this money would be spent in the following ways:

- Immediately create bookmobile service in every county in the State not presently receiving any adequate library service.

- Hire specialized consultants to provide individual guidance and hold seminars and workshops throughout the State.

- Enlarge central processing to include automation as soon as possible. Develop a book-form union catalog and distribute copies to every library within the State.

- Hire additional professional librarians at the State level and develop extensive training procedures for librarians at the local level.

In summary, the State agency in Utah is extremely well organized under dynamic and talented leadership. The emphasis on bookmobiles to extend library service as quickly as possible to the maximum number of people (most of whom previously had no, or minimal, service) represents highly effective usage of LSCA funds.

VI. BIBLIOGRAPHY

Utah State LSA and LSCA Title I annual plans, reports, and programs submitted to USOE during the period 1958-1968 (miscellaneous titles).

Annual Reports of Utah Public Library Service during the period 1958-1967 (miscellaneous titles and pagination).

Utah State Library. Library Laws of Utah; 1963. Salt Lake City, Utah, 1963, 16 pp.

REGION IX:

Alaska
Arizona
CALIFORNIA
Guam
Hawaii
Nevada
Oregon
WASHINGTON
American Samoa
Trust Territory of Pacific Islands

Helen Luce, Library Services
  Program Officer, AVLP
  Federal Office Building
  50 Fulton Street
  San Francisco, California 94102

CHAPTER XIV
CALIFORNIA

I. SOURCES OF INFORMATION

The following organizations and persons were visited to obtain information
for this study (see Figure C-1 for a map of the State):

Date	Place Visited	Persons Visited
7/9/68	California State Library Sacramento	Mrs. Carma R. Leigh, State Librarian
7/10/68	USOE Regional Office San Francisco Region IX	Kent Bennion, Director, AVLP Helen Luce, Library Services Program Officer
7/15/68	Latin American Library Fruitvale Branch Oakland Public Library	William H. Brett, 3rd Asst., City Librarian Barbara Winn, Director, Latin American Library
7/16/68	Service Center Project Richmond Public Library Richmond	John D. Forsman, Head Librarian Rosemary Townes, Asst. City Librarian Lucy Wilson, Director
7/17/68	San Joaquin Valley Library Information Service Fresno Central Library Fresno	Glenys Cobeen, Director Mrs. Alice F. Reilly, Director
7/18-19	49-99 Cooperative Library System, Stockton	Mrs. Margaret K. Troke, Director, Library Services, and Staff
7/23/68	Los Angeles Public Library Los Angeles	Harold L. Hamill, City Librarian Katherine Laich, Asst. City Librarian
7/23/68	Los Angeles Public Library Bookmobile Project Southwest Los Angeles	Miss Betty Purdy, Area Supervisor Marianne Adler, Project Director Frances Carter, Children's Librarian Ann Levine
7/23/68	Los Angeles County Library Los Angeles	William S. Geller, Head, Los Angeles Public Library John Bailey, Coordinator, "Way Out Project"

Date	Place Visited	Persons Visited
7/24/68	Venice Branch Los Angeles Public Library Venice	Joyce Elliot, Branch Librarian Donald Roberts, Staff Member
7/24/68	Black Gold Library System Ventura - Santa Barbara Santa Barbara	Mrs. Catherine L. Chadwick, Librarian Mrs. Elizabeth Hutchinson, Asst. Librarian Marjorie Lipney, Adult Service Coordinator Mrs. Patricia Hurst, Director, Foster Library
7/24/68	Santa Barbara Public Library Santa Barbara	Robert Hart, Librarian Nadine Greenup, Reference Librarian
7/25/68	San Diego Public Library San Diego County Library San Diego	Clara E. Breed, City Librarian Arthur B. Murray, County Librarian
7/25/68	Lincoln Heights Branch Los Angeles Public Library	Joseph L. Buelna, Young Adult Specialist and also with Children's Specialist
7/25/68	Inland Library System San Bernardino	Colin Lucas, City Librarian Kenton White, Film Librarian Elizabeth Martin, Reference Librarian Gertrude Odell, Reference Librarian
7/26/68	Lassen County-Washoe County Library System Phone Call	Elizabeth Hallum, Lassen County Librarian
7/29/68	North Bay Cooperative Library System Santa Rosa	Mrs. Edna F. Hanna, Administrator
7/30/68	City-County Library Ukiah-Mendocino Counties Library, Ukiah	Frieda Winter, City-County Librarian
7/30/68	California State Library Sacramento	Mrs. Phyllis I. Dalton, Asst. State Librarian
7/30/68	California Legislative Analysts Office Sacramento	Clinton Jordan, Analyst for Education

Date	Place Visited	Persons Visited
7/31/68	San Mateo County Library System San Mateo Belmont	Virginia L. Ross, County Librarian, Director
7/31/68	East Palo Alto Project San Mateo County	Mrs. Jill Karpf, Branch Librarian, East Palo Alto, San Mateo County Library
7/31/68	North Sacramento Valley Library System	Mrs. Lois Bewley, Coordinator
7/31/68	Tehema County Library Red Bluff	Mrs. Alice Mathisen, Librarian
7/31/68	Butte County Library Oroville	Ursula Meyer, Librarian
7/31/68	State Finance Department Sacramento	Paul H. Holmes, Budget Analyst
7/31/68	California State Library Sacramento	Mrs. Phyllis Dalton, Assistant State Librarian
7/31/68	San Francisco Public Library San Francisco	John Anderson, Administrator Harold D. Martelle, Jr., Asst. Director Richard Coenenberg, Coordinator, BARC Project
7/31/68	Mill Valley Public Library Mill Valley	Mrs. Dorothy M. Thomas, Librarian
7/31/68	Marin County Public Library San Rafael	Mrs. Virginia Keating, Librarian Bruce Bajema, Asst. Librarian

Date	Place Visited	Persons Visited
8/1/68	Metropolitan Cooperative Library System Pasadena	Marjorie Donaldson, Librarian, Pasadena Public Library, Director, Metropolitan Cooperative Library System Raymond H. Holt, Librarian, Pomona Public Library John Lustic, Librarian, Monrovia Public Library
8/1/68	Petaluma Public Library Petaluma	Edna R. Bovett, Librarian
8/1/68	Sonoma County Library Santa Rosa	David Sabsay, Director
8/1/68	El Dorado - Alpine County Bookmobile Project El Dorado	Elsie Weaver, Asst. County Librarian, El Dorado County Agnes Moody, Clerk, El Dorado County Library
8/1/68	Alpine County Bookmobile Woodfords	Cleo McManus, Alpine County Bookmobile-Librarian George Clary, Superintendent of Schools, Alpine County
8/2/68	Inglewood Public Library Inglewood	John W. Perkins, City Librarian

Much valuable information was also obtained from the publications listed in the Bibliography, Section VI of this chapter.

Figure C-1. Map of the State of California

II.   BACKGROUND FOR LSCA OPERATIONS

THE STATE AGENCY

The California State Library is the official agency designated by law to receive, disburse, and administer all funds granted to the State for the improvement and extension of library services under the Library Services Act (LSA) and, later, under the Library Services and Construction Act (LSCA). The State Library is a division of the State Department of Education, but the State Librarian is appointed by the Governor. Under the existing conditions, the State Library operates effectively as a semi-autonomous agency. Budget management of the State Library is carried out by the Fiscal Office of the Department of Education; the Library, however, is responsible for preparing its own budget and presenting it to the Legislature.

The State Librarian, Mrs. Carma Leigh, assisted by the Assistant State Librarian, Mrs. Phyllis Dalton, is responsible for the management and administration of the entire State Library, including all of its functions, programs, and services. The California Public Library Commission, also appointed by the Governor, acts as a body of consultants to the State Librarian and her staff.

Some functions of the agency, as listed in the Martin Report[1], are as follows:

- Service to government

- Maintenance of collections

- Service to the general public

- Indirect service through other libraries

- Information and statistical services

- Library and consultant services

- Fiscal agency for State and Federal aid

---

[1] Martin, Lowell A. and Roberta Bowler. Public Library Service Equal to the Challenge of California, June 30, 1967, California Office of State Printing, Sacramento.

HISTORY OF STATE AID TO CALIFORNIA LIBRARIES

From the beginning of her tenure, the present State Librarian, with the support of the California Library Association and other leading library figures in the State, waged a campaign for a public library assistance law. The library professionals recognized that local support of libraries was not adequate to provide for the needs of library users. Indeed, with the rapid increases in population, all service resources were very much strained.

Following the recommendations of the California Public Library Commission, the State Librarian and library leaders throughout the State formulated a Master Plan for Public Libraries in California. This plan was written and adopted by the California Library Association at Coronado in 1962. As an outgrowth of the recommendations of the Commission Report and the Master Plan adopted by the Association, the Legislature approved the California Public Library Services Act of 1963 (PLSA), which provided grants for three purposes:

- Planning Grants, for planning of library systems.

- Establishment Grants, for establishing library systems.

- Per Capita Grants, for per capita support of library system operation.

PLSA is similar in intent to the Federal Library Services Act (LSA). The Federal support of public libraries began in 1957-58 with LSA and the funds were used for special demonstration projects designed to initiate new forms of library service and organization. Most of those early demonstrations are now established systems, with local funds having supplanted Federal funds.

Figure C-1, page   , shows public library systems extending beyond one county, as established subsequent to the passage of PLSA. Areas singled out for specific study grants are shown in Figure C-2.

RELATIONSHIP OF STATE AGENCY TO OTHER ORGANIZATIONS

The State Library Association

The role of the California Library Association in helping establish both the California State Master Plan for library development and the California State Plan (a requirement for qualification for LSCA funds), was discussed earlier. The Association has from time to time served as an effective lobby within the State for the improvement of libraries--school, college, and university as well as public. Such support by the library profession has been of great value to the State Library and all of its several programs.

Figure C-2. Planning and Study Grant Areas

LIBRARY FUNDING

When LSCA was passed in 1964, Federal funds were increased. It was also at this time that State aid under PLSA was begun. These combined funds were used for planning and establishing new library systems. LSCA Title I funds have increased in California, keeping pace with PLSA funds. The following table shows funding under both acts for the past four fiscal years.

Table C-1. LSCA and PLSA Funding in California 1965-1968

Fiscal Year	LSCA Title I*	PLSA**
1965	$1,825,848	$ 800,000
1966	1,816,318	1,000,000
1967	2,666,778	800,000
1968	2,666,778	1,200,000

*Source: Regional Office, Region IX, USOE
**Source: California State Library

California also uses local tax monies (approximately $2,800,000 in Fiscal Year 1968) as matching funds under LSCA.

III.   LSCA PROGRAM

OVERVIEW OF ACTIVITIES

The central idea or philosophy of the California State Library regarding the use of State aid and Federal funds for library services is that those funds should in one way or another support the development and maintenance of library systems. For a library to qualify for a grant, it must be part of a system, or it must be planning a system configuration or affiliation of some sort. The grants are made on a flexible, pragmatic basis.

Planning Grants. As a rule, a planning or survey grant is given for one year in a specific amount. It is usually not renewable, but may be if the State Librarian or Assistant State Librarian feels it is warranted. Such grants are intended to establish the parameters for a system or a demonstration project.

Establishment grants. These are usually funded for two years with the option of extending the grant resting with the Assistant State Librarian, in conjunction with the State Librarian. There is a methodical attempt to elicit sufficient popular support for an establishment project so that local government will assume the funding after the program has manifested its usefulness. Much publicity is used to stimulate local support--radio, television, speeches, news articles, visits to officials, and so on.

Per capita grants. These are continuing allocations intended to maintain a system or a special service that has been demonstrated successfully. Such grants are provided when it is not feasible for a local entity to assume financial responsibility because of low tax base or small population.

An attempt is made to ensure that projects and programs are not duplicative and that a variety of projects are established.

The Library has allocated funds to at least 48 projects since LSA and LSCA funds became available. These projects cover every geographic area of the State, from sparsely settled rural mountain areas to densely populated urban areas, and from wealthy farming districts to poverty-stricken city districts. The SDC survey team was fortunate in being able to visit a majority of these projects as well as many system headquarters.

Projects are funded to demonstrate the feasibility of standard library services, special kinds of library service, cooperative library systems, and so forth. The intent of these demonstrations is to use LSCA funds to establish, by exhibition, the feasibility of a service. It is expected that after a given period has elapsed (usually two years), local funds will assume the support of the service.

ALLOCATION OF LSCA TITLE I FUNDS

The criteria for allocating PLSA and LSCA funds are straightforward. The State Librarian and the Assistant State Librarian (who administers these funds) first determine whether a project is in accord with the California Master Plan for library service and with the California State Plan submitted to the United States Office of Education (USOE). One of the most important requirements is that the project must seek to tailor its programs to the community needs; but this must be done so that the program will carry the community beyond where it was at the time the project began. That is, it ought to be an extension or broadening of service to the community, rather than a maintenance of service at status quo. Other selection criteria for each project are as follows:

> Is there a possibility for it to become a cooperative project
> (a project in cooperation with another)?

- Is there, in the judgment of the Assistant State Librarian, a demonstrated need for it?

- Is it innovative? (If it is innovative and different, it is more likely to be funded.)

- Is there local support for (interest in) the program?

- Is the program one that is likely to be successful? (That is, will it fill the demonstrated need and gain popular support?)

- Finally, is there a likelihood that the local government unit will be willing to assume funding for the program after the Federal demonstration funds are expended?

The State Library allocates State aid and LSCA funds to a variety of classes of projects. A brief discussion of these projects will illustrate the range of service within the State.

Bookmobiles

One important method used in providing and extending library service to some areas, especially rural areas, is the bookmobile. There are several bookmobile programs in operation in California. For example, the Alpine County Demonstration is providing service on a continuing basis to a rural mountainous county that was previously without a library. This project also makes available the part-time services of a professional librarian from another county.

The Los Angeles Public Library sponsors a bookmobile program designed to bring library services to the culturally deprived. The project seeks to reach these patrons by bringing the library to their community and by offering enrichment programs such as storytelling and motion pictures.

San Diego County has instituted bookmobile service (one of the first in the State) in the northern part of the county as a part of the development of strong regional library service.

Enrichment

Inherent in most of the LSCA projects that are funded in California is the expectation that each program will enrich the service provided to patrons.

The enrichment program of the State Library provides a good example of this concept. In accordance with the needs of the State, the agency has used a part of the Federal funds to enrich its holdings and to enhance its ability to provide more adequate service throughout the State. Among the areas of benefit are the following:

- Supporting the Consultant Service of the State Library, enhancing further the ability to provide specific advice and help through visits, telephone conversation, and correspondence.

- Supplying supplementary book services through interlibrary loan from the collection of the State Library.

- Supplying reference and information services from the staff of the State Library.

- Strengthening the overall resources and collections of the State Library by: microfilming of early California newspapers; purchase of library materials for use in serving public libraries throughout the State; and conducting or authorizing studies relative to the developing library needs of the State.

Central Processing

There are two levels of central processing in the California system: the State level and the local system level. At the State level, the State Library operates a Central Processing Center for 28 subscribing libraries. Federal monies are used as a revolving fund for operating costs until reimbursement is made by the member libraries. The centralized service relieves member libraries of many clerical tasks and enables their professional personnel to devote more time to expansion and enrichment of reader services. At the local level, the Black Gold System (for example) processes system acquisitions for its members. The benefits of the service are roughly the same as those provided by the State Central Processing Center.

Mechanization

The California State Librarian has recognized the need for some form of mechanization or computer support of the library. A project has been initiated to establish computer processes in the California State Library. The University of California has been engaged to provide scientific, professional, and engineering services to develop computer control of the California State Library Processing Center for serial control and book catalog production. This will specifically benefit the 28 member libraries of the processing center.

The Disadvantaged

One important theme in the California plan is extension of service to the
disadvantaged. There are four classes of disadvantaged--the culturally
disadvantaged, the ghetto disadvantaged, the urban disadvantaged, and the
rural disadvantaged.

Projects for the culturally disadvantaged are designed to extend service
to the segment of the population that is handicapped by some cultural
difference that makes it difficult for them to compete with the majority
community. One project serving this class of disadvantaged is the
Fruitvale Library Project, oriented toward a Mexican-American population in
the Fruitvale District of Oakland. This library provides Spanish-language
books and materials to the local community as well as to 11 other branches
within the Oakland System. The project staff cooperates actively with
other community agencies so as to ensure maximum effect among the Spanish-
speaking people. The Lincoln Heights Project in Los Angeles is another
example of a program designed to reach a Mexican-American population.

Projects for the ghetto disadvantaged are designed to serve the residents
of an urban ghetto. Usually, these people are primarily Black. In some
instances, they are functional illiterates. An example of this kind of
project is the Venice Branch project of the Los Angeles Public Library
System. Personal contact and personal commitment are indispensable to the
success of this kind of program. Services range from the typical library
programs to dance and jazz concerts, as well as an annual Cinco de Mayo
Festival, which involves all elements of the community. One obvious
weakness of this kind of program is that its success depends so very heavily
on the dedication and personalities of the members of the project staff
and their ability to innovate continually.

Another project designed to provide service to Black ghetto residents is
the Richmond Public Library Service Center Project. The project is located
within the lobby of the State of California Service Center in the largely
Black district of Richmond. The project staff is attempting to do away
with the stereotyped image of the library as only a dispenser of books.
This stereotype has long affected the relationships between libraries and
their communities: the populace, city council, civic groups, etc. The
Richmond Project staff, located in the Service Center of the hub of many
activities, is working systematically to change this image, and to present
the library as a communication center, a resource center, and an agent for
social change.

The urban disadvantaged are in some ways similar to the ghetto disadvantaged,
but by no means completely so. Largely, these people are characterized
by their inability or refusal to accept the services of the public library.
They behave as though they are not aware that library services and materials

are available to them. One of the programs designed to reach such a group is the Los Angeles Public Library Demonstration of Service to Shut-Ins. The program is designed to provide service to persons--largely the elderly-- who are confined to their homes. This very laudable project is far more expansive than regular library service because of the necessity of having individual messengers visit the shut-ins to provide service.

Projects for the rural disadvantaged are designed to establish or extend library service to residents of rural depressed communities and farm labor camps. An example of this kind of program is the San Joaquin Valley Library System Service to the Rural Disadvantaged. A bookmobile has been purchased as the physical means of providing books, audiovisual programs, story hours, etc., to farm labor camps, depressed rural communities, and previously unserved small communities where known pockets of culturally deprived persons reside. These patrons often are "invisible" and there is no easy way to reach them or even to estimate their numbers. In contrast, the ghetto disadvantaged are relatively visible and can be more or less easily counted.

IV.   DESCRIPTION OF REPRESENTATIVE USES OF LSCA FUNDS

In conformance with the California State Plan governing LSCA expenditures, allocations have been made to support a number of cooperative library systems. Some representative systems are described below.

The North Bay Cooperative Library System

The first and perhaps the best known such system in California is the North Bay Cooperative Library System. Begun as a project in May 1960, it is now a permanently established system. The areas served--just north of San Francisco Bay--include Solano and Lake Counties and parts of Napa, Sonoma, and Marin Counties, with a total estimated population of 500,000.

The 16 city and county libraries in the system are demonstrating that it is possible to achieve good library standards by having each library contribute to the service, rather than by having services provided by one large central library. Telephone and teletype service joins them together; there is a processing center and a storage area for book service; film service is provided to all member libraries; and adult and children's services are shared by the whole system. Member libraries have from the beginning of the program shared the cost of centralized services. The system is now strong. By legal action it has established itself as a permanent public agency, and was given an LSCA Title II grant to construct a system headquarters. This headquarters will be limited to administrative and indirect services for all libraries in the system.

LSCA Title I grants are used to help support the following functions:
processing, materials transportation, regional storage center, film service,
consultative and administrative functions, and communication.

There are three types of libraries in the North Bay System: (1) (such as
the Marin County, Sausalito, and Mill Valley libraries) which are funded
separately and which have no legal or financial relationships with one
another; (2) affiliate libraries for which towns pay both county and city
taxes; and (3) local libraries that contract with the County Library for
services.

The North Bay Cooperative has been investing its State and local funds in
capital goods and in projects whose termination would not affect the system
as a whole.

The Serra Regional Library System

In 1963 a State-funded study (by Joseph Wheeler, a private consultant) was
made to consider the plans for some form of consolidated cooperative library
system for the southernmost part of California. Wheeler's study resulted
in a document, published in 1965, entitled Proposed Regional Library System
for the San Diego Area. Wheeler proposed a general plan; however, the
Serra System as it now exists did not completely follow the plan indicated.
At present the Serra Regional Library System consists of the Carlsbad City
Library, the Chula Vista Public Library, the Coronado Public Library, the
National City Public Library, the Oceanside Public Library, and the San
Diego City Library. Any library may apply for membership in the Serra
System. Minimum standards for participation must be met, however, and
the applicant's City Council must concur by means of a joint powers agreement.
(The San Diego County Library is not a member because it does not meet the
minimum standards for participation.) An executive group of librarians
from each community meets once monthly to deal with administration and
operation of the system.

This system is financed by a grant from the State of California under LSCA.
In 1965-1966, a State grant of almost $97,000 was received, plus $57,000
from LSCA--a total of $154,000. In 1966-1967, the total grant amounted to
$156,000. In 1967-1968, a reduced amount under the new formula for State
grants was received in the amount of $62,000. In 1968-1969, the State
grant has diminished further to $52,000. This money is being spent to
enrich collections and to improve services to patrons in all of the member
libraries.

The Serra System uses a variety of means for book distribution: their own
vehicle; the Greyhound bus; and, for isolated areas, the U. S. Mail.
Originally they had provided long-distance phone service free, but they are
now charging for it. For reprints they charge 10¢ per xeroxed page, with a
reduction for multiple copies.

One interesting aspect of their work is that they do provide a fair amount of service outside the country, mainly to organizations, agencies, and individuals in Baja California. The service is the same as that within the area and the only requirement is that the requester apply for a card giving name and address.

Chula Vista, near the Mexican border, represents an area of declining circulation. The older residents are moving out and being replaced by Mexican-American families who have recently come to the United States. They have added a "floating" librarian to attempt to work with some of these incoming groups.

The Director indicated that one of the system's greatest needs was for training, for both professionals and library aids. Although there is the usual number of workshops, the system is operating with help that is not as skilled or experienced as she would like; and the lack of training presents difficulties, especially in providing reference services.

49-99 Cooperative Library System

The 49-99 System, with headquarters in Stockton, gets its name from the two major highways (State 49 and U. S. 99) that bisect it. About 494,000 people are served by the system. There are large numbers of Negroes, Mexicans, Portuguese, and East Indians. The system has been in operation for 18 months. The first 6 months were devoted to planning and establishing operating procedures and guidelines for the system; the past 12 months have been the effective operational period of the project. The 49-99 System, began as a project funded by LSCA money, is now supported by PLSA as well as by LSCA Title I funds. It is part of a larger experimental system that has been in operation for two years.

The 49-99 System is a network of libraries and stations, among which there is a free exchange of library books and materials. One may, for example, check out a book in one county and return it, without penalty, to any station within another county in the system. There are three deliveries per week per station. This system seems to be working very well. In addition, patrons may call upon the 49-99 System to interact with libraries throughout the State for services that are not available at their local branches or within the 49-99 System.

Each of the county libraries serviced by the 49-99 System has about eight branches. The branches, of course, work through their own local county libraries; although the system deals more directly with the county units themselves, all of the other divisions or branches of the county are an important part of the system.

As nearly as possible, the 49-99 System has followed the recommendations found in several of the survey studies funded both by State and LSCA projects. Particular emphasis has been placed on the projects that have been funded with the State Library funds granted by the State Librarian for this purpose.

PLSA funds have been used for buildings and capital equipment. A formula contained in the State law governs the level and type of funding for such purposes, taking into account the need of the county, the effort of the local officials or the local system, and the population involved. The per capita allotment, based on the State formula, then takes into consideration all of these aspects.

LSCA Title I funds, however, play a large role in providing services not covered by local funds. These are, of course, distinct from capital improvements and not covered by Title I. There are three LSCA projects that are an important part of the 49-99 System. They are as follows:

- The record collection, which is large and which has been expanded with LSCA funds. Each member library within the system has its own collection and there is a circulating collection, such that every library will receive every record within the collection on a rotating basis. And, on special call, libraries may request records that are not in their current files.

- The foreign language book collection, containing volumes in different languages.

- The collection of books in large (oversize) print. These are provided for the partially sighted or patrons who have weakened vision. Such magazines as Reader's Digest, Life, and Look can also be found in this collection.

Since many of the small libraries do not have professional librarians on their staffs, a training program is conducted by the Stockton Library staff, who serve as instructors and consultants. An attempt is made to give specialty training to librarians in the small outlying libraries. The training is not structured in the form of a course with specific start and end dates. It is given the year round, and anyone who wishes may enter it at any time.

One indication of the utility and worth of the 49-99 System is its success in establishing programs for children. When the system began, there were absolutely no children's programs in the rural counties. Under the direction of the 49-99 System, and as a part of its services to its public, the rural counties now have such programs. On our visit to the system we were able to observe that the reading program for children, even in the smallest counties in terms of population, showed evidence of being viable. We could see the number of children who were registered in the summer reading program, and who had received awards for having read a certain number of books during the summer. Though all of the counties do have children's programs, not all the rural counties or elements of the system have the same kind of program, nor do the programs all have the same effect. For example, Amador, Calaveras, and Tuolumne Counties use children's programs more than do some of the others; they also use the 49-99 System itself more than other counties.

One important project developed through the use of the system is the microfilming of a large collection of periodicals, newspapers, and other such resources. The system calls upon college and university libraries, public and county library systems, and special library systems throughout the area to make inputs to system headquarters for its periodicals collection.

Another important activity is the development of a union catalog of periodicals that presently contains 5,000 to 8,000 titles. This catalog is also being placed into a microfilm system.

The system's librarians are beginning to observe greatly increased library usage, particularly districts of the system and in some of the minority areas within the metropolitan area of Stockton. New users are coming into the library to browse, to get information, to check out books, to read books within the library without checking them out.

There is strong evidence that government officials, supervisors, and library boards and commissions do support the 49-99 System, and that there is sufficient fiscal support for the system to carry on without LSCA funds.

The Inland System

The Inland Library System includes the city libraries of Corona, Colton, San Bernadino, Upland, and Barstow. The San Bernardino County Library, which has many branches and bookmobiles, is also a part of the system. The Inland System has received three LSCA grants. The first initiated the system, the second increased audiovisual capability within the system, and the third created a reference system. Local funds have not decreased as a result of the Federal funds. On the contrary, funding has increased from a 1966 book budget of $35,000 to a $60,000 budget in 1967 and to $70,000 for 1968.

We visited the system at the San Barnardino Public Library, the headquarters for the audiovisual and reference systems. As a part of the service to the patrons, the system has developed a film collection. These are mostly entertainment films. Teachers occasionally choose films to show at the

schools; in general, however, there are few instructional films. The
collection is small: only 263 films. The librarian feels that money
currently going into the film collection would be better spent in joining
a network that would provide access to a large number of films. Much of
what is being accomplished with films is similar to what the librarians
from the disadvantaged areas through the State think is needed for their
patrons--that is, a visual presentation that gets patrons into the library.
The present audiovisual services do, however, appear to stimulate interlibrary
interaction and to attract new users to the system. To this extent, the
film collection seems to perform the same function here as in some
disadvantaged areas.

Lassen County (California)-Washoe County (Nevada) Library System

The arrangement that Lassen County has with Washoe County in Nevada is
partially funded by LSCA Title I and partially by Title III. Lassen
County--geographically, culturally, and economically--is more closely
related to Nevada than to California. Susanville, the county seat, is on
the eastern, or desert, side of the Sierra Nevada. We asked the Director
whether the initiative to join with Washoe County had come from the State
Library or from Lassen County, and were told that the pressure was completely
from Lassen County itself. For three years the county had been urged by the
State Library to become part of the Northern California Library System. For
three years they had refused and asked instead to become allied with Washoe
County and its system. Permission and funding were given in 1967.

We asked the Director whether local funding was expected to decrease as a
result of the Federal support. She answered that the supervisors insisted
she not cut back on spending of local monies because of the LSCA funds;
indeed, the supervisors gave more money than had been received before.

As in some of the other demonstration projects, this system is using the
funds to accumulate capital in the form of collections. Most of the money
for the first year is going into capital; a smaller amount is going into
capital for the second year, and more into operation. The Director expects
that the local population will continue to support the service once the
demonstration period is over. The problems in Lassen County are quite
different from those of the more populous areas; people are scattered,
some as far as 80 miles from the library, and supplying library service
to such a sparse population calls for a different technique.

San Mateo County Library System

For more than 10 years prior to the funding of the LSCA Young Adult Program
of the San Mateo County System, the County Librarian and her staff had
attempted to establish some service to young adults in the county. She and
her staff felt that large numbers of young people, teenagers and adults in

their early twenties, were not being serviced by traditional library practices. She felt there was a great need for some innovative service to attract these nonusers and she repeatedly proposed such a service to the County Manager, who repeatedly turned her down because he felt that no such need had been demonstrated.

In 1965, the Young Adult Program had its real funding beginning. The Young Adult Department of the San Mateo County Library is now completely supported by county funds. The programs are developed to meet the special needs of young adults as those needs are defined by the young people themselves. An attempt is made to talk to as many high school groups as possible throughout the county, either in the high school itself or in the branch libraries. Also, school officials and school librarians are informed about county library programs, so that they can work together to satisfy the library needs of the youngsters throughout the county.

Librarians say they have had a difficult time in explaining--to the supervisors, the County Manager, and the city councils in the several independent cities served by the system--that it is necessary to allow enough time to assess needs as well as to estimate ways in which these needs have been met, and that funds for the project should not be cut off without permitting such an evaluation.

North Sacramento Valley Library System

The initial impetus for the North Sacramento Valley System formation came from a group of county and city librarians, who began meeting in the fall of 1964 for the purpose of creating this system. Their tentative plans were furthered by an independent chain of circumstances: two $25,000 PLSA grants were provided during Fiscal Years 1965 and 1966 for a survey of library services throughout Northern California. This survey was performed by the Public Administration Service and published in 1966 in a report entitled Public Library Services in Northern California. The study provided background information on the social and economic features in the entire Northern California area and also made specific recommendations concerning the nature of library service that should be established in this area. As a direct result of this report, the North Sacramento Valley System was initiated as the first portion of the Northern California plan.

It is interesting to observe the way this multicounty system was created in California. The process consists of a 1-year planning period in which librarians of the member libraries would generally meet for a full day once a month to discuss the necessary implementation arrangements, legal questions, procedures, and the whole array of issues involved in operating such a system. The system planner, who was hired to coordinate and who was the operating arm of this group, would obtain information on costs for various alternative arrangements such as central processing, the acquisition of vehicles of different types, the cost of teletypes or TWX systems, and so forth. She was operating as an administrative person providing the decision-making group with the necessary information from which to consider alternative approaches during the planning phase.

A major problem in the development of the North Sacramento Valley System was the absence of any large central library around which the system could be built. There were several intermediate-sized libraries--the Municipal Library in Chico, the Butte County Library, and the Shasta County Library-- that could provide a base for further development but none, in itself, was a substantial resource library. One of the issues involved in creating the system was the advisability of selecting and adding to one of the intermediate- sized libraries and making it the central resource library for the system. The system, with Chico as its headquarters, has now been operating for approximately two years.

The Metropolitan Library System

The Metropolitan Library System of 12 member libraries, located in the northeast part of the Los Angeles metropolitan area, was originally called the San Gabriel Valley Library System. After a period of operation as the San Gabriel Valley Library System, (originally comprising seven libraries) the system was expanded to include an additional five libraries.

The important purposes of the Metropolitan Library System are:

·   To strengthen the reference service for the member libraries.

·   To allow uniform library services to be given to patrons within the system.

·   To provide better public information regarding the holdings of the several libraries.

The Metropolitan Library System is funded with two LSCA grants: $20,000 for reference materials; $75,000 for other system needs. The two grants are combined into a single fund, and since the project has been expanded to include 12 libraries, there is $176,000, including local monies, that has been funded for the period through February 1970.

There is another LSCA fund of $20,000 for planning a study of business and industrial aspects of library services. All of the librarians in the system are excited about the possibilities of such services. Practically speaking, the businessmen within the communities are the ones who can throw their support--through the Chamber of Commerce and service clubs--to any

program, whether it is for libraries, schools, or whatever; and their
support will make a great difference. If the libraries can demonstrate
that they can serve the needs of the business community, they will be
making friends.

Though the executive function rests with the Director, the Metropolitan
Library System relies heavily on its 12-member council, one member from
each of the libraries. The council meets monthly and operates through a
number of committees set up for the various aspects of the program--for
example, the audiovisual committee, the reference committee and the books
acquisitions committee. All recommendations made by the council are
reviewed by a 3-member executive committee. The recommendations of this
committee then go to the Director, who then makes the final decision based
on the recommendations received.

V.   EVALUATION

PROGRAM STRENGTHS

California has developed a strong public library program under difficult
circumstances. Funding under the 1963 California Public Library Services
Act (PLSA) has never been adequate to meet the minimum needs of the
public libraries of the State, nor has the funding ever reached the level
called for by the formula within the law. This low level of support has
been felt (and is now being felt) throughout the State. Nevertheless,
under the skillful management of the State Librarian and the Assistant
State Librarian, California has profited by these meager funds. California
can be proud of the general management of both State and LSA/LSCA funding
for the public library assistance program.

PROBLEM AREAS

A possible weakness of the library development in California is the lack of
a systems development plan. Though the State's Master Plan is based on the
concept of library systems and though many grants have been made for establishment and support of various systems, there is nonetheless a dearth of
specific definitions, guidelines, and provisions for coordination. Many of
the existing cooperative relationships have developed without sufficient
counsel. Local library directors state that they want and need more systematic guidance in defining a system. A number of considerations should be
taken into account, in addition to natural geographic configurations. The
State Library has funded several surveys that have addressed this problem,
but a statewide systems plan is yet to be created.

CONCLUSIONS

If the LSCA program in California were to be discontinued, aid to local
libraries would be diminished, and the development of regional library
systems would be slowed. The overall library program, however, would
continue as a result of wide public support.

VI.   BIBLIOGRAPHY

California State LSA and LSCA Title I annual plans, reports, and programs submitted to USOE during the period 1957-1968 (miscellaneous titles).

Boaz, Martha, Dr. New Directions in Library Service. University of Southern California, Calif., 17 pp.

California Library Commission. Reports, California Public Library Commission; Pursuant to 1957 Statutes of California Chapter 2328. University of California, Berkeley, Calif., 1959. Contains:

Report No. 1.   Wight, Ed. A. General Report.
Report No. 2.   Koepp, Donald W. Titles Added in 1957 to a Group
                of California Public Libraries.
Report No. 3.   Hardkopf, Jewel C. Personnel Utilization in a
                Group of California Public Libraries.

California State Library. "California State Plan for Libraries Programs Under the Library Services and Construction Act, as Amended." News Notes of California Libraries. Calif., 62:3, Summer 1967, pp. 289-335.

California State Library. News Notes of California Libraries. Various issues including Statistical and Directory issues such as: Spring, Winter 1968; Spring, Fall, Winter, Summer 1967; Spring, Fall, Winter, Summer 1966. Sacramento, Calif.

California State Library. "Public Library Service Standards for California." News Notes of California Libraries. Calif., 58:2, Spring 1963, pp. 291-302.

California State Library. "Summary of State Library Services Act and Library Services and Construction Act Program in Ten-Year Period." News Notes of California Libraries. Calif., 62:3, Summer 1967, pp. 337-343.

California State Library. "Summary Reports: Programs Under the Public Library Development Act of 1963." News Notes of California Libraries. Calif., Fall 1964, pp. 431-488.

Governor's Conference on Libraries. Sacramento, Calif., 26-29 May 1968.
Contents:

A Master Plan for the Development of Public Library Service in the State of California. Pp. 101-112.

Current Approaches to Standards for Information Science and Library Problem Areas. 10 pp.

How Obsolete is Your Community College Library--All Materials. 7 pp.

Libraries in the California State Colleges. 7 pp.

Libraries of the University of California. 17 pp.

Library Programs to Serve the Future. 5 pp.

Special Librarianship: Information at Work. 15 pp.

The Challenge of Leisure: A Southern California Case Study. 96 pp.

Wilson Library Bulletin. April 1968, pp. 796-828.

Holt, Raymond M. "Services to 'Match our Mountains'; A Review of Public Library Services in Northern California; A Plan for the Future." News Notes of California Libraries. Calif., 62:3, Summer 1967, pp. 343-352.

Holt, Raymond M. and Rostvold, Gerhard N. San Gabriel Valley Community Libraries Face Tomorrow. San Gabriel Valley, Calif., October 1965, 14 pp.

Klausner, Margaret and Wheeler, Evanne. A Survey With Recommendations Prepared Under Provision of the Library Service Act. Amador County, Calif., 1959, 26 pp.

Los Angeles City Schools. Office of Urban Affairs, School-Community Relations Unit: Orientation to East Los Angeles. Los Angeles, Calif., September 1967, 23 pp.

Los Angeles Public Library. Report of Library Services and Construction Act Project #2842. Los Angeles, Calif., 1 January - 30 June 1967, 165 pp.

Martin, Lowell A. and Bowler, Roberta. _Public Library Service Equal to the Challenge of California_. California State Library, Sacramento, Calif., 30 June 1965, 132 pp.

Marysville Public Library. _Public Library Services in Northern California: A Plan for the Future_. Oroville, Calif., 12 pp.

Prentiss, S. Gilbert. _A Critique of a Report of Public Library Services in Northern California_. Public Administration Service, April 1966, 19 pp.

Public Administration Service. _Public Library Services in Northern California: A Plan for the Future_. San Francisco, Calif., 1966, 161 pp.

San Joaquin Valley Library System. _Film Catalog_. Fresno, California, 1968, 44 pp.

Swank, R. C. _Interlibrary Cooperation Under Title III of the Library Services and Construction Act_. June 1967, 78 pp.

Troke, Margaret Klausner and Gardner, Aurora West. _A Survey With Recommendations Prepared Under Provisions of the Library Services and Construction Act_. Calaveras and Tuolumne County, Calif., June 1966, 25 and 26 pp.

Wheeler, Joseph L. _Proposed Regional Library System for the San Diego Area_. San Diego Public Library, Calif., February 1965, 76 pp.

CHAPTER XV
WASHINGTON

I.   SOURCES OF INFORMATION

The following organizations and persons were visited to obtain information
for this study (see Figure W-1 for a map of the State):

Date	Place Visited	Persons Visited
8/19/68	USOE Regional Office San Francisco Region IX	Helen Luce, Library Services Program Officer Dr. Pedro Sanchez

8/20/21	Washington State Library
	Olympia
		Maryan E. Reynolds, Washington
		  State Librarian
		David Taylor, Associate State
		  Librarian
		Dorothy Doyle, Library Consultant
		Dorothy Cutler, Director,
		  Library Development
		Mrs. Josephine Pulsifer,
		  Supervisor, Technical
		  Services

8/22/68	Timberland Library
	  Demonstration Project
	(Grays Harbor, Mason, Pacific,
	Lewis and Thurston Counties)
		Mrs. Louise E. Morrison, Director
		David Taylor, Associate State
		  Librarian

8/22/68	Grays Harbor County Library Montesano	Mrs. Ruth Greer, Librarian

8/22/68	Aberdeen Public Library
	Aberdeen
		Mrs. Rosalie Spellman, Librarian
		  and Area Supervisor, Grays Harbor
		  and Pacific Counties

8/22/68	Pacific County Library Raymond	Mrs. Bertha Hager, Librarian Don Cox, Trustee, Pacific County Board
8/22/68	Centralia Public Library Centralia	Mrs. Mary Stough, Coordinator of Services to Children Dr. William Lawrence, Member, Library Advisory Board

Date	Place Visited	Persons Visited
8/23/68	Washington State Library Olympia	
8/26/68	Washington State Library Olympia	
8/27/68	North Central Regional Library Wenatchee	Michael Lynch, Director
8/28/68	Moses Lake Public Library Moses Lake	Mrs. Marie Kennedy, Librarian Chester Waggener, Moses Lake City Manager Mrs. Eric D. Peterson, retired Library Board Member Mrs. Susan Dennis, Library Board Trustee
8/28/68	Grand Coulee Public Library Grand Coulee	Mrs. Lorna Thomas, Librarian Mrs. Etheta Anderson, Library Board Member Mrs. J. H. Heidt, Library founder and pioneer
8/28/68	Omak Area Library	Mrs. Rachael Steiner, Omak Area Librarian Mrs. Marilyn Wilson, Library Board Building Chairman, Past Board Chairman Mr. James Markel, Board Chairman Mrs. Vesta Sackman, Board Member Mrs. Betty Miller, Board Member Mr. Saul Herrera, Board Member Mr. James Baxter, Wenatchee Area Bookmobile Driver
8/28/68	Winthrop Public Library	Mrs. Barbara Duffy, Librarian Mrs. Sue Schaufler, Board Chairman Mrs. James (Kathy) McCauley, Board Member
8/29/68	Seattle Public Library Seattle Yesler Branch Seattle Public Library	Mr. Roman Mostar, Assistant Librarian Branch Librarian, Seattle Public Library
8/29/68	University of Washington Seattle	Dr. William Schill, College of Education

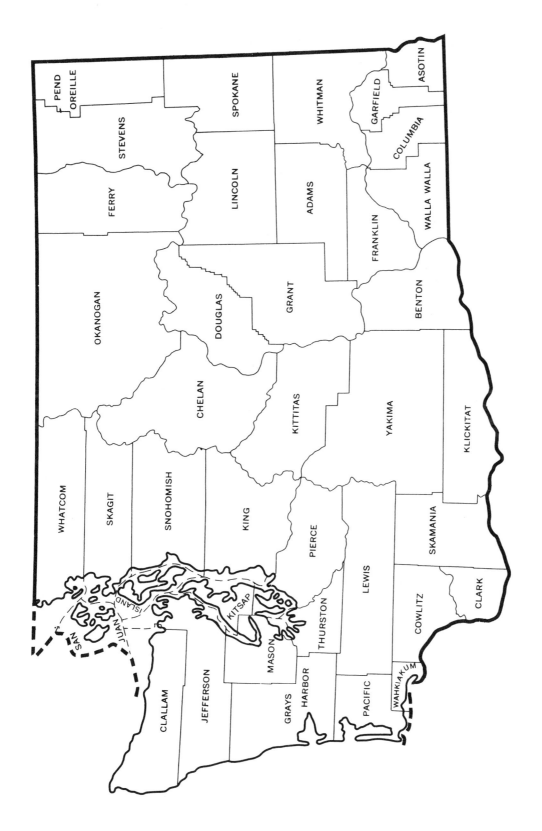

Figure W-1. Map of the State of Washington

Much valuable information was also obtained from the publications listed in the Bibliography in Section VI of this chapter.

II. BACKGROUND FOR LSCA OPERATIONS

The Washington State Library Commission is the official agency designated by State law to receive, disburse, and administer all funds granted to the State for improving and extending library services under the Library Services Act (LSA), and the Library Services and Construction Act (LSCA). The State Library Commission, an executive commission appointed by and responsible to the Governor, appoints the State Librarian, who serves as secretary to the Commission and operates the State Library. The State Librarian, presently Maryan E. Reynolds, is a member of the Governor's cabinet. (See Figure W-2.)

The Commission is chartered to provide book services to areas where no libraries exist, and (through the State Library) to act as a supplementary book source for, and focal point of, an interlibrary loan system among the libraries of the State. The Commission also provides consultant services to public officials on library matters, to libraries in all communities, and to citizens' groups desiring to establish or improve library service. The Commission seeks to promote cooperation, coordination, integration, and regionalization by:

1. Providing improved supplementary book services and consultant services to unserved and inadequately served areas of the State;

2. Providing grant funds to assist in establishing new libraries, to improve existing services, and to continue and extend services for more efficient operations; and

3. Holding demonstrations, within any or all of the regions and for specified periods of time, that may lead to the establishment of locally operated and supported library systems. These demonstrations are predicated upon providing good library service to unserved or inadequately served areas. They consist in establishing new service and in extending existing services into new areas.

The Commission provides assistance, through merger and demonstration grants, to existing library units that may consolidate for more effective service.

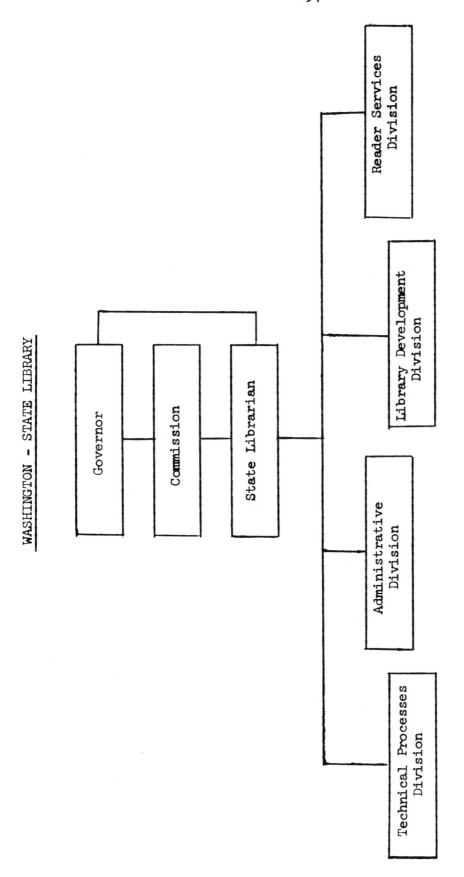

WASHINGTON - STATE LIBRARY

Figure W-2. Organization of the Washington State Library

The following divisions of the Washington State Library are involved in the State's Library Extension Program, designed to implement the Washington State Plan (which is discussed below):

1. Library Development Division. This division has primary responsibility for projects under LSCA Title I. Consultants in the Division work with library boards, government officials at the municipal levels, Friends of the Library, lay groups, and other persons interested in establishing, extending, and improving library service in their locales. The Division also administers the Washington Library Film Circuit.

2. Administration Division. This division has direct supervision of the State Plan, and the operation of the Library in all of its functions.

3. Reader Services Division. Mail service to unserved areas, inter-library loan, institutional library service, distribution of Washington State documents to depository libraries, supervision of Federal depository and the State depository system, service to departments of government, supplementary reference service to libraries so requesting.

4. Technical Processes Division. Responsibility for acquisitions, cataloging and processing of all State Library materials (including institutional), centralized cataloging and processing for Timberland Regional Library, book catalog production for Timberland Regional Library and North Central Regional Library. Consultants also provide advice on automation, cataloging, processing and various other library functions.

HISTORY OF STATE AID TO WASHINGTON LIBRARIES

After a study made by Charles Bowerman in 1948,[1] the Washington State Library Commission adopted a long-range regional plan for library development in the State. The State was divided into 12 regions, each of which was to receive standard library service. (The North Central Regional Library and the Timberland Demonstration, discussed later, are instances of massive assistance to two of the 12 regions. A key feature of the regional library plan, which is basic to the overall State plan for public library service, is that each of the 12 regions must have a population base and a tax base large enough to allow it to maintain demonstrated library services. This requirement ensures

---

[1]Bowerman, Charles, Proposed Regional Library Plan, University of Washington, 1948.

that when library services have been shown to be feasible (in terms of both cost and use), the likelihood of their support's being assumed by the local patrons will be high. A map of the 12 regions is shown in Figure W-3.

This regional plan for public library service was adopted by both the Washington State Library Commission and the Washington Library Association as the long-range Regional Plan for the library development in the State. As the Regional Plan was adopted before the passage of LSA, the State Library Commission decided to use the Federal funds to further implement this operational plan. In determining which areas are inadequately served or are without service, the American Library Association Standards adopted in 1956 are applied to all libraries that request grants under LSCA.

LIBRARY FUNDING

Washington has State funds which are used for all aspects of its promotion and development of library service throughout the State and its various subdivisions. These funds are used to match the Federal Library Services and Construction Act.

For purposes of reporting to the United States Office of Education regarding the allocation of LSCA and State matching funds, the State Library uses six project categories (discussed below under LSCA PROGRAM) to cover all of the several kinds of grants and services supported under the State plan.

Table W-1. LSCA and State Matching Funds for Fiscal Year 1968[2]

Project Categories	LSCA Funds	State Matching Funds
I. Service to Public Libraries	$230,958	$288,426
II. Demonstration Projects	$195,531	$244,259
III. Service Grants	$ 74,298	$ 92,815
IV. Consultant Programs	$ 54,011	$ 67,471
V. Governor's Conference on Libraries	$ 4,404	$ 5,501
VI. Regional Governor's Conference	$ 6,757	$ 8,440
	$565,959	$706,912

[2]Source: Washington State Library.

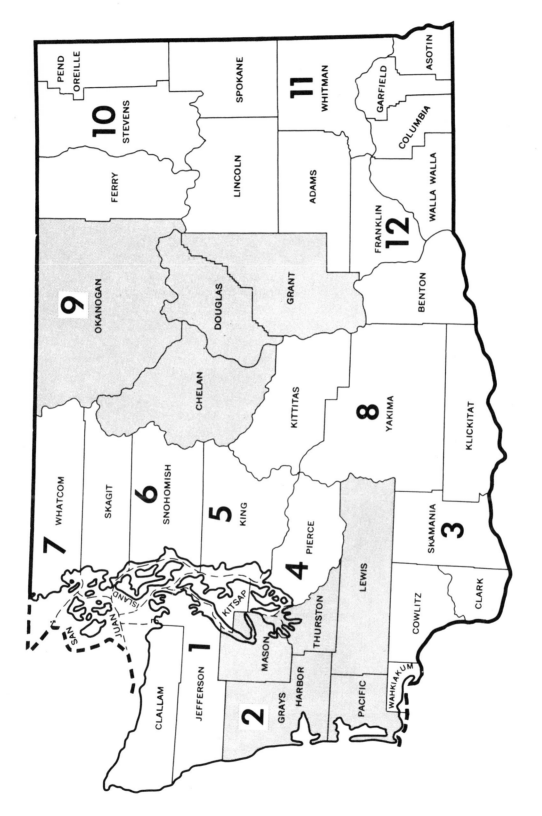

Figure W-3. Regional Plan for Library Development in the State of Washington

III.   LSCA PROGRAM

OVERVIEW OF ACTIVITIES

The State Library has a five-member Commission which sets policy and has final responsibility for all programs. All LSCA projects are under its general direction, acting through the State Library. Categories I, IV, V, and VI are at the State level. The Demonstration Projects vary in exact administrative structure and method of financing, depending upon the individual situation. Merger grants are made to the requesting library and are for one time only.

Service to Public Libraries (Project Category I)

The entire population of the State of Washington is served through the State Library by programs funded and administered under the project category. Through the system of interlibrary loans, the State Library serves as an auxiliary and supplementary resource to the public libraries of the State. Service to citizens who do not have access to public libraries is also provided under this program. The general resources of the State Library--including nonfiction books, Federal documents, documents from other States, microfilmed newspapers, maps, and other materials--are made available to libraries and individual citizens.

Demonstration Projects (Project Category II)

Several types of demonstrations are possible under the Washington State plan. One type of demonstration is exhibiting the advantages of bringing into one strong single administrative system, already existing libraries while at the same time extending service to unserved areas. The Timberland Library Demonstration, discussed later in this chapter, is an example of this type of demonstration.

Another type of demonstration involves applying advanced technology to library needs. The MARC Project, an example of this type, is also discussed later.

Service Grants (Project Category III)

Service grants are provided to public libraries upon request for funds for any one of several types of special service grants.

Consultant Programs (Project Category IV)

The Consultant Program of the Library is, according to professional librarians in the State, one of the strongest and most effective of all the services of the State Library. Though the consultant staff is not large, the consultants are extremely competent, experienced, and dedicated. Their services are available to all public libraries, to all library boards, and to government officials.

Governor's Conference on Libraries (Project Category V)

A Governor's Conference on Libraries was held September 20, 1967, as a result of a report to the Washington State Library Commission from the Executive Committee of the Washington Library Trustees Association. The theme of the Conference was "Libraries--A Force for Progress." Its major purpose was to bring to the attention of the public (through publicity, addresses, sessions open to all, etc.) the vital and expanding role of libraries in all areas of educational, cultural, and economic development in the State. It is anticipated that further such conferences may be held.

Regional Governor's Conference on Libraries (Project Category VI)

Six Regional Conferences, patterned after the statewide Governor's Conference, were held in 1967. Their purpose was to bring to the attention of the public the role of libraries in the growing educational needs of communities and to gain ultimate financial support for all types of libraries within the State. The Regional Conferences, also, are expected to be repeated at some future date.

GRANTS FUNDED UNDER THE WASHINGTON STATE PLAN

Under the terms of the Washington State plan, the following types of grants are supported:

Demonstration Grants

Demonstration grants encompass a pre-demonstration preparatory period, service demonstration period, and post-demonstration. The objective is to hold the service demonstration period within a two to four-year span. A vote of the people is required to assure the formation of a library district with the authority to levy a tax for library service.

Demonstrations may consist of any library service or combination of services in accord with and in furtherance of the State plan, such as establishing new service, extending existing services into new areas, and merging services.

· Evolutionary Grants

Libraries as well as library systems may apply for special grants
when entering into an evolutionary plan of cooperation, i.e., a
written, binding agreement to implement a plan of service for the
population served by the contracting libraries.

· Merger Grants

Merger grants are given only once. Merger grants are made under the
following circumstances: when a city and a library district merge
to form a regional library, when two or more library districts
merge to form an intercounty library district, when there is a
contractual agreement between an incorporated city or town and a
library district, and when libraries join the Washington Library
Film Circuit as new members.

· Establishment Grants

An establishment grant is made to a new library or library district,
to a library system introducing service to an unserved area when
that area becomes a part of the system, and to a library system
establishing a formal branch program in an area that has not been
served previously.

· Extended Service Grants

Extended service grants are made to libraries bearing special burdens
of service outside their own jurisdictional area of support.
Interlibrary loan service, service to the blind, institutional
service, and use of modern library techniques such as mechanization
and automation are supported. These grants may be continued at the
discretion of the State Librarian.

· Education for Librarianship Grants

Grants are made upon request to libraries for recruitment, scholarships and internships in library service, support for specialized
instruction for librarians, and workshops for librarians and library
trustees. Such grants may be renewed or extended depending upon the
circumstances.

· In-Service Training Grants

Grants are made for projects that improve the efficiency of libraries
in the following ways: workshops for library employees, volunteer
training programs and community education in the use of libraries.
These grants may be continued or renewed as required.

• Research and Planning Grants

Grants are made for studies designed to advance the development of library service in the State of Washington. These grants may be continued, renewed or extended as required.

IV.   DESCRIPTION OF REPRESENTATIVE USES OF LSCA FUNDS

In providing services to public libraries under Project Category I during Fiscal Year 1968, a total of $519,380 was spent by the State Library. Of this sum, $230,958 were LSCA funds; $288,426 were State funds. These monies were spent by and through the State Library in its statewide public library service program.

A summary of requests for services during one fiscal year may be helpful in judging the scope and range of the services the State Library provides to public libraries:

Circulation Requests	105,631
Reference Requests	39,506
Mail Requests	23,322
Documents Distributed	287,493
Consultant Visits and Talks	272

There is one major project that is operated out of the State Library under Project Category (MARC Pilot Project) and a number of projects that are funded for operation on a regional or local level.

MARC Pilot Project

Washington State Library is one of 16 libraries participating in the Library of Congress Project MARC. Machine Readable Catalog data are supplied to the Library on magnetic tape. To use these data, the State Library staff has created some computer programs and has adapted other programs supplied by the Library of Congress. Procedures have been developed for producing an experimental catalog of the current book acquisitions of the King County Library System, the North Central Regional Library, and the Timberland Library Demonstration. This catalog, currently in use in these systems, can be updated without excessive cost. It is arranged in three parts:

Register: The Register is a listing of full LC information in the order in which acquisitions are input to the system. The Register is reprinted only when it is worn out.

Author-Title-Subject Catalogs: These catalogs provide adequate finding information on books, giving author, short title, publisher, date, the library holding the book, and the call number. Each entry refers to the register number for full information.

<u>Adult-Juvenile Titles</u>: Adult and juvenile titles are produced in a combined volume. Separate volumes can be produced if they are desired.

<u>Timberland Library Demonstration Project</u> (Region 2)

The Timberland Library Demonstration Project began preparation in 1962 and started operations (under adverse administrative conditions) in 1964 funded by a demonstration grant and managed on the regional level. Based on a favorable vote of the people in the general election of November 5, 1968, the Demonstration was legally established as the Timberland Regional Library on January 1, 1969.

The Demonstration Project covers Lewis, Pacific, Thurston, Mason, and Grays Harbor Counties. Libraries in all five counties were visited in the course of the survey. The headquarters of the Demonstration Project is in the South Puget Sound Regional Library in Olympia. The Director of the South Puget Sound Regional Library is also the Director of the Demonstration Project.

Because of administrative problems in the early months of the project's operation, the State Librarian decided to call in an outside consulting firm, Nelson Associates, to advise on the continuance of the project and upon the question of submitting the Demonstration proposition to the voters in the general election in November 1966. The consulting firm found that a number of problems had made it impossible for the project to fully demonstrate standard library service as originally intended. The firm made two important recommendations: (1) that the Demonstration be extended to the termination date of December 31, 1968; and (2) that the question of establishing the system not be submitted to a vote until the November 5, 1968, general election. Both of these recommendations were followed by the State Librarian. As a result of the extension, which allowed a more adequate display of standard library services, the vote in the November 1968 general election was favorable.

In visiting the libraries we made stops throughout the five counties. Most of the towns in the area are small and rural; few of them could be considered medium-sized cities. For example, the combined population of several of the towns that are adjacent to each other is something like 30,000.

The goals of the Demonstration Project have been well met. There was sufficient support to get the Demonstration Project accepted. As a result, library services for the five county population of 192,864 have been greatly expanded. Rural areas previously without libraries now receive Bookmobile service. The Demonstration offers "Direct-to-Borrower" mail service, and it has made possible extended Bookmobile routes and strengthened existing library collections. Central processing and ordering are provided, and facilities for information and self-education of professional staffs are available. But the full impact of the effect of this well-planned and well-executed Demonstration can best be shown by the following summary:

	Pre-Demonstration Years 1962 - 1964	Demonstration Years 1965 - 1967
Circulation	3,621,887	4,176,356
Materials Added	63,382	119,447
Film Service (borrowed)	622	13,034
Attendance at Film Showings	25,340	284,840
Phonograph Record Circulation	45,506	79,456

Since the Timberland Regional Library was established by a favorable vote in the general election in 1968, State and Federal funds will be available to maintain the same level of service until local tax funds become available in 1970.

The acceptance of the tax encumbrance by the electorate of the region is clear evidence of the salutary effect of LSCA funds in this area of the State.

North Thurston Library (Lacey)

Library service began in the Lacey area in December 1965 from a bookmobile parked at a location on Market Square. During 1966 the bookmobile circulated nearly 12,000 items. In December 1966, larger quarters were obtained, and the book collection was increased from approximately 2,000 volumes to about 4,500. Circulation in 1967 was 33,592 and a good reference collection was added to the library.

In 1968 the town of Lacey began to participate in supporting the library. The library was moved to a larger building with 2,400 square feet. In the first quarter of 1968, circulation was 13,234, which is more than the annual total for 1966. A projection of circulation figures through December 31, 1968, would indicate a total circulation of 50,000.

This library is a part of the Timberland Demonstration and, as such, received LSCA support.

Seattle Public Library--Extended Service Grant

The Seattle Public Library received an extended service grant to support a program begun in 1955 for statewide library service to the blind. LSCA funds help maintain the service but are not sufficient to materially improve it. This had been extended to the physically handicapped and partially sighted on a low-key basis with plans to escalate as soon as funds permit. Funds granted to the Seattle Public Library are used to defray expenses incurred in giving service to persons outside the city of Seattle.

Shoreline Branch--Establishment Grant

The King County Library System was granted LSCA funds totalling $28,262 in Fiscal Year 1967 to help in establishing an area center and branch library. The Shoreline facility was dedicated on December 4, 1966. Use has been outstanding: In 9 months of 1966, the Richmond Highlands Library circulated about 41,000 volumes. In 9 months of 1967, the Shoreline area center library (which replaced Richmond Highlands) circulated about 137,000 volumes.

Spokane County (Cheney) Rural Library District Establishment Grant

An LSCA grant of $34,439 was made to the District to assist in establishing a branch facility in Cheney, an incorporated town of over 4,000 population previously without library service. Before this grant was made the town had contracted (in 1966) with the District for service, beginning with bookmobile service.

Washington Library Film Circuit--Merger Grant

An LSCA merger grant of $17,079 was granted to the Film Circuit in Fiscal Year 1967 to maintain and upgrade the level and quality of its services to member libraries. The grant was justified on the basis of the addition of three new libraries to the circuit.

Yakima Valley Regional Library Research and Planning Grant

In Fiscal Year 1967 an LSCA grant of $17,940 for research and planning was made to the Yakima Valley Regional Library. The consulting firm of Nelson Associates was retained to conduct a survey of the total library resources and services available to Yakima, Kittitas, and part of Eastern Klickitat County.

North Central Regional Library--Merger Grant

In Fiscal Year 1967, an LSCA merger grant of $32,345 was made to the North
Central Regional Library, in support of the project for the Integration of
the Book Collection at North Central Regional Library. The four projects
covered by the grant are:

- Integration of standard files,

- Integration of locally owned Northwest materials,

- Reprocessing of locally owned titles to conform with book
  catalog, and

- Production of a Wenatchee-area shelf list.

North Central Regional Library (Region 9)

The NCRL System is one that is not primarily supported by LSCA funds at
this time. It was established under LSA funds as the Demonstration Project
and subsequently supported by the people. It is, however, one of the very
fine instances of the impact of LSA funds on expanded library service, and
no report on public libraries in the State of Washington, (and no attempt to
describe the effect of LSA/LSCA funds on public library development in the
State of Washington) would be complete without a discussion of this system.

The North Central Regional Library District covers Ferry, Okanogan, Chelan,
Douglas, and Grant Counties. The North Central Regional Library (NCRL),
originally the Columbia River Demonstration Project, was established in
November 1960, upon the adoption of the establishment proposition by the
voters in the District. It was the first LSCA demonstration project in
the State.

Since the 2-mill taxing has been available to support the NCRL System, the
LSCA funds are given to other regions of the State and not to the NCRL as
operating funds. (At no time was it planned to continue funding regions.
The objective was local tax support.) (Some LSCA funds presently go to the
NCRL in the form of the merger grant described above.) The impact of the
LSA funding on NCRL is quite clear; the people in the area have accepted
standard library service as developed by the NCRL System.

The five-county NCRL System (approximately equal in size to the areas of
Maryland and Connecticut combined) has a total population of 133,300. The
Regional Library serves 89 percent of these people--approximately 119,800.
The library presently has a per capita checkout of books at the rate of
7.1; the State average for libraries of this size is 6.1. It seems clear
that the Regional Library is serving the population at a rather high rate.
During 1967, for example, the NCRL circulated 853,242 books, magazines,
records, films, pamphlets, and paperback books.

The following four member libraries are typical of those in the area
served by NCRL:

Moses Lake Public Library

Moses Lake is one of the areas where most of the standard library services
were not available until LSA funded the Demonstration Project in 1958. In
our visit to Moses Lake Public Library we were told that the people in the
community are very proud of the library and use it frequently. The film
service, the audiovisual aids--indeed all of the additional services other
than just the circulation of books--are widely used. We were told that the
people would be most unhappy if the library service were withdrawn. One of
the big strengths here is the outstanding well-qualified librarian who
would not have come unless it had been a part of the regional library.

Grand Coulee Public Library

At Grand Coulee, the more traditional library services are provided. The
librarian does not have a library degree, but she does have considerable
experience. Most of the reference questions are forwarded to the regional
headquarters in Wenatchee for disposition. Circulation of materials is
quite adequate. The people in the community are very strong in supporting
the library. They would not tolerate any termination of the contract with
the regional system because they are now accustomed to standard library
service.

Omak Public Library

The entire board of the Omak Library discussed with us the Regional Library
System and the attitude of the people regarding their membership in the
NCRL System. The board and the people are unanimous in their praise of
the service. They made it quite clear that under no circumstances would
they accept withdrawal of membership in the NCRL System; they are accustomed
to it and willing to pay for it.

The Winthrop Area

In the very small town of Winthrop we discussed the use of local library
services and their impact on the community. There was unanimous support
of the library.

V.   EVALUATION

PROGRAM STRENGTHS

The success enjoyed by the State of Washington in the use of LSA and LSCA
funds is due in large measure to early and careful planning, and to the
leadership of the State Librarian and her staff. Washington has made very

effective use of LSA and LSCA allotments. All major demonstrations supported by LSA/LSCA funds have been accepted by the local patrons, and local regional libraries have been established. Although massive amounts of money have been spent on two major demonstrations (North Central Regional Library and Timberland Demonstration Project), no part of the State has been neglected in the use of funds.

The establishment of libraries according to the Regional Plan has been slow; however, it has been well planned. Some library service has been provided throughout the State but major efforts have been zeroed in on specific problems until solved.

PROGRAM WEAKNESSES

It has taken the State Library 26 years to succeed in establishing two regional library systems. At that rate of development, using the demonstration approach described in the State plan, many years will pass before standard library service will be provided to all of the State. Moreover, even in the two regions where demonstration projects have been accepted, only a thin veneer of standard services in fact exists; the multicounty units may be too lacking in adequate library personnel, with great distances separating remote communities, to make the ideal of standard library services a reality. Alternative approaches, such as single-county units and special-purpose projects, would permit a broader range of activities to be undertaken, but they have not been used.

Another weakness of the present approach is that a demonstration of a multicounty regional library system could be rejected by the people. If it were, much time and large sums of money would have been irretrievably lost, and the State Library would be faced with physically removing its capital resources from the area, at further expense. Years would probably pass before the population in such an area would again request the State's assistance.

CONCLUSIONS

If the LSCA program in Washington were to be discontinued, aid to local libraries would be diminished, and the development of regional library systems could be slowed. The overall library program, however, would continue as a result of wide public support.

VI.   BIBLIOGRAPHY

Washington State LSA and LSCA Title I annual plans, reports and programs submitted to USOE during the period 1957-1968 (miscellaneous titles).

Becker, Joseph and Hayes, Robert M. A Proposed Library Network for Washington State; Working Paper for the Washington State Library. Wash., September 1967, 50 pp.

Leivestad, Kristy. Washington Library Film Circuit Handbook. Washington State Library, Olympia, Wash., 1968-1969.

Washington State MARC Catalog: King County Library System, North Central Regional Library, Timberland Library Demonstration, 1967. (Olympia, Washington State Library) 2 v.

Washington State Library. Principles and Rules and Regulations for Library Services and Construction Act Programs in Washington State. Olympia, Wash., April 1965.

CHAPTER XVI
GENERAL FINDINGS OF THE STUDY

GOALS AND OBJECTIVES OF THE STATE PROGRAMS

The objective of the LSCA Title I programs in each of the 11 States was to extend public library services to areas "without such services or with inadequate services." Since each of the 11 States library administrative agencies has determined that all of the population of that State has either inadequate public library service or no public library service, the further extension of public library service can, within the provisions of LSCA Title I, be offered to the population of any political subdivision in each State.

The State library administrative agencies have chosen a number of strategies to achieve their objectives. These various methods are described in this section. (Table XVI-1 shows specific States employing each of these strategies.)

1. Stimulating Local Tax Support. Since the amount of the LSCA Title I monies is insufficient to meet the objective of adequate public library service, nine of the States have used these funds to stimulate additional local tax support for public library services. Two different methods of stimulating such support have been used. One is the demonstration grant, through which the State will fund (or partially fund) new library service in a community with the understanding that the community will either assume additional (or total) finanical responsibility for this service after the demonstration period has ended, or in the absence of local support, the State will remove the service. The second stratagem has been to make LSCA support contingent upon the level of local support. As illustrated in Table XVI-1, seven states have used demonstration projects; three require a level of local tax support.

2. Formation of Systems. Nine of the States have used LSCA Title I funds to induce public libraries to join systems, so that these libraries might increase their services by sharing material and professional resources. The concept of the amalgamating small libraries with larger libraries into a larger association has been attractive to these States as the method by which each library could greatly augment its strength at only moderate additional cost.

3. Attracting Professional Librarians. Seven States have used LSCA Title I monies to increase the number of trained professional librarians serving the public libraries of the State, by

   . Offering scholarships for professional training to those who would contract to serve in the public libraries of the State,

Table XVI-1. Methods Used by the 11 States to Extend Library Services with LSCA Title I Funds

	\$ Massachusetts	New York	North Carolina	South Carolina	Ohio	Wisconsin	Kansas	Arkansas	Utah	California	Washington	TOTAL
1. Stimulating Local Support												10
a. Demonstrations	X	X			X	X			X	X	X	(7)
b. Requirement of local matching funds			X	X				X				(3)
2. Formulation of Systems	X	X		X	X	X	X	X		X	X	9
3. Attracting Professional Librarians	X	X	X	X	X	X		X				7
4. Institutes	X	X		X	X	X	X	X	X	X	X	10
5. Surveys	X	X			X	X					X	5
6. Holdings and Reference Services	X	X		X	X	X	X	X	X	X	X	10
7. "Disadvantaged" Projects	X	X		X	X	X				X		6
8. Cooperation with Schools		X		X*								2
9. Public Relations	X	X	X	X					X		X	6
10. Consultant Services	X	X	X	X	X	X	X	X	X	X	X	11
11. Central Processing	X	X	X	X	X	X	X	X	X	X	X	11
12. Central Holdings	X	X	X	X	X	X	X	X	X	X	X	11
13. Networks	X	X	X			X	X					5

S T A T E S

*Until ESEA was passed.

. Supplying additional LSCA funds to those library systems whose pay scale is such as to make public library service in the State more attractive, and/or

. Supporting LSCA programs which would cause undergraduate college students to select library training as their field of postgraduate college training.

4. Institutes. Ten of the 11 States have chosen to strengthen the capabilities of the local libraries by providing training to and institutes for local librarians and local library trustees. Continuing education is necessary for the continual improvement of library staff performance. Most of the libraries have neither the funds nor the resources to provide this education. At many of the libraries, proper funding depends upon the knowledgeable activity of the trustees. The institutes conducted by the State with LSCA funds are directed to filling the educational need.

5. Surveys. Five of the States help local libraries plan for the further extension of services by providing LSCA grants for surveys of local needs. These surveys usually employ the advise of outside experts whose expenses and fees are funded through Title I funds.

6. Holdings and Reference Services. Ten of the States have made specific grants for improving book collections, reference services, and audiovisual holdings. Immediate help can be given to local libraries by giving funds that increase the book holdings of that library. Similarly, libraries are encouraged to increase their audiovisual holdings through the use of Title I grants. Augmenting the reference service is often achieved through grants for paying research personnel as well as through grants to be used to increase the reference holdings.

7. "Disadvantaged" Projects. Six States have sought to extend library services to those who have not used such services. These efforts have taken the form of outreach programs to the "disadvantaged." In the States we examined, the term "disadvantaged" has included not only the urban black citizens, but also the Spanish-speaking citizens, the rural farm workers, and the Indians.

8. Cooperation with Schools. Two States have LSCA programs that give grants for cooperating with schools so that better library services might be extended to students. The student population forms a major user group of the libraries. Cooperation by libraries with schools has been used to make the libraries' holdings more applicable to the immediate needs of the students.

9. Public Relations. Six States fund public relations from LSCA Title I monies so that the public might be aware of services extended by the libraries.

10. Consultant Services. All of the States offer consultant services to local libraries so that the ability of local libraries to extend services may be augmented. The smaller libraries have the need for guidance and leadership that can be offered by librarians who have a broader view of library problems and the solutions that others have successfully applied to these problems. A major LSA and LSCA activity on the part of the State library administrative agencies has been to provide such guidance and leadership.

11. Central Processing. All of the States provide central processing services so that both the personnel and financial resources of the local libraries might be utilized to better extend library services. The unit cost of technical processing decreases as a larger volume of materials are processed. Most libraries do not process a large enough volume of materials to make processing reasonably inexpensive. Therefore, the States provide technical processing services for the smaller libraries. Central ordering has also allowed the States to get volume discounts for the participating libraries. This has been achieved without the States' doing centralized book selection.

12. Central Holdings. All of the States provide a resource of central holdings upon which local libraries can draw in extending service to local library users. Most libraries can never expect to have sufficient holdings to satisfy all of their clients' needs. The State has made its holdings a resource which these libraries can draw upon.

13. Networks. Five States have created networks with LSCA funds (sometimes Title III funds) so that local libraries can draw upon greater resources in extending their services to each of their owner groups of users. The State libraries form one of the natural nodes of such networks; usually, non-public libraries form other natural nodes.

ADMINISTRATION OF STATE PROGRAMS

All public libraries (and State Libraries) of the 11 States visited are eligible to receive LSCA Title I funds. The legally designated State administrative agencies have chosen different ways of identifying recipients and allocating these funds.

Some States, which already had master plans for the use of State monies, chose to use the Federal funds to augment existing State appropriations for these plans. Other States authorized the library administrative agency to develop LSCA program plans for the State. Two other states were guided in forming their original LSCA plans by committees of librarians from the State.

With respect to disbursement of funds, some of the 11 States chose to have local librarians propose projects for ad hoc consideration by the State library administrative agency, while other States have formulas for the disbursement of funds. Utah has created a State Library that is in effect the local library for most of the State; most of Utah's Title I funds are used for this purpose.

A major decision for the States whether LSCA Title I money should be considered as continuing funding or funding with a terminal date. Many of the States used the money as if it would continue indefinitely; these States made long-range plans for extending library service.

Other States, more conservative in their approach, considered the authorization as having a terminal data, even viewing the annual appropriations as tentative until money was actually allocated. Thus, some of the States (for example, New York) chose to benefit from LSCA by using the money for noncontinuing efforts. Others, such as Washington, funded demonstration projects, which could be continued with local monies after the LSCA funding had been discontinued.

The 11 States differed so widely in their use of LSCA funds that the SDC team was necessarily cautious in making generalizations. The very knowledge-able Library Services Program Officers further informed us that the 11 States could not be considered typical of their Regions and that, in general, it would be difficult to single out any State within any Region as typical.

North Carolina uses the Federal money to augment a State grant-in-aid program already in existence; these combined State and Federal monies are used as grants to county libraries, to improve local library services. New York, which also has a State aid program, awards the Federal money competitively to its 22 system libraries on the basis of project proposals from these libraries.

Utah had had no State Library before LSA, and in most areas of the State there had never been libraries; Federal monies were used here to create a State Library that would extend services to the population of this vast area. Massachusetts, on the other hand, with long-established public libraries in every township in the State, used LSCA and State monies to enrich these libraries through special-purpose grants, the coordination of an interlibrary loan and reference service, and the support of regional public library systems.

The State of Washington, like Utah, had had large areas without library services. Even before LSA, the State had embarked on a program to help these areas start library system if they showed willingness and ability to support libraries after a two-year demonstration period. Washington, then, chose to use LSCA monies to accelerate the State Library's program.

Kansas began with local demonstrations under LSA and moved to develop regional systems with LSCA. In addition, it developed an information network providing public libraries with access to the either major collections within the State.

California chose to use LSA money to achieve two different goals: to reduce the number of counties without county library service, and to encourage formation of systems joining areas that already had library service. Under LSCA, these two goals were modified so that cities could extend library services to those who had been without such service, and so that city systems could provide reference services to other systems with less adequate reference sources.

Wisconsin, much of whose considerable rural population had had inadequate library service, has adopted the concept of the library system; LSA and LSCA monies have been used to develop systems linking each local library user to a larger array of library materials and professional services.

The Ohio State Library Board has allocated LSCA funds for three general categories: State Library-directed programs that extend and supplement library service in rural areas, projects that foster intra-county and multicounty cooperative efforts, and special projects that include programs for the urban disadvantaged.

The Arkansas Library Commission has used LSCA funds to strengthen State agency activities (workshops, technical processing, cataloging, consulting, etc.) that serve participating libraries. LSCA money has also strengthened multicounty libraries by funding additional staff, books, equipment, and supplies.

The South Carolina State agency has chosen to augment their own State grant-in-aid funding with LSCA Title I funds. This money is used to strengthen local library capabilities on an incentive basis requiring certain minimum standards and specified local support.

FINANCIAL RESOURCES AND USE OF MATCHING FUNDS

A variety of resources are available for carrying out LSCA Title I programs. In addition to the Federal funds, there are State and local monies which often are directly utilized in the same effort. Some states require the expenditure of local money (though this money may not be accounted for as a local contribution).

The funds that have been identified by the States as matching funds are not necessarily used as part of the LSCA program by that State. As an example, California identifies the budget of one of its bi-county libraries as part of the funds that the State uses to match the LSCA Title I allocation. The ability of the States to show non-project library expenditures as matching funds has rendered the requirement of matching funds according to a per centum formula meaningless. Any State can show that there are sufficient public library expenditures in that State to more than equal the matching fund requirement established for it. As a consequence, LSCA Title I funds are distributed (after $100,000 is allocated to each State) according to the population of that State without any regard to the relative wealth of that State. The following paragraphs summarize the procedures of the States for the matching funding required under LSCA Title I.

The North Carolina State government appropriates money that is more than enough to meet the matching requirement imposed by the formula. This money is mingled with LSCA, Title I money and is then allotted by the State Library according to the State Plan.

The New York State government allocates a large amount of money to be disbursed among the 22 library systems of the State. This amount is far beyond what is required for New York's matching funds. The State money, however, is not mingled with Federal money in individual projects; rather it is listed as a separate project.

Utah uses the money appropriated to the State Library for its matching requirement. This money is mingled with LSCA money to fund the State Library's services.

California meets its matching requirement by adding the budget of a bi-county library to a part of the State Library's budget. The State's own support for libraries is not listed as part of California's matching monies.

Under LSA, Kansas initially used only State appropriations for matching purposes. This amount, however, was not sufficient to entitle it to the full appropriation authorized under the law. The budget of the Wichita Public Library was therefore included to augment the matching funds. With the additional LSCA money that was received as a result, sufficient library activity was stimulated so that this State can now use money from regions that have been formed as a result of LSCA activity to show local money as its matching budget.

Ohio matches with local library money, State aid, and some of its Federal Appalachia funds.

Wisconsin currently uses as matching funds both State appropriations and monies from local libraries that benefit from LSCA funding.

Arkansas matches with State aid money and partially supplements these funds with the operating budget of the State agency.

Washington and Massachusetts use State aid money to provide matching funds for LSCA Title I; both States combine Federal and State funds for allocation.

South Carolina currently uses, for matching funds, both State grant-in-aid appropriations and local monies from areas that have received substantial benefit from LSCA funding.

ASSIGNMENT OF RESPONSIBILITIES

The formal assignment of responsibility for the LSCA program in each State is the head of the State library administrative agency. Authority, however, is actually exercised at two levels: at the State agency and at the level of the local library organization which receives grants from the State agency.

In States with a small population (such as Arkansas, South Carolina, Kansas, or Utah), the head of the State agency has retained actual responsibility. In other States such as California, North Carolina, New York, or Wisconsin, the responsibility for LSCA Title I programs is delegated to a lower level within the State library administrative agency.

In all States but Utah there is a further delegation for the expenditure of funds at the local level to the library or library system which receives the local grants from the State. Continuing eligibility to receive grants depends on operation of the local libraries according to the standards created at the State level.

Standards for local operation differ with the States. In general, these standards are not harsh. Since the goal of the States is either to stimulate greater local support for library services or to provide services where such services have been inadequate, the State library administrative agencies have had to be tolerant of the capabilities of local personnel. Formal qualifications of personnel range from those possessed by competent heads of urban libraries to those of bookmobile drivers responsible for extending service to a large geographical area. No State is satisfied with the number of trained professional librarians actually engaged in public library service in that State, and in no case did the State agency have the capability to increase trained staffing to the desired level. Not only is the flow of available money for personnel dependent largely on local tax sources, but the total supply of new personnel is dependent on the insufficient output of the library schools.

LSCA PROGRAM SUCCESSES AND PROBLEMS

MAJOR PROGRAM SUCCESSES

The Library Services Act of 1957 was restricted to rural areas and communities with less than 10,000 population. At the time LSCA was passed, there were fears that it might result in rural areas' being slighted. The study showed that this has not happened; LSCA has maintained the momentum of rural development that began with LSA; in fact, it has had its greatest impact in areas that are too sparsely populated to be able to support library services from local taxes.

The program successes in the different States vary according to the different approaches taken by the State library administrative agencies; some of the differences in approach are the result of differences in population density (e.g. Massachusetts as compared to Utah), others are the result of the different degrees of library development that existed at the time LSA was enacted (e.g. New York had already encouraged the formation of library systems, while Kansas used Federal funds to foster the creation of library systems).

States, such as California, that have used LSCA funds to support innovative projects have a larger number of successes than States such as Utah, that have used the funds to support a single project. This section isolates what seemed to the survey group the one or two most important accomplishments that were achieved in each State under LSA/LSCA funding.

Massachusetts

Massachusetts, which already had public libraries for all of the citizens of the State, used its LSCA funds to strengthen the capabilities of these libraries, which now have the greatest per capita support of those in any of the 50 States. It also completed the establishment of three library systems that tie these libraries together and that can use the Boston Public Library as the library of last resort.

New York

New York had already passed State-aid-to-libraries legislation that accomplished most of the goals that the other States have chosen. Therefore, New York sought to improve services through local-library projects, which have been very successful. Prominent among New York's successes have been the projects that have sought new ways to serve the "disadvantaged" non-user of large urban libraries. While New York has given the largest amounts of funds to the "disadvantaged", however, it has also extended library service to the population of its large rural areas.

North Carolina

North Carolina has sought to improve services by stimulating county tax
support and through offering central service. County government support
has increased twentyfold since North Carolina started its program (16 years
before LSA) and threefold since the passage of LSA; central processing is
performed for 55 libraries serving more than 60% of the population of the
State.

South Carolina

South Carolina, which had very rudimentary library services before LSA,
has used LSCA funds in such a way that very few areas are now left totally
unserved by some form of library service.

Ohio

Ohio, a State with many large urban libraries, has hitherto had a weak State
library administrative agency. Under LSCA, Ohio has created a comprehensive
State plan for library development.

Wisconsin

Wisconsin, through the use of LSA and LSCA funds, now has the beginnings of
a public library regional system configuration and the network linkages to
make it operationally effective. Wisconsin has also used its funds to maintain a strong extension service that provides direction and assistance in
public library development.

Kansas

LSA and LSCA have been instrumental in Kansas in creating seven regional
library systems and the Kansas Information Circuit. The regional library
systems have grouped the libraries in each of the seven geographical areas
together; the Kansas Information Circuit has given these seven regions a
mechanism for identifying and sharing each other's resources.

Arkansas

Arkansas has used LSCA funds to enable county and regional libraries to add
new books selected by local librarians and purchased and processed centrally
at the Arkansas Library Commission. A central shelf list of books purchased
with both Federal and local funds is maintained to speed interlibrary loans.

Utah

LSA was the stimulus that caused Utah to create a State Library; this library renders some library service to 90% of the geographical area of the State (an area previously without any library service).

California

LSA and LSCA have been the source of funds to establish library services in California that benefit groups who previously were non-users. Two different types of library service were established: experimental outreach programs to the urban "disadvantaged", and extension library services in rural areas, which were achieved through the fostering of systems.

Washington

LSA and LSCA have funded demonstrations of library service that have resulted in the extension of library service to large geographical regions that previously had been without library service.

MAJOR PROBLEM AREAS

The problems that are listed below are not due to the management of LSCA programs by the States; rather, they are due to more general circumstances that cannot be altered by good management of LSCA programs.

The first major problem is that of insufficient funds. The average state-wide per capita operating expenditures for public library systems serving communities with at least 25,000 inhabitants for fiscal year 1965 are shown below.[1]

The figures are higher than the true State per capita expenditures in that the population without library service is not included.)

State	Per Capita Operating Expenditure
Arkansas	$1.07
California	3.46
Kansas	2.29
Massachusetts	4.24
New York	3.75
North Carolina	1.15

---

[1] Figures are taken from STATISTICS OF PUBLIC LIBRARIES Serving Communities with at Least 25,000 Inhabitants 1965 U.S. Department of Health, Education, and Welfare OE-15068

State	Per Capita Operating Expenditure
Ohio	$3.37
South Carolina	0.91
Utah	2.79
Washington	3.17
Wisconsin	3.47

None of the 50 States has the $5.00 per capita expenditure listed as the minimum for adequate library service by the American Library Association.

The second major problem is one of insufficient numbers of personnel. The shortage of trained professional personnel was acute in South Carolina and Utah; in none of the 11 States was the number of professional personnel near the need. Though the shortage of nonprofessional personnel might be solved rather quickly if the first problem, that of insufficient funds, were solved, the shortage of professional personnel would still remain until the library schools could attract, and then graduate, students seeking service in the public libraries.

The third major problem was that of a lack of coordination between public libraries and school, university, and other institutional libraries. Even though many of the State agencies are within State education agencies, public libraries in those States remain largely independent of the other libraries in the State.

The fourth major problem was a lack of understanding of how to provide service to persons who do not presently use the library. The outreach programs to the "disadvantaged" suffer from a failure to know what services will reach those whom the library is presently seeking to serve for the first time. Libraries have long depended on those who seek their services.

During the course of this survey, we observed a number of projects and programs in large urban areas. The titles of many of these projects included the word "disadvantaged." Although many "disadvantaged" projects are located in ghetto neighborhoods, it is not necessarily true that all persons living in those neighborhoods are economically or educationally disadvantaged. Many ghetto residents choose not to use the public library because they feel alienated from the society that library represents. A number of public libraries that we visited in the course of our survey seem to have sensed this alienation, and are inventing many laudable ways to reach the "alienated patron" who refuses to seek or accept library service. Research is needed to determine which of these well meaning efforts are effective.

The fifth major problem is a lack of understanding on the part of the public of the services the library is already offering. Reference service is an important example of this. Most people do not realize that the library offers more in reference collection.

The sixth major problem is a lack of ability on the part of the public libraries to react quickly to demands for more services. Budgets must be drawn up and approved so far in advance that, for most public libraries, large increases in services would prematurely exhaust their funds.

The seventh major problem is a lack of suitable measures of library performance. Circulation statistics, which are the usual measure of library performance were viewed as inadequate by those we interviewed. It was felt that circulation figures cannot by themselves, give libraries sufficient information on their communities' needs to permit libraries to respond best to those needs.

ADMINISTRATION OF LSCA BY USOE

By law, USOE has limited administrative power over the States. Section 502(a) of LSCA authorizes the U.S. Commissioner of Education to administer the Act under the supervision and direction of the Secretary of Health, Education, and Welfare. However, Section 2(b) of the Declaration of Policy is explicit in reserving most administrative privileges to the States and their local subdivisions. Section 501 gives the Commissioner the responsibility for determining whether the State plans comply with the requirements of the Act; it does not give him the authority to determine what plans a State might adopt. If any State is dissatisfied with the Commissioner's final action with respect to the approval of its State Plan, the State may appeal to the United States Court of Appeals. The judgment of that court affirming or setting aside the action of the Commissioner is subject to review only by the U.S. Supreme Court.

The activities of the Division of Library Services and Educational Facilities (DLSEF), which is the USOE agency responsible for LSCA, consist mainly in being sufficiently well informed about the States' activities that compliance with the Act can be determined. DLSEF keeps itself informed about the States' activities primarily through statistical reports prepared by the States and submitted on forms designed by USOE. The statistical information collected in this manner is sufficient to keep DLSEF reasonably well informed about what is being done in the States, but does not include the enormous amount of information that is collected by the States for their own (primarily legislative) purposes. While this more extensive information is usually sent to DLSEF and does greatly enhance DLSEF's awareness of the States' activities, it is not in a consistent--and therefore comparable --format, because it has been collected by different agencies to meet different requirements. With this extensive information, DLSEF has kept itself well informed about how public library funds are being spent.

DLSEF is presently within the Bureau of Adult, Vocational, and Library Programs, whose administrators are oriented primarily toward activities other than those of libraries. In addition, library services within USOE are fragmented. Figure XVI-1, taken from the January 1, 1968, issue of Library Journal, highlights nine activities spread among USOE bureaus. These nine activities, in turn, are spread among five different officers reporting to the Commissioner of Education. A further reduction in the cohesiveness of DLSEF's library-services activities came through regionalization. Figure 2 shows the map of the nine HEW regions. Figure 1 indicates that these nine regions report through still a sixth person to the Office of the Commissioner. Despite regionalization, communication has continued among the Library Program Officers as well as between the Library Program Officers and DLSEF. Communication has been hampered, however, by distance and low travel budgets. In addition, the Library Program Officers are not administratively under the control of DLSEF; they report directly to the Regional Director of Adult, Vocational, and Library Programs, and through him, to the Regional Assistant Commissioner, who reports to Field Services.

The disadvantage of regionalization from a central-headquarters point of view is matched by its disadvantages from the point of view of some of the State Librarians, who felt quite strongly that services had deteriorated as a result of regionalization. They felt that before regionalization, when they needed information, they were able to get it from somebody knowledgeable at USOE, even if their own Program Officer was out.

Regionalization has also broken the historical continuity of DLSEF's files. Current files are being collected in the nine regional offices, while the older files remain in Washington. The communication among Regional Program Officers has been weakened. Although they can talk to one another by phone, many of those who have not been with USOE and worked together for a long time have not had as much opportunity to establish a rapport among them. This break in communication has affected the amount of knowledge that each Program Officer has concerning LSCA's activities throughout the country.

IMPLICATION OF THE STUDY

DEPENDENCY OF THE STATES ON FEDERAL FUNDING

Both LSA and LSCA were enacted as temporary measures to run a limited number of years. The States, have as a result of varying circumstances (political, economic, even historical) adopted different attitudes toward

LIBRARY PROGRAMS IN THE U.S. OFFICE OF EDUCATION, BY THE OPERATING UNIT AND PROGRAM[1]*

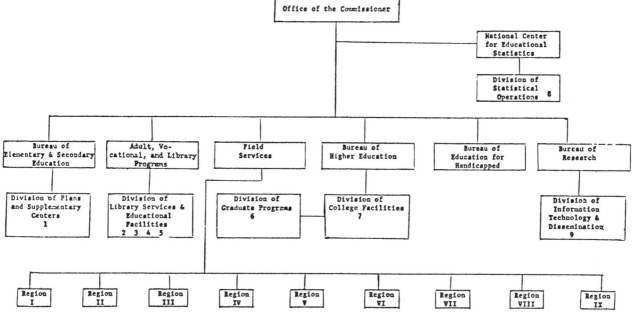

1/ Not a complete chart for Office of Education, presents only location of library programs.

PROGRAM CODE

1. Instructional Resources Branch
Elementary & Secondary Education Act, Title II (School Library Resources)

2. Library Program and Facilities Branch
Library Services and Construction Act

3. Library Resources & Training Branch
Higher Education Act, Title II-A & B
(College Library Resources and Library Training)

4. Library Planning and Development Branch
(Consultative, Advisory and Planning Services by type of library)

5. Library and Information Science Branch
(Consultative Advisory Development Services for Library Education)

6. Graduate Facilities Branch
Higher Education Facilities Act, Title II

7. Program Operations Branch
Higher Education Facilities Act, Titles I and III

8. Adult Vocational and Library Studies Branch
(Library Statistics)

9. Library and Information Science Branch
Higher Education Act, Title II-B, (Library Research)

I-IX Regional Library Program Officers of the Bureau of Adult, Vocational, and Library Programs

Figure XVI-1.   Library Programs in the
U.S. Office of Education

*Library Journal, January 1968, p. 45.

the eventual termination of the funding. New York has strongly resisted any temptation to become dependent upon Federal money. Funds are granted to systems for only a short period of time and are not mingled with State aid. The only real breakdown in New York's effort to remain independent has been the insistence of some of the urban disadvantaged projects on continuing, rather than temporary, funding. North Carolina, on the other hand, has so mingled Federal and State money that any interruption in Federal support would be catastrophic to most of the rural libraries of the State.

California, like New York, has attempted to avoid the continuing funding of projects. If Federal money stops, the libraries of California would certainly not receive a fatal blow, but local pilot or demonstration projects initiated by the State Library would be interrupted. The State of Washington would be able to continue its general expansion of services, but the rate of development would be slowed by loss of Federal money. Massachusetts would lose a source of support for its libraries; these libraries would continue to exist, but they would provide less adequate service to their patrons.

In Utah, most of the extension of library service to the outlying rural population would cease. Kansas, through the receipt of Federal money, has been stimulated to create regional systems that would continue after the loss of Federal money, new statewide services, however, would not develop. The Wisconsin State Library would lose the leadership that allows it to support rural projects; these projects would be damaged, and further development efforts would be retarded. Ohio would lose its chance to implement its proposed State Master Plan and would have to reduce its State Library staff. Libraries in Arkansas would suffer a serious blow. The libraries of South Carolina would continue to exist, but they would lose a substantial source of support.

IMPLICATION FOR FEDERAL PLANNING

Continuation of Federal Funding

The reports on the individual States indicate that the State library have managed well the Federal funds that have been entrusted to them. Good management by itself does not call for a continuation of Federal support; it merely means that mismanagement cannot be used as a reason for discontinuing that support. One of our concerns, however, was whether Federal money should continue to be offered for library services, and, if so, at what level.

The American Library Association in its 1965 National Inventory of Library Needs, stated that an additional 439 million dollars was required for the operating expenditures of public libraries. This is far more than one might expect to come easily from State and local taxing bodies, which may look favorably upon libraries but that must weigh library needs against the needs of other public agencies. Nevertheless, competing with other demands, libraries are receiving increased tax support. From a national point of view, it matters little what tax procedures the citizens of the individual States have adopted. New York, for example, chooses to have generous statewide support for its library systems; California chooses to support its libraries through local tax monies; other States have used different procedures. Localities differ as to whether they use ad valorem taxes, intangibles taxes, liquor taxes, or other forms of revenue. In some States the county has primary support responsibilities; in other States, these responsibilities reside with the municipality. These differences are of local interest but not of national concern. What is of national concern is that the citizens of these States feel that library services are worthy enough of additional non-Federal tax support to give this support against other demands for tax monies and against demands to keep the tax burden from increasing. In effect, this collective response provides a continuing national referendum on tax support for libraries.

The results of this referendum should be used to determine the level of Federal support for libraries just as they are being used to determine the levels of non-Federal support. We suggest that the total local and State support for public libraries for Fiscal Year 1968 be taken as a base on which to measure increased non-Federal tax support, and that the $35 million allocated under LSCA Title I for Fiscal Year 1968 be the base for measuring additional or reduced Federal support for library services. Any increase in LSCA Title I support beyond $35 million would be equal to the increase in non-Federal tax support for public library operating expenditures. The additional Federal money would be distributed by the same formula that is presently embodied in Federal law. In effect, the Federal government would match State expenditures according to formula, rather than the States matching Federal grants. The continuing local and State tax decisions would indicate whether public library services had grown so lavish as to no longer require additional tax support or whether they were still so far short of the needs of the citizenry as to merit additional support despite the other requirements for tax money. This would lead to reductions in Federal support when, in the eyes of either the citizens or their local representatives, libraries required less non-Federal tax support. This form of what may be called "responsive federalism" would be dependent both upon the aggregate of the actions of the citizens of the 50 States, and on the actions of the citizens of the individual States; the maximum total Federal allocation would be determined by the increased support of public libraries by the 50 States. Each State would set its own limit on the amount of Federal support that it would receive.

The differences between the poorer States and the richer States would still be continued. The retention of the 66 percent maximum and 33 percent minimum for the Federal share would still see the poorer States receiving almost four times as much Federal matching for each additional dollar of State spending than the richer States would obtain. However, if any State felt that, compared to all needs, its library services did not require additional non-Federal tax monies, it would also fail to receive the additional amount of Federal tax monies. Such tax monies would not be allocated among the other States, but would remain in the Federal Treasury as monies authorized for library services for which there was not sufficient demonstrable need for allocation. Thus, in general, the full amount allocated in any year by the Commissioner of Education would probably not reach the actual amount of increase by the several States.

These additional monies, as the earlier monies, would still be administered by the State library administrative agencies. They should be given without further categorization. The State agencies have not only been competent, but they have been fair; they have been aware of, and responsive to, the needs of their States. Under the formula suggested above, even more incentive would be given to these agencies to so spend the money as to elicit additional local and State support for public libraries.

A National Role for USOE

The main body of this report testifies to the fine work that the 11 States studied have done in managing LSCA Title I funds. There appears to be little need for USOE to concern itself with the management of these funds within the States to any greater degree that it now does. There is a need, however, for USOE to assume a stronger national role in library services--principally by undertaking some of the tasks that would benefit libraries throughout the nation, and that can now be performed only by several States acting in concert. The areas in which greater efforts by USOE are needed are outlined below. USOE is, of course, currently doing many of these things; they are mentioned here because our study of 11 States indicated that even greater efforts are needed.

1. Research. Though USOE performs a research function for libraries in its Division of Information Technology and Dissemination, we found States spending money on library research that, if fruitful, will have implications far beyond State boundaries. Some of this research was in the area of recruitment, some in the area of finding effective means of providing library services to the urban disadvantaged. All were expensive beyond the immediate return possible to the local library, and all would benefit libraries in all of the States.

Major research is also needed to establish the criteria that individual libraries, State agencies, and USOE can use in determining whether changes in service are producing or inhibiting the further extension of service by the libraries to both the users and nonusers. Such research must be preceded by a determination of needs that are presently not satisfied.

2. Technology. Problems of automation have begun to confront many of the States. Smaller States, such as North Carolina, that have a need for automation of technical services cannot provide the capital to create an effective system. Though they could provide the operating expenses for such systems, they will be without them until USOE provides the technology, one of the richer States provides a working system (New York, California, and Washington are working in this direction), or such a system appears on the commercial market.

3. Librarian Recruitment, Training, and Education. Despite the efforts already expended by USOE, there still remains an imposing shortage of qualified library personnel. USOE should increase its efforts to relieve the States of some of the burden of training.

4. Interstate Communication Channels and Intrastate Library Coordination. Though the State agencies perform a fine task of coordinating the public libraries within their States, there is a lack of interstate communication. Interlibrary loans require knowledge of where holdings are. The Federal Government should serve as a central communication point for interstate borrowing, and could provide interstate accounting for library purposes. This would also permit contact between public libraries and the large number of Federal libraries. Interstate compacts are now required to allow such direct permanent cooperation.

Though school, university, and public libraries receive substantial infusions of Federal funds, there is little or no coordination among these libraries. To create this coordination would be natural at the Federal level. However, the fragmentation of library services within USOE inhibits both the creation of interstate communication channels and library coordination. (Title III of LSCA is meant to enhance such cooperation, but has not received sufficient funding or national guidance to allow its effect to be felt in most of the States.)

The National Advisory Commission on Libraries stated among its recommendations:

To provide the essential overall leadership, the National Advisory Commission on Libraries specifically recommends the appointment of an Associate United States Commissioner of Libraries responsible directly to the Commissioner of Education.

We concur with that recommendation.

If such a role were delegated to USOE, there would be more meaningful function for the Regional Library Services Program Officers. They could provide State Libraries within their Regions not with leadership, but with the services and products with which State agencies might be of better service to the libraries of their States.

IMPLICATIONS FOR STATE PLANNING

1. Flexible Funding. The State library administrative agencies should work toward a change in the type of funding that libraries receive. The present long-term budgetary allocations prevent libraries from increasing their service beyond what the budget will allow. Budgets that can be increased to meet larger demands would reduce the present tendency to continue giving only a little more than had previously been offered.

2. Publicity. More vigorous public-relations work is required to inform the public of the large number of services that can be provided by libraries. Such public relations can be coupled with immediate service. The bookmobiles that were observed were exceedingly effective in publicizing a wide range of services.

3. Interfaces with Non-public Libraries. The State library adminis-trative agency directors should foster greater interaction between the public libraries and the other libraries in the State. In States where the State library agency is part of the State educational agency, such increased cooperation already has an administrative framework within which to develop.

IMPLICATIONS FOR THE METHODOLOGY OF FUTURE STUDIES

Consideration of the methodology of the present study raises two important questions, now that one can look back at the successful aspects and the troublesome aspects of the study. The first question is, "What does the survey team wish it had done differently in the present study?"; the second question is, "What methodology would the survey team recommend for future studies?" The following paragraphs address these questions.

It might have been more desirable to visit the States in a different order. The survey team had assumed that the States were so much alike that an initial training period in California would be sufficient preparation for obtaining all the necessary information in each of the other 10 States; the consequence of this assumption was that no State could be revisited to obtain further data required to verify insights acquired after one of the other States was visited. In retrospect, it would have been more productive to have first spent one week in each of the 11 States, and then, after a consideration of all the data, to have returned to each State for the second week of data collection.

The order in which the data were collected for each State was highly satisfactory for making an independent case study of each State. First, documentation concerning the State's LSCA program was studied; second, the Library Services Program Officer for the State was interviewed; third, the State library administrative agency was visited; fourth, local libraries chosen by the State library administrative agency was visited. After an interval of one week, local libraries selected by SDC were visited, and then final interviews were held at the State capital. In retrospect, however, we do feel that the time spent on each of the information-gathering activities should have been budgeted differently. The amount of time spent at the local libraries was greater than the optimal amount; the time spent at the State library administrative agencies was sufficiently productive that less time could have been spent at local libraries. On the other hand, far more interview and documentary information was gathered than we were able to study profitably during the analysis period of the survey. The time saved by eliminating visits to some of the local libraries should have been used for analysis.

The writing of the final report was scheduled to begin after all of the 11 States had been visited for the second time. Sufficient questions arose during the writing of the report that we felt that we should have started the writing immediately after we had completed the first visits to the States; the questions that arose during the initial writing could then have been addressed during the second visits.

If another study of the effects of LSCA Title I were to be funded, the information that this present study had already gathered is such that the techniques of the present study (even as modified in retrospect) should not be replicated. Instead a different approach should be used. After the present study was completed, it was clear that the availability and quality of library service are a function of three factors: the amount of funding available to a library, the number of trained professional librarians, and the formal networks that had been created for sharing services and holdings among libraries. A future study of LSCA might well compare the effects of these factors in libraries that have received LSCA funds with their effects in libraries that have not received LSCA funds. Such a study would require that less be spent on travel and interview, and more be spent on analyses of the statistics that have already been compiled at the State level. These analyses would seek to determine when Federal funding had merely become an additional source of library support and when it had actually stimulated localities and States to assume additional responsibilities.

This survey has clearly demonstrated the need for a broader and more systematic analysis of the overall impact of Federal funds upon State and local expenditures for libraries. Further analysis will require the application of empirical measures for assessing this impact. Some possible empirical indices should include: (a) State and local legislation (new or amended), (b) library appropriations (increase or decrease) at both State and local governmental levels, and (c) degree of political support for, and the attitude toward, library programs at State and local levels. These kinds of indices would provide some insight into the impact of LSCA funds within a particular State or individual jurisdiction.

Another by-product of this research is the obvious realization that the LSCA program does not operate in a vacuum. The LSCA program naturally responds to, and becomes a product of, various social, economic, and political forces. Not all of these forces are readily identifiable or apparent to administrators of LSCA projects, either in the initial program planning and development stage or in the actual implementation period. The inability to identify crucial variables which might affect an LSCA project is evident when one observes the differential strategies employed by States in administering their LSCA program.

This study identifies and examines a number of "causal" variables affecting the execution of LSCA projects. Future research efforts should focus upon providing a comprehensive planning framework for identifying and assessing the effects of these causal variables as they relate to the implementation of the entire LSCA program.

APPENDIX A

LIBRARY SERVICES AND CONSTRUCTION ACT

APPENDIX A
LIBRARY SERVICES AND CONSTRUCTION ACT*

AN ACT

To promote the further development of public library services.

Be it enacted by the Senate and the House of Representatives
of the United States of America in Congress assembled, That this
Act may be cited as the "Library Services and Construction Act."

DECLARATION OF POLICY

Sec. 2. (a) It is the purpose of this Act to promote the
further extension by the several States of public library services
to areas without such services or with inadequate services, to
promote interlibrary cooperation, and to assist the States in
providing certain specialized State library services.

(b) The provisions of this Act shall not be so construed as
to interfere with State and local initiative and responsibility in
the conduct of public library services. The administration of
public libraries, the selection of personnel and library books and
materials, and, insofar as consistent with the purposes of this
Act, the determination of the best uses of the funds provided under
this Act shall be reserved to the States and their local subdivisions.

TITLE I--PUBLIC LIBRARY SERVICES
AUTHORIZATION OF APPROPRIATIONS

Sec. 101. There are authorized to be appropriated for the
fiscal year ending June 30, 1967, $35,000,000; for the fiscal year
ending June 30, 1968, $45,000,000; for the fiscal year ending
June 30, 1969, $55,000,000; for the fiscal year ending June 30, 1970,
$65,000,000; and for the fiscal year ending June 30, 1971, $75,000,000,
which shall be used for making payments to States which have submitted
and had approved by the Commissioner of Education (hereinafter
referred to as the Commissioner) State plans for the further extension
of public library services to areas without such services, or with
inadequate services.

---

* as amended by the "Library Services and Construction Act Amendments
  of 1966," Public Law 89-511, approved July 19, 1966, and by Public
  Law 90-154, approved November 24, 1967.

ALLOTMENT TO STATES

Sec. 102. From the sums appropriated pursuant to section 101 for each fiscal year, the Commissioner shall allot $25,000 each to Guam, American Samoa, the Trust Territory of the Pacific Islands, and the Virgin Islands and $100,000 to each of the other States, and shall allot to each State such part of the remainder of such sums as the population of the State bears to the population of the United States, according to the most recent decennial census.

STATE PLANS

Sec. 103. (a) To be approved under this section, a State plan for the further extension of public library services must--

(1) provide for the administration, or supervision of the administration, of the plan by the State library administrative agency, and provide that such agency will have adequate authority under State law to administer the plan in accordance with its provisions and the provisions of this Act;

(2) provide for the receipt by the State treasurer (or, if there be no State treasurer, the officer exercising similar functions for the State) of all funds paid to the State pursuant to this Act and for the proper safeguarding of such funds by such officer, provide that such funds shall be expended solely for the purposes for which paid, and provide for the repayment by the State to the United States of any such funds lost or diverted from the purposes for which paid;

(3) provide policies and methods of administration to be followed in using any funds made available for expenditure under the State plan, which policies and methods the State library administrative agency certifies will in its judgment assure use of such funds to maximum advantage in the further extension of public library services to areas without such services or with inadequate services;

(4) provide that the State library administrative agency will make such reports as to categories of expenditures made under this Act, as the Commissioner may from time to time reasonably require; and

(5) provide that any library services furnished under the plan shall be made available free of charge under regulations prescribed by the State library administrative agency.

(b) The Commissioner shall approve any plan which fulfills the conditions specified in subsection (a) of this section.

(c) The determination of whether library services are inadequate in any area within any State shall be made by the State library administrative agency of such State.

PAYMENTS TO STATES

Sec. 104. (a) From the allotments available therefor under section 102, the Secretary of the Treasury shall from time to time pay to each State which has a plan approved under section 103 an amount computed as provided in subsection (b) of this section, equal to the Federal share of the total sums expended by the State and its political subdivisions under such plan during the period for which such payment was made, except that no payments shall be made to any State (other than the Trust Territory of the Pacific Islands) from its allotment for any fiscal year unless and until the Commissioner finds that (1) there will be available for expenditure under the plan from State or local sources during the fiscal year for which the allotment is made (A) sums sufficient to enable the State to receive under this section payments in an amount not less than $25,000 in the case of the Virgin Islands, American Samoa, the Trust Territory of the Pacific Islands or Guam and $100,000 in the case of any other State, and (B) not less than the total amount actually expended, in the areas covered by the plan for such year, for public library services from such sources in the second preceding fiscal year, and (2) there will be available for expenditure for public library services from State sources during the fiscal year for which the allotment is made not less than the total amount actually expended for public library services from such sources in the second preceding fiscal year.

(b) The Commissioner shall from time to time estimate the amount to which a State is entitled under subsection (a), and such amount shall be paid to the State, in advance or by way of reimbursement, at such time or times and in such installments as the Commissioner may determine, after necessary adjustment on account of any previously made overpayment or underpayment.

(c) For the purposes of this section the "Federal share" for any State shall be 100 per centum less the State percentage and the State percentage shall be that percentage which bears the same ratio to 50 percentum as the per capita income of such State bears to the per capita income of all the States (excluding Puerto Rico, Guam, American Samoa, the Trust Territory of the Pacific Islands, and the Virgin Islands), except that (1) the Federal share shall in no case be more than 66 per centum or less than 33 per centum, and (2) the Federal share for Puerto Rico, Guam, American Samoa, and the Virgin Islands shall be 66 per centum, and the Federal share for the Trust Territory of the Pacific Islands shall be 100 per centum.

(d) The "Federal share" for each State shall be promulgated
by the Commissioner between July 1 and August 31 of each even-numbered
year, on the basis of the average of the per capita incomes of each of
the States and of all of the States (excluding Puerto Rico, Guam,
American Samoa, the Trust Territory of the Pacific Islands, and the
Virgin Islands), for the three most recent consecutive years for which
satisfactory data are available from the Department of Commerce. Such
promulgation shall be conclusive for each of the two fiscal years in
the period beginning July 1 next succeeding such promulgation: Provided,
That the Commissioner shall promulgate such percentages as soon as
possible after the enactment of this Act.

(e) No portion of any money paid to a State under this title
shall be applied, directly or indirectly, to the purchase or erection
of any building or buildings, or for the purchase of any land.

TITLE II--PUBLIC LIBRARY CONSTRUCTION
AUTHORIZATION OF APPROPRIATIONS

Sec. 201. There are authorized to be appropriated for the
fiscal year ending June 30, 1967, $40,000,000; for the fiscal year
ending June 30, 1968, $50,000,000; for the fiscal year ending June 30,
1969, $60,000,000; for the fiscal year ending June 30, 1970, $70,000,000;
and for the fiscal year ending June 30, 1971, $80,000,000, which shall
be used for making payments to States, which have submitted and had
approved by the Commissioner, State plans for the construction of public
libraries.

ALLOTMENTS

Sec. 202. From the sums appropriated pursuant to section 201
for each fiscal year, the Commissioner shall allot $20,000 each to Guam,
American Samoa, the Trust Territory of the Pacific Islands, and the
Virgin Islands, and $80,000 to each of the other States, and shall
allot to each State such part of the remainder of such sums as the
population of the State bears to the population of the United States,
according to the most recent decennial census. A State's allotment under
this subsection for any fiscal year shall be available for payments
with respect to the administration, during such year and the next
fiscal year, of its State plan approved under section 203, and for
payments with respect to construction projects approved under such
State plan during such year or the next fiscal year.

STATE PLANS FOR CONSTRUCTION

Sec. 203. (a) To be approved for purposes of this title a State plan for construction of public libraries must--

(1) meet the requirements of paragraphs (1), (2), (4), and (5) of section 103(a);

(2) set forth criteria and procedures for approval of projects for construction of public library facilities which are designed to insure that facilities will be constructed only to serve areas, as determined by the State library administrative agency, which are without library facilities necessary to develop library services;

(3) provide assurance that every local or other public agency whose application for funds under the plan with respect to a project for construction of public library facilities is denied will be given an opportunity for a fair hearing before the State library administrative agency; and

(4) provide assurance that all laborers and mechanics employed by contractors or subcontractors on all construction projects assisted under this Act shall be paid wages at rates not less than those prevailing on similar construction in the locality, as determined by the Secretary of Labor in accordance with the Davis-Bacon Act, as amended (40 U.S.C. 276a-276c-5), and shall receive overtime compensation in accordance with and subject to the provisions of the Contract Work Hours Standards Act (Public Law 87-581); and the Secretary of Labor shall have with respect to the labor standards specified in this paragraph the authority and functions set forth in Reorganization Plan Numbered 14 of 1950 (15 F.R. 3176; 5 U.S.C. 133z-15) and section 2 of the Act of June 13, 1934, as amended (40 U.S.C. 276c).

(b) The Commissioner shall approve any plan which fulfills the conditions specified in subsection (a) of this section.

PAYMENTS TO STATES

Sec. 204. (a) From its allotment available therefor under section 202 each State shall be entitled to receive (1) an amount equal to the Federal share (as determined under section 104) of projects approved under its State plan (as approved by the Commissioner pursuant to section 203) during the period for which such allotment is available, and (2) an amount equal to the Federal share of the total of the sums expended by the State and its political subdivisions for the administration of such State plan during the period for which such allotment is available.

(b) The Commissioner shall from time to time estimate the amount
to which a State is entitled under subsection (a), and such amount shall
be paid to the State, in advance or by way of reimbursement, at such
time or times and in such installments as the Commissioner may determine,
after necessary adjustment on account of any previously made overpayment
or underpayment.

TITLE III--INTERLIBRARY COOPERATION
AUTHORIZATION OF APPROPRIATIONS

Sec. 301. There are authorized to be appropriated for the
fiscal year ending June 30, 1967, the sum of $5,000,000; for the fiscal
year ending June 30, 1968, $7,500,000; for the fiscal year ending
June 30, 1969, $10,000,000; for the fiscal year ending June 30, 1970,
$12,500,000; and for the fiscal year ending June 30, 1971, $15,000,000;
which shall be used for making payments to States which have submitted
and had approved by the Commissioner State plans for establishing and
maintaining local, regional, State or interstate cooperative networks
of libraries.

ALLOTMENTS

Sec. 302. From the sums appropriated pursuant to section 301
for each fiscal year the Commissioner shall allot $10,000 each to Guam,
American Samoa, the Trust Territory of the Pacific Islands, and the
Virgin Islands, and $40,000 to each of the other States, and shall
allot to each State such part of the remainder of such sums as the
population of the State bears to the population of the United States
according to the most recent decennial census.

PAYMENTS TO STATES

Sec. 303. From the allotments available therefor under
section 302, the Secretary of the Treasury shall from time to time
pay to each State which has a plan approved under section 304 an amount
equal to the Federal share which for the fiscal year ending June 30,
1968, shall be 100 per centum of the total sums expended under such
plan (including costs of administering such plan), and for any fiscal
year thereafter shall be 50 per centum of such sums, except that the
Federal share for the Trust Territory of the Pacific Islands shall be
100 per centum.

STATE PLANS FOR INTERLIBRARY COOPERATION

Sec. 304. (a) To be approved for purposes of this title a
State plan must--

(1) meet the requirements of paragraphs (1), (2), (4), and (5) of section 103(a).

(2) provide policies and objectives for the systematic and effective coordination of the resources of school, public, academic, and special libraries and special information centers for improved services of a supplementary nature to the special clientele served by each type of library or center;

(3) provide appropriate allocation by participating agencies of the total costs of the system;

(4) provide assurance that every local or other public agency in the State is accorded an opportunity to participate in the system;

(5) provide criteria which the State agency shall use in evaluating applications for funds under this title and in assigning priority to project proposals; and

(6) establish a statewide council which is broadly representative of professional library interests and of library users which shall act in an advisory capacity to the State agency.

(b) The Commissioner shall approve any State plan which meets the conditions specified in subsection (a) of this section.

TITLE IV--SPECIALIZED STATE LIBRARY SERVICES
PART A--STATE INSTITUTIONAL LIBRARY SERVICES
AUTHORIZATION OF APPROPRIATIONS

Sec. 401. There are authorized to be appropriated for the fiscal year ending June 30, 1967, the sum of $5,000,000; for the fiscal year ending June 30, 1968, $7,500,000; for the fiscal year ending June 30, 1969, $10,000,000; for the fiscal year ending June 30, 1970, $12,500,000; and for the fiscal year ending June 30, 1971, $15,000,000; which shall be used for making payments to States which have submitted and had approved by the Commissioner State plans for establishing and improving State institutional library services. For the purposes of this part the term "State institutional library services" means the providing of books, and other library materials, and of library services to (A) inmates, patients, or residents of penal institutions, reformatories, residential training schools, orphanages, or general or special institutions or hospitals operated or substantially supported by the State, and (B) students in residential schools for the handicapped (including mentally retarded, hard of hearing, deaf, speech impaired, visually handicapped, seriously emotionally disturbed, crippled, or other health impaired persons who by reason thereof require special education) operated or substantially supported by the State.

ALLOTMENTS

Sec. 402. From the sums appropriated pursuant to section 401 for each fiscal year the Commissioner shall allot $10,000 each to Guam, American Samoa, the Trust Territory of the Pacific Islands, and the Virgin Islands, and $40,000 to each of the other States, and shall allot to each State such part of the remainder of such sums as the population of the State bears to the population of the United States according to the most recent decennial census.

PAYMENTS TO STATES

Sec. 403. From the allotments available therefor under section 402, the Secretary of the Treasury shall from time to time pay to each State which has a plan approved under section 404 an amount equal to the Federal share (as determined under section 104, except that the Federal share for the fiscal year ending June 30, 1968, shall be 100 per centum) of the total sums expended by the State under such plan (including costs of administering such plan).

STATE PLANS FOR STATE INSTITUTIONAL LIBRARY SERVICES

Sec. 404. (a) To be approved for purposes of this part a State plan must--

(1) meet the requirements of paragraphs (1), (2), (4), and (5) of section 103(a);

(2) provide policies and objectives for the establishment or improvement of State institutional library services;

(3) provide assurance that all eligible State institutions will be accorded an opportunity to participate in the program pursuant to this part;

(4) provide criteria which the State agency shall use in evaluating applications for funds under this part and in assigning priority to project proposals;

(5) provide assurances satisfactory to the Commissioner that expenditures made by such State in any fiscal year for State institutional library services will not be less than such expenditures in the second preceding fiscal year; and

(6) establish a council which is broadly representative of State institutions eligible for assistance under this part which shall act in an advisory capacity to the State agency.

(b) The Commissioner shall approve any State plan which meets the conditions specified in subsection (a) of this section.

(c) No portion of any money paid to a State under this part shall be applied, directly or indirectly, to the purchase or erection of any building or buildings, or the purchase of any land.

PART B--LIBRARY SERVICES TO THE PHYSICALLY HANDICAPPED
AUTHORIZATION OF APPROPRIATIONS

Sec. 411. There are authorized to be appropriated for the fiscal year ending June 30, 1967, the sum of $3,000,000; for the fiscal year ending June 30, 1968, $4,000,000; for the fiscal year ending June 30, 1969, $5,000,000; for the fiscal year ending June 30, 1970, $6,000,000; and for the fiscal year ending June 30, 1971, $7,000,000; which shall be used for making payments to States which have submitted and had approved by the Commissioner State plans for establishing and improving library services to the physically handicapped. For the purposes of this part the term "library services to the physically handicapped" means the providing of library service, through public or other nonprofit libraries, agencies, or organizations, to physically handicapped persons (including the blind and visually handicapped) certified by competent authority as unable to read or to use conventional printed materials as a result of physical limitations.

ALLOTMENTS

Sec. 412. From the sums appropriated pursuant to section 411 for each fiscal year, the Commissioner shall allot $5,000 each to Guam, American Samoa, the Trust Territory of the Pacific Islands, and the Virgin Islands, and $25,000 to each of the other States, and shall allot to each State such part of the remainder of such sums as the population of the State bears to the population of the United States according to the most recent decennial census.

PAYMENTS TO STATES

Section 413. From the allotments available therefor under section 412, the Secretary of the Treasury shall from time to time pay to each State which has a plan approved under section 414 an amount equal to the Federal share (as determined under section 104, except that the Federal share for the fiscal year ending June 30, 1968, shall be 100 per centum) of the total sums expended under such plan (including costs of administering such plan).

STATE PLANS FOR SERVICES TO THE PHYSICALLY HANDICAPPED

Sec. 414. (a) To be approved for the purposes of this part a State plan must--

(1) meet the requirements of paragraphs (1), (2), (4), and (5) of section 103(a);

(2) provide policies and objectives for the establishment or improvement of library services to the physically handicapped;

(3) provide assurance that all appropriate public or nonprofit libraries, agencies, or organizations for the physically handicapped will be accorded an opportunity to participate in the program pursuant to this part;

(4) provide criteria which the State agency shall use in evaluating applications for funds under this part and in assigning priority to project proposals;

(5) provide assurances satisfactory to the Commissioner that funds available from sources other than Federal sources in any fiscal year for expenditures under State plans for library services to the physically handicapped will not be less than actual expenditures from such source in the second preceding fiscal year; and

(6) establish a council which is representative of eligible agencies which shall act in an advisory capacity to the State agency.

(b) The Commissioner shall approve, after consultation with the Librarian of Congress where appropriate, any State plan which meets the conditions specified in subsection (a) of this section.

(c) No part of any money paid to a State under this part shall be applied, directly or indirectly, to the purchase or erection of any building or buildings, or the purchase of any land.

TITLE V--GENERAL
WITHHOLDING

Sec. 501. If the Commissioner finds after reasonable notice and opportunity for hearing to the State agency administering or supervising the administration of a State plan approved under this Act, that the State plan has been so changed that it no longer complies with the applicable requirements of this Act or that in the administration of the plan there is a failure to comply substantially with the provisions required to be included in the plan, he shall notify such State agency that further payments will not be made to the State under this Act (or, in his discretion, that further payments will not be made with respect to portions of or projects under the State plan affected by such failure) until he is satisfied that there is no longer any such failure to comply. Until he is so satisfied, no further payments shall be made to such State for carrying out such State plan (or further payments shall be limited to parts of or projects under the plan not affected by such failure).

ADMINISTRATION

Sec. 502. (a) The Commissioner shall administer this Act under the supervision and direction of the Secretary of Health, Education, and Welfare, and shall, with the approval of the Secretary, prescribe such regulations as may be necessary for the administration of this Act.

(b) The Commissioner is also authorized to make such studies, investigations, and reports as may be necessary or appropriate to carry out the purposes of this Act, including periodic reports for public distribution as to the values, methods, and results of various State demonstrations of public library services undertaken under this Act.

(c) There are hereby authorized to be appropriated for expenses of administration such sums as may be necessary to carry out the functions of the Secretary and the Commissioner under this Act.

(d) (1) The Commissioner shall not finally disapprove any State plan submitted under this Act, or any modification thereof, without first affording the State submitting the plan reasonable notice and opportunity for a hearing.

(2) If any State is dissatisfied with the Commissioner's final action with respect to the approval of its State plan submitted under Title I, Title II, Title III, or part A or B of Title IV, or with respect to his final action under section 501, such State may appeal to the United States Court of Appeals for the circuit in which the State is located, by filing a petition with such court within sixty days after such final action. A copy of the petition shall be forthwith transmitted by the clerk of the court to the Commissioner or any officer designated by him for that purpose. The Commissioner thereupon shall file in the court the record of the proceedings on which he based his action, as provided in section 2112 of title 28, United States Code.

(3) Upon the filing of the petition referred to in paragraph (1) of this subsection, the court shall have jurisdiction to affirm the action of the Commissioner or to set it aside, in whole or in part,

temporarily or permanently, but until the filing of the record the Commissioner may modify or set aside his order. The findings of the Commissioner as to the facts, if supported by substantial evidence, shall be conclusive, but the court, for good cause shown, may remand the case to the Commissioner to take further evidence, and the Commissioner may thereupon make new or modified findings of fact and may modify his previous action, and shall file in the court the record of the further proceedings. Such new or modified findings of fact shall likewise be conclusive if supported by substantial evidence.

(4) The judgment of the court affirming or setting aside, in whole or in part, any action of the Commissioner shall be final, subject to review by the Supreme Court of the United States upon certiorari or certification as provided in section 1254 of title 28, United States Code. The commencement of proceedings under this subsection shall not, unless so specifically ordered by the court, operate as a stay of the Commissioner's action.

REALLOTMENTS

Sec. 503. The amount of any State's allotment under section 102, 202, 302, 402, or 412, for any fiscal year which the Commissioner determines will not be required for the period for which such allotment is available for carrying out the State plan approved under section 103, 203, 304, 404, and 414, respectively, shall be available for reallotment from time to time, on such dates during such year as the Commissioner may fix, to other States in proportion to the original allotments for such year to such States under such section 102, 202, 302, 402, or 412, as the case may be, but with such proportionate amount for any of such other States being reduced to the extent it exceeds the amount which the Commissioner estimates the State needs and will be able to use for such period of time for which the original allotments were available for carrying out the State plan approved under section 103, 203, 304, 404, or 414, as the case may be, and the total of such reductions shall be similarly reallotted among the States not suffering such a reduction. Any amount reallotted to a State under this subsection from funds appropriated pursuant to section 101, 201, 301, 401, or 411 for any fiscal year shall be deemed part of its allotment for such year under sections 102, 202, 302, 402, and 412, respectively.

DEFINITIONS

Sec. 504. For the purposes of this Act--

(a) The term "State" means a State, the District of Columbia, Puerto Rico, Guam, American Samoa, the Trust Territory of the Pacific Islands, or the Virgin Islands;

(b)   The term "State library administrative agency" means the official State agency charged by State law with the extension and development of public library services throughout the State;

(c)   The term "public library" means a library that serves free all residents of a community, district, or region, and receives its financial support in whole or in part from public funds;

(d)   The term "construction" includes construction of new buildings and acquisition, expansion, remodeling, and alteration of existing buildings, and initial equipment of any such buildings; including architects' fees and the cost of the acquisition of land;

(e)   The term "Secretary" means the Secretary of Health, Education, and Welfare.

****

APPENDIX B

FEDERAL ALLOTMENTS AND REQUIRED
MATCHING EXPENDITURES FROM
STATE AND LOCAL SOURCES FOR
TITLE I - PUBLIC LIBRARY SERVICES
FISCAL YEAR 1968

DEPARTMENT OF HEALTH, EDUCATION, AND WELFARE
Office of Education
Washington, D. C. 20202

The Library Services and Construction Act, Public Law 89-511

Federal Allotments and Required Matching Expenditures
from State and Local Sources for Title I
Public Library Services
Fiscal Year 1968

States and Outlying Parts	Federal Allotment 1/	State and Local Matching	Federal Percentage	State Percentage
TOTALS	$35,000,000	$36,244,179	--	--
Alabama	633,492	333,376	65.52	34.48
Alaska	136,935	194,627	41.30	58.70
Arizona	312,656	246,657	55.90	44.10
Arkansas	391,716	201,793	66.00	34.00
California	2,666,778	4,057,322	39.66	60.34
Colorado	386,437	383,818	50.17	49.83
Connecticut	514,029	863,696	37.31	62.69
Delaware	172,884	272,923	38.78	61.22
District of Columbia	224,762	456,335	33.00	67.00
Florida	908,640	715,091	55.96	44.04
Georgia	743,951	472,451	61.16	38.84
Hawaii	203,338	232,635	46.64	53.36
Idaho	208,959	152,875	57.75	42.25
Illinois	1,746,355	2,558,193	40.57	59.43
Indiana	861,433	892,656	49.11	50.89
Iowa	550,334	495,531	52.62	47.38
Kansas	455,789	426,838	51.64	48.36
Kentucky	596,161	351,329	62.92	37.08
Louisiana	631,904	380,438	62.42	37.58
Maine	258,291	178,601	59.12	40.88
Maryland	606,374	731,314	45.33	54.67
Massachusetts	940,815	1,195,459	44.04	55.96
Michigan	1,377,606	1,604,225	46.20	53.80
Minnesota	657,518	608,644	51.93	48.07
Mississippi	455,712	234,761	66.00	34.00

P.L. 89-511 - Title I - Fiscal Year 1968 (Cont'd)

States and Outlying Parts	Federal Allotment1/	State and Local Matching	Federal Percentage	State Percentage
Missouri	$ 805,469	$ 745,598	51.93	48.07
Montana	210,196	170,043	55.28	44.72
Nebraska	330,484	291,428	53.14	46.86
Nevada	146,589	248,530	37.10	62.90
New Hampshire	199,116	177,072	52.93	47.07
New Jersey	1,090,767	1,607,815	40.42	59.58
New Mexico	255,312	175,449	59.27	40.73
New York	2,840,719	4,318,351	39.68	60.32
North Carolina	844,066	496,572	62.96	37.04
North Dakota	203,285	137,340	59.68	40.32
Ohio	1,685,152	1,774,409	48.71	51.29
Oklahoma	480,232	334,964	58.91	41.09
Oregon	388,844	394,326	49.65	50.35
Pennsylvania	1,948,566	1,947,008	50.02	49.98
Rhode Island	240,363	253,297	48.69	51.31
South Carolina	489,102	251,961	66.00	34.00
South Dakota	211,135	132,453	61.45	38.55
Tennessee	682,542	390,806	63.59	36.41
Texas	1,664,458	1,242,892	57.25	42.75
Utah	245,448	192,461	56.05	43.95
Vermont	163,671	116,108	58.50	41.50
Virginia	747,843	577,180	56.44	43.56
Washington	565,959	637,441	47.03	52.97
West Virginia	403,825	233,525	63.36	36.64
Wisconsin	745,365	717,856	50.94	49.06
Wyoming	153,903	139,861	52.39	47.61
American Samoa	28,275	14,566	66.00	34.00
Guam	35,949	18,519	66.00	34.00
Puerto Rico	483,704	249,181	66.00	34.00
Virgin Island	30,242	15,579	66.00	34.00
Trust Territory	36,550	--	100.00	--

1/Distribution: Basic allotment of $100,000 to the 50 States, District of
Columbia, and Puerto Rico, and $25,000 to the other outlying areas; the
remainder distributed on the basis of total population, April 1, 1960
(except Trust Territory, 1958).

APPENDIX C

CHECKLISTS

CHECKLIST FOR INTERVIEW WITH THE
LIBRARY PROGRAM OFFICER IN THE REGION

1. What is the organization of the State Library Office?

2. Is it an independent agency or part of some other agency such as

    the Department of Education?

3. What is the makeup of its staff? How many consultants does it

    have to send out to the field?

4. What relevant political events or issues might have affected the

    Title I Program?

5. Who really runs LSCA Title I in the State?

6. What do you think will happen when and if the present State Library

    hierarchy disappears?

7. Tell me what to look for when I go into the State.

8. What are the significant projects in the State?

    a. Unique

    b. Successful

    c. Unsuccessful

9. **Whom should I talk to who is _not_ getting LSCA funding?**

10. Can a case be made for a Regional Program determination and/or

    administration of library services rather than that which exists

    within State determination and control?

11. What is the role of the Regional Officer in relationship to the

    State Library?

12. What is the role of the Regional Library Program Officer and USOE

    Headquarters?

13. How do you think that the Regional setup will evolve?

14. How much capability do you have to respond to the library requests

    from the State?

15. What sort of help can you (or headquarters) give to the State

    Librarian and how effectively can you provide this help under the

    decentralized arrangement?

16. What sort of communication exists between the Regional Program
Officers?

17. What sort of purview do you have over the State Annual Program?

18. To what extent do you approve or disapprove of individual projects?

19. What effect do you think you will have over future Annual Programs
from the individual States?

20. How much travel money do you have:

    a. to travel with within your Region?

    b. to travel to interact with other Regional Program Officers?

21. How easy are phone communications for you to maintain contact
with the States or for the States to maintain contact with you?

22. Are the States in which you are not physically located any better
off than when you were in D.C.?

23. Since conclusions will be drawn about 56 States from those who read
our report, could you describe the State that we are going to visit
in relation to the other States in your region?

24. How adequate is the present information flow from the State

libraries in order for you to do your job?

25. To what extent do local projects contact you?

26. To what extent do you then contact the local projects?

CHECKLIST FOR INTERVIEWS WITH LOCAL PROJECT PERSONNEL

1. Get a description and a history of the local project.

2. Is the local project going to continue if Federal funding disappears?

3. What is the minimum time for support for this project for realistic long-lived effect?

4. Suppose Federal funds disappear, what are you going to do?

5. Do you reach a catastrophe date when local funding will not be able to continue the project, for instance when a bookmobile finally is worn out or a reference collection is hopelessly out of date?

6. How do you decide which programs to submit to the State?

7. Can we have a copy of the plan that was submitted to the State?

8. Can we have a copy of some of the plans that were rejected by the State?

9. Can you tell us something about the plans that were rejected by the State?

10. To what extent are the criteria for submitting a plan determined

by the State?

11. To what extent is the funding determined such that there is least

damage to the local organization when Federal funding disappears

(e.g., major portion of Federal funding goes into capital

improvements)?

12. If the end of Federal funding terminates the project, why is it

that local or State funding won't keep the project going?

13. What reception has the project received in the community?

14. How do you measure the effect of the project on the community?

    a. quantitative?

    b. qualitative?

    c. How secure do you feel about your measures?

15. What portion of the community is this project directed towards?

16. What are the attitudes of the local library funding body towards

the project (e.g., supervisors, city council)?

17. How is the public relations for the project done?

18. NOT A QUESTION. Uncover how much the project is dependent or

    was dependent on one strong person.

19. NOT A QUESTION. What is the quality of local library personnel?

20. What level of training do the personnel have?

21. How was Federal money spent?

    a. salaries

    b. books

    c. training

    d. capital improvement

22. Are there recognized professional library associations in the State?

23. Tell me about the recognized professional library associations.

24. Tell me about the informal groupings of the library personnel.

25. Do you get together with other library personnel in the State?

    How does this affect the spending of LSCA Title I funds?

26. Tell me about your reaction to the training and internship programs

    if any.

27. Who determines the selection criteria? What controls are exercised during acquisition to make sure that these selection criteria are adhered to?

28. What standards do you follow in providing minimum library services? Do you follow ALA standards? If so, what does this mean in terms of operational descriptions of your service?

29. Are you able to secure funding from other Federal agencies or private foundations?

30. Is your library (or library personnel) part of any community planning groups?

31. How are funds obtained for membership in the system (special library assessments?)?

32. Are there legal ceilings on library assessments?

CHECKLIST FOR INTERVIEWS WITH STATE LIBRARY PERSONNEL

1. Get a background and history of the State plan and how it evolved.

2. Determine the organizational structure of the State Library.

3. Is the position of the State Library within the State government dysfunctional in terms of getting money?

4. With respect to the requests that you get for money from projects within the State, how do you decide who is going to get money and who will be turned down?

5. With respect to the requests from somebody to whom money will be granted, how do you decide which projects to fund and which not to grant?

6. Of the Title I money that you receive:

    a. What fraction goes to strengthening the State's own collection which is available to the rest of the State?

    b. What fraction goes to strengthening State services that are outwardly oriented such as consultant services or central processing for other libraries?

    c. What percentage goes to out-and-out grants?

7. How detailed a plan do you require of those who ask for funding?

8. How much lead time do you give them for building the plan?

9. What followup do you do on the spending that takes place at the

    local projects?

10. Do you have records indicating what the local groups spent before

    they received Federal money, and afterwards if it were a demonstration

    project which terminated?

11. Can we have a copy of the statistics on spending?

12. What happens to the grand plan when the present decision makers

    at the State Library leave?

13. What relationship exists between the State Library and the Program

    Officer?

14. Does the Program Officer affect local projects?

15. How useful is the Program Officer to you in getting help from the

    U.S. Office of Education in Washington?

16. Do you think your State will be favorably or unfavorably affected

    by decentralization?

17. What standards do you follow in providing minimum library services?

    Do you follow ALA standards? If so, what does this mean in terms

    of operational descriptions of your service?

18. To what extent are the consultants full time extension oriented?

19. Are the consultants geographically oriented or skill oriented?

20. To what extent does the State Library create the local plan?

21. What if you received a block grant, how would you divide the money

    between the titles?

22. How were the regions chosen?

CHECKLIST FOR INTERVIEWS WITH STATE FINANCE
DEPARTMENT OR THE LEGISLATIVE FINANCE PERSONNEL

1. Obtain a history of the State financing of libraries.

2. With the same amount of money that has been appropriated by the
    State without Federal money coming in, would less have been
    appropriated by the State or have the Federal funds stimulated
    State spending?

3. What if Federal funding ended, would the State pick up the difference?

4. What if there were a block grant of all Federal funding to the States,
    would the Library get a proportional share or is the Library a local
    and Federal darling but not of particular interest to the State?

5. What is the relationship of the State Library to the Finance
    Department?

6. Describe the relationship of the State Library to the Legislative
    bodies?

7. What is the general attitude about the Library as a useful adjunct
    to the Capitol?

8. What is the general attitude about the State Library as a guiding

   and leading force throughout the State Library System?

9. How effective is the State Library or the professional library

   associations in the State in lobbying for State funds?

APPENDIX D

WASHINGTON, D.C. VISITS

APPENDIX D

WASHINGTON, D.C. VISITS

Date	Place Visited	Persons Visited
8/22/68	U. S. Office of Education	Frank Kurt Cylke, Acting Chief of the Library and Information Sciences Research Branch Ray M. Fry, Director, Division of Library Services and Educational Facilities Elizabeth H. Hughey, Acting Chief, Library Programs and Facilities Branch Michelle R. Vale, Evaluation Specialist Dorothy A. Kittel, Library Extension Specialist, Title III Betty Jones, Research Assistant
10/24/68	American Library Asso. Washington Office	Germaine Krettek, Director
	Mr. Dunbar's home	Ralph M. Dunbar, former Director of the Division of Library Services, USOE
	Dept. of Health, Education, and Welfare	Samuel Halperin, Asst. Secretary of Health, Education, and Welfare for Legislation
10/25/68	Library of Congress	John Lorenz, Deputy Librarian
	Senate Office Building	John S. Forsythe, General Counsel, Senate Committee on Labor and Public Welfare

APPENDIX E

GENERAL BIBLIOGRAPHY

APPENDIX E

GENERAL BIBLIOGRAPHY

American Library Association. ALA Bulletin. Chicago., Ill., Monthly (various issues).

American Library Association. National Inventory of Library Needs. Chicago, Ill., 1965, 72 pp.

American Library Association, American Association of State Libraries. Standards for Library Functions at the State Level. Chicago, Ill., 1963, 37 pp.

American Library Association, Public Library Association. Costs of Public Library Service in 1956; A Supplement to Public Library Service. Chicago, Ill., 1956, 15 pp.

_____. Costs of Public Library Service in 1959; A Supplement to Public Library Service. Chicago, Ill., 1960, 15 pp.

_____. Costs of Public Library Service in 1963; A Supplement to Public Library Service. Chicago, Ill., 1964, 15 pp.

American Library Association, Public Library Association. The Small Public Library: A Series of Guides for Community Librarians and Trustees. Chicago, Ill., 1962.

American Library Association, Standards Committee. Interim Standards for Small Public Libraries: Guidelines Toward Achieving the Goals of Public Library Service. Chicago, Ill., 1962.

American Library Association, Standards Committee. Minimum Standards for Public Library Systems, 1966. Chicago, Ill., 1967, 69 pp.

Assembly of State Librarians. Summary Proceedings of the Assembly of State Librarians. Washington, D.C.: Library of Congress, 1959, 45 pp.

_____. Proceedings of the Second Assembly of State Librarians. 1959, 12 pp.

_____. Proceedings of the Third Assembly on the Library Functions of the State. 1956, 85 pp.

Beach, Fred F., Dunbar, Ralph M, and Will, Robert F. The State and Publicly Supported Libraries: Structure and Control at the State Level. U.S. Office of Education, Washington, D.C., 1956, 85 pp.

Buckland, M.K. and Woodburn, I. Some Implications for Library Management of Scattering and Obsolescence. University of Lancaster, Lancaster, U.K., 1968, 25 pp.

Bunge, Charles A. "Statewide Library Surveys and Plans, Development of the Concept and Some Recent Patterns." Library Quarterly. 36:25-37 (January 1966).

Bunge, Charles A. "Statewide Public Library Surveys and Plans, 1944-64." ALA Bulletin. 59:5 (May 1965), pp. 364-374.

Carl, Herbert A., ed. Statewide Long-Range Planning for Libraries; Report of Conference/September 19-22, 1965/Chicago, Illinois. U.S. Office of Education, Washington, D.C., 1966, 57 pp.

Cohen, Nathan M. State Library Extension: Resources and Services 1960-61. U.S. Office of Education, Washington, D.C., 1966, 90 pp.

Coplan, Kate and Castagna, Edwin. The Library Reaches Out; Reports on Library Service and Community Relations by Some Leading American Librarians. Oceana Publications, Dobbs Ferry, N.Y., 1965, 403 pp.

Frantz, John C. Library Services Act--Library Services and Construction Act: The Past is Prologue. Illinois State Library, 47:1, January 1965, pp. 3-12.

Frantz, John C. and Cohen, Nathan M. The Federal Government and Public Libraries: A Ten-Year Partnership Fiscal Years 1957 - 1966. Illinois State Library, Ill., 1967, 25 pp.

Fry, Ray M. "New Team at the Top." Library Journal. R. R. Bowker, N.Y., N.Y., 1 January 1968, pp. 43-47 (reprint).

Hans, Warren J. "Statewide and Regional Reference Service." Library Trends. 12:405-12 (January 1964).

Humphry, John A. and Humphry, James III. Library Service in Louisiana: Keeping Pace With Progress in the State. Louisiana Library Association, Louisiana, 1968, 116 pp.

Leigh, Carma and others. "The Role of the State Librarian." Wilson Library Bulletin. 42:8 (April 1968) pp. 796-828.

Martin, Lowell A. Library Development Under the Library Services Act and the Library Services and Construction Act; An Informal Report to the U.S. Commissioner of Education. Washington, D.C., July 1966, 36 pp.

Monnypenny, Phillip. The Library Functions of the States; Commentary on the Survey of Library Functions of the States. American Library Association, Chicago, Ill., 1966, 178 pp.

Moon, Eric. "Route '66: A Selective Review and Commentary on the (Mostly American) Library Scene and its Events of the Past Year." Library Journal. 92:1 (1 January 1967) pp. 51-63.

Nelson Associates, Inc. American State Libraries and State Library Agencies: An Overview with Recommendations. A report prepared for the National Advisory Commission on Libraries. N.Y., N.Y., November 1967, 31 pp.

Nyren, Karl. "The National Dimension." Library Journal. 92:1 (1 January 1967) pp. 64-71.

Stout, Donald E., ed. The Impact of the Library Services Act: Progress and Potential. (Allerton Park Institute, No. 8), University of Illinois, Graduate School of Library Science, Urbana, Ill., 1962, 120 pp.

U.S. Congress. "Extension of Remarks." Congressional Record. Washington, D.C., 114:173 (21 October 1968), pp. 9356-9366.

U.S. Congress, House of Representatives. Extension of Library Services Act. Hearings, March 29, April 6, 7, 1960. 165 pp.

U.S. Congress, House of Representatives. Library Services Act. Hearings, June 26, 27, and 29, 1962. U.S. Printing Office, Washington, D.C., 243 pp.

U.S. Congress, House of Representatives. Library Services and Construction Act Amendments. Hearings, May 20, 1966. U.S. Printing Office, Washington, D.C., 371 pp.

U.S. Congress, Senate. Amending the Library Services Act of 1956. Report Together With Minority Views. U.S. Printing Office, Washington, D.C., 1963, 18 pp.

U.S. Office of Education. Amendment of Guide for Preparing a State Plan for Library Programs. Office of Education, Washington, D.C., 1968, 3 pp.

U.S. Office of Education. State Plans Under the Library Services Act, a Summary of Plans and Programs for Fiscal 1957, Submitted Under Public Law, 84th Congress. Office of Education, Washington, D.C., 1953, 84 pp.

_____. Supplement 1. Summary of Programs for Fiscal 1958. 82 pp.